SUNYATA
BOOKS

SEATTLE

THE SINGING EARTH

BARRETT MARTIN

For information about permissions to reproduce selections from this book, translation rights, or to order bulk purchases, go to www.sunyatabooks.com.

Cover art by Erin Currier
Author photo by Dean Karr

Martin, Barrett
The Singing Earth
ISBN 978-0-692-85174-6

1. Biography & Autobiography—Composers & Musicians. 2. Music—Ethnomusicology.

SUNYATA
BOOKS

WWW.SUNYATABOOKS.COM

THE SINGING EARTH

This book is dedicated to all the musicians
who carry the soul of the world in their hearts.

PRELUDE

A UNIVERSE MADE OF SONG

Me and my first drum set, Olympia, WA, 1977

"All a musician can do is to get closer to the sources of nature, and so feel that he is in communion with the natural laws."

—John Coltrane

When I was a little boy around the age of seven, I would occasionally awaken in the middle of the night and wander outside our house to listen to the fragrant forest that surrounded my childhood home. The forest was alive—it seemed to vibrate with sound, color, texture, and smell. I could hear the frogs croaking in the distant swamp, the occasional night bird, and the whirring of leaves when a warm breeze rustled through the trees. This was all before I knew I would become a musician, but looking back, I realize that the forest was already singing to me in its own way, with its own song, and it was utterly captivating.

I've never lost my love of forests and the wilderness, but by the time I was 21 I was a professional musician playing in cities around the world. I was still hearing the music of the Earth, but now it included the sounds of communities, cities, and entire countries, all of which resonated with a certain frequency that was unique and particular to each place. Often it came to me as a rhythm, sometimes it was a melody, and occasionally it was just the general feeling or mood of a place that sounded like a rich jazz chord. Other times the place sounded dangerous, but there is a certain excitement in that too, where life and death seem to exist in a tentative balance. Over the course of many years of traveling, I came to realize that the Earth is singing to us all the time, in a language that has no boundaries, with deep cultural and spiritual significance to each of us. A huge amount of information is transmitted in this way, and part of our evolution as a species is learning how to listen and understand these messages.

When I first started traveling as a musician, we toured in a 1973 van, the engine of which my brother and I rebuilt in our grandfather's garage. We put 50,000 miles on that van during my first two years of touring across the United States and Canada, and this eventually culminated in an extensive tour of Europe with a different van that had been converted from an old milk truck. Over the years I joined different bands and moved up to newer vans and eventually, modern air-conditioned tour buses. I took more transoceanic flights and slept in more hotel rooms than I can count (and I once slept outside on a fire escape in Philadelphia because of an all-night party that was keeping me awake). I can't say that it was a glamorous life because mostly it was just hard work, traveling through time and space for many years, just to play music for people. However, the most rewarding experiences I had were the incredible landscapes I saw, and the amazing people I met when we finally arrived at our destination.

I've heard it said countless times that the 22 hours a musician travels in a day is what we get paid for, and the two hours we play for an audience is what we give away. I totally agree with that sentiment, because music is a gift that needs to be shared and we all benefit from it. But it wasn't always touring that took me to the most interesting places; in fact, it was when I put on a backpack and started walking into a rainforest, a desert, or a city where I had never played a show that I had the most extraordinary experiences.

During these global travels I spent long periods of time in countries where I could immerse myself in the music and culture of the people I was visiting. All told, I've spent about 30 years studying and playing music around the world, and fortunately I wrote a huge number of letters, emails, and journal entries, which I draw upon for the stories in this book. I also use the word verse instead of chapter, as I think it's an interesting way to arrange these writings, like a long, global songline that circumnavigates the Earth. Each verse can stand as its own story, but I also think you'll find that each story connects to the next, as I look at the power of music, environment, community, culture, and spiritual understanding in each of these different places.

Needless to say, my adventures (and sometimes, misadventures) changed me deeply at a personal and spiritual level, and my hope is that you will find something revealing in these pages that inspires you in your own life. Perhaps you'll go to one of these countries, or maybe an entirely new place altogether and thus begin your own adventure. The most important thing I hope you'll take from these stories is the importance of our planet, her natural environments, her people, and how they shape our cultures, musics, and spiritual understandings. As they say, every journey begins with a first small step, and that is when you find the real journey is an internal one.

As I approach half a century of life on this planet, I often wonder what it is that my generation will leave behind besides mountains of garbage, oceans full of plastic, and a political and economic landscape that is dismal at best. When I look back at my grandfather's generation, the Greatest Generation as they were called, they left behind a world free from the tyranny of fascism. The next generation, the Baby Boomers, seem to have done quite well for themselves materially, but largely at the expense of the world's natural resources, which are quickly drying up and burning away. The two youngest generations, Generation X (my generation) and the Millennials, have been left with a landscape of industrial pollution, corrupt and predatory economic systems, ignoble politicians who only represent special interests, and an increasingly militarized society where a citizen is more likely to die at the hands of power than be protected by it. Yet despite all of this I have optimism, because there is music, beautiful music, everywhere.

Fortunately, the musicians of my generation cultivated the immense power of music and, combined with the digital revolution, we used both tools as social instruments to allow our voices to be heard around the world. I think that might be the greatest gift my generation could leave behind; our music and our social messaging, in addition to cleaning up a bit of the environmental, economic, and political waste we have been left with. There is also another very important part of this movement, and that is the preservation of our sacred, natural environments. Music is how I experienced the world's greatest landscapes at their deepest level, and that is a repeating theme throughout this book—the protection of our shared Earth.

If I were a farmer (perhaps the most noble of professions), I'd probably write a book about the different agricultural zones around the world. If I were a biologist, perhaps this book would be about wildlife habitats from the Amazon to the Arctic. But I'm a musician, and music is the thing I know best, so this book is about music and the people who make it, in several countries across six continents. These are their stories.

In one of the many Hindu creation myths, the Great Lord Shiva sits at the center of the universe in complete meditative bliss until he awakens and decides to Create. He strikes his Drum Of Creation and BOOM—the universe explodes into existence. It's the Big Bang, which physicists believe happened about 14 billion years ago, but a new theory suggest that there may have been countless previous Big Bangs, and infinitely more Big Bangs to come. They estimate that the universe might be closer to a trillion years old, or perhaps even, eternal. I like this idea, because if you think about all those Big Bangs happening over the course of eternity, its like the universe has a constant rhythm that has been going on—forever.

Perhaps because I'm a drummer by profession, I can understand this idea of an eternally, rhythmic cosmos. I feel rhythm in my body all the time, every day of my life, and I just take it for granted. I have also been fortunate to play with some of the best bands and singer-songwriters of my generation, and there's a very special relationship that exists between drummers and singers, which I learned about in West Africa. It is how drummers essentially represent the Earth, the foundation of life, and singers represent the voice, or the Spirit of the universe. The two need each other symbiotically in order to express themselves, and I've found this to be a great metaphor that has many parallels in this world, which I explore throughout this book.

I have also seen how music can forge incredibly strong communities, such as the Seattle music scene that I came from, as well as the way music enlightens and educates people about culture, social justice, and the evolution of human consciousness. I've come to believe, as many anthropologists and sociologists do, that music is actually a survival mechanism that brings us together and evolves us, just as it did in ancient history when we first began to organize ourselves into nomadic tribes. Through music we find validation within the communities we create; it's a kind of sonic fabric that wraps us up and keeps us warm around a collective, ancient fire that we periodically stoke with new ideas. It is music that keeps us alive, and it is most certainly where the idea of a nomadic band of musicians first came into existence—we took the music with us as we moved across the landscapes of the Earth.

Where did music come from in the first place? And how did we come to conceive of sequential rhythms and melodies that evolved into organized musical statements? We can imagine a bunch of prehistoric cave people clacking some old bones together and thus creating the first rhythmic sequences, rhythms that they might repeat every night. The human mind likes that sort of thing, the repetition of rhythm, and it becomes a familiar, comforting thing. But where does melody come from, or the more complex idea of creating musical instruments, with scales and sophisticated chord structures? How did we even come to conceive of the great Invisible Art of music?

One obvious theory comes from the birdcalls we heard as early humans, which influenced how our evolving minds and vocal chords might create melodies. Another theory is posited by Dr. Bernie Krause, who has an extraordinary story about this very subject in his book, The Great Animal Orchestra. In it, he recounts an experience he had with a Native American elder from the Nez Perce tribe in the state of Oregon, in the Pacific Northwest. There, near a frozen lake with an abundance of reeds along its banks, Dr. Krause and his companions heard an enormous howling sound, much like a gigantic pipe organ as he described it. It turns out that the sound was created by the wind blowing across the tops of the frozen, broken reeds along the banks of the lake, a sound that is much like blowing across an empty bottle, except in this case, amplified by thousands of reeds. The Nez Perce elder then cut a reed from the banks, bored some finger holes in it, and began to play a melody, showing Dr. Krause how Nature directly taught us the art of flute making. I'll explain this more in a later story about music in the Middle East, and how the sound of the reed flute is analogous to the spiritual evolution of man.

It turns out that the oldest known musical instrument that we know of is, in fact, a flute made of vulture bone (a reed flute just wouldn't last very long). This flute was made by a prehistoric Neanderthal musician and it was found buried in a German cave. It's been carbon dated to about 35,000 years old and it even has carved ornamentation around the finger holes. We know that human beings have been making music for at least that long, and likely much longer, starting with those first rudimentary sticks, stones, and bones, the human voice, and these primitive flutes.

In West Africa, they say the first holy trinity happened when we made drums by stretching animal hides (the animal kingdom) across hollow logs (the forest kingdom) and then man (the human kingdom) united all three by striking the drums. This evolution in instrument making would also create the first complex rhythms, songs, and dances, as well as the ceremonies we would celebrate with these new forms of expression. It is also said that the pursuit of musical wisdom over the course of one's life will result in the revelation of mystical truths. I wholeheartedly believe this to be true, and when we think about our 35,000-year-old flute maker, we can see that they took the art of music making very seriously indeed.

Humans have used music since our earliest ceremonies, for the changing of the seasons, for the harvest celebrations, for initiations, marriages, births, war, and especially death. These ceremonies helped us to create stronger, more stable communities and social order in a world that is generally unpredictable. I see this in my own life, where my best friends and musical collaborators were people I bonded with decades ago through the music that defined our generation. I have also come to realize that music is synonymous with intelligence, wellness, healing, and the foundation of strong spiritual communities. Musicians are some of the brightest, most intuitive people you will ever meet, and that's because they live and breathe within the sacred realm of sound, rhythm, and spirit.

You probably understand this already, where the music you loved as a young person brought you together with like-minded people who you might still be friends with today, or perhaps even married to. That's a beautiful thing, a musical community that you and your friends created through music and relationships, and it should be celebrated. Music has been the greatest transformative force in my life; it has alternately healed me, educated me, and allowed me to see much of this amazing world. It has also given me great insight into other cultures. For example, when I was doing anthropology fieldwork in the Peruvian Amazon, I worked with the indigenous Shipibo tribe, near the headwaters of the Amazon River. In their cosmology, every human being has a song that is unique to them, which they radiate out like a beacon to the world. This song determines everything about a person, from the way we speak, walk, work, dance, make love, interact with other people, and even the general disposition of our personality. The Shipibo shamans say that when a person becomes sick, it is because their song has been disrupted, which can usually be traced back to a specific, traumatic event. The song can be restored and healed with time and effort, and that role might be played by a parent, a friend, a teacher, a lover, or even a musician or band. Other times a shaman is needed to "re-sing" the song and heal the person of their psychic malady. I'll talk about that more later, but I think it's a very important way to start our journey—by thinking about how each of us has as an individual song that we project out into the world.

This is also why I believe we must honor the old indigenous traditions of the planet, whose cultures hold the oldest and highest forms of wisdom, much of which is contained in their music. I have learned through personal experience that wise action comes from listening to the indigenous caretakers of the Earth, those who have lived countless generations dedicated to its understanding and preservation. Their languages and songs contain information about the Earth's many environments, ecosystems, and all of life's complexities, long before it became scientific study. By learning from these people and their deep knowledge of the Earth, we can come to a deeper understanding of ourselves, our relationship with our different environments, and how we can exists in a state of balance with our planet.

We live in dynamic, transformative times; indeed these are revolutionary times. The Earth is in a terrible state of environmental destruction, the rainforests are burning, the coral reefs are bleaching out, and the oceans have been fished down to about 10 percent of their capacity. There are entire species of animals that could disappear within our lifetimes because someone wants to carve up the last elephant tusk.

At the same time, technology is outpacing every other form of industry and we are becoming more self-aware and informed about our shared Earthly existence. This is a great thing, and we can use that technology in a positive way. But we can't eat a software program, clothe ourselves in an app, or take shelter in a website. Technology is simply a tool for a higher means. The question is, what kinds of tools do we want to make, and how are we going to apply those tools so that we can protect our planet, preserve its multitude of cultures, and allow humanity to flourish in a state of balance with our Earth?

We can return to our daily routines in front of computers, inside fluorescent-lit cubicles, on the assembly lines of factories, in the classrooms, or perhaps in the forests and fields where life still grows. Our lives may have become more specialized and even isolating at times, but we must always remember our organic, elemental connection to one another and our shared Earth. Music is the best way for us to feel that connection, and for me, it all started in my little corner of the planet, way up here in the Pacific Northwest.

1. Barrett Martin Group "Calling The Spirits"

VERSE 1

SEATTLE: THE LEADEN SKIES OF GRUNGE

Thin Men on a Seattle rooftop, 1988. Left to right: Barrett Martin, Ben Floresca, Tom Gnoza, Pat Pedersen

"Do not pray for an easy life, pray for the strength to endure a difficult one."

—Bruce Lee

I have to acknowledge that my musical career would have had a much different trajectory if I hadn't had the good fortune of growing up in the Pacific Northwest, moving to Seattle right as a verdant music scene was just starting to grow. Dozens of books and countless newspaper and magazine articles have devoted their pages to the Seattle music scene, so my addition to the commentary is more of a personal one, the way I experienced it. By the time I arrived in Seattle in 1987, there had already been nearly a century of musical innovation going on in the Pacific Northwest. The alternative music revolution that I was a part of was just one style of music in a very long tradition of great music that has emanated from the forests, mountains, basements, and bars of this special place. It must also be said that this musical region is not just limited to Seattle, but extends from Vancouver, BC in the north, all the way south to Portland, Oregon in the south, and includes many smaller towns and communities in between. Music up here in the PNW is a way of life. We live and breathe it, and it defines our character in the most unique of ways.

It all started with the Coast Salish indigenous tribes, which are numerous and noted by the early pioneers for their drumming, dancing, and singing abilities. Much later, in the early 20th century, came the blues and jazz of the Mississippi Delta, which transplanted itself onto Jackson Street in downtown Seattle in the 1920s, 30s, and 40s. I've spent a fair amount of time in the Mississippi Delta and have noticed many similarities between the Delta and the Pacific Northwest. And perhaps that's why the working class roots of blues and jazz have always had such a strong hold up here. Because like the Mississippi Delta, Washington State has a huge river running through it, the Columbia River, which supports the agricultural and shipping economy between eastern and western Washington. And like the Delta region, the Northwest is peppered with small working class towns that survive on everything from farming, to forestry, to fishing, and the same small business that every little town has. I also think there's a natural salt-of-the-earth feeling that exists in both regions, where the people love the land, the waterways, and the natural habitats that exist in these places. As a result, very distinct styles of music have emerged in both the Delta and Washington state, and even if the branches of the tree have diverged, the roots go back to the same source—indigenous and African American music mixed with a working class ethos.

In the 1950s, rock & roll emerged here, there, and everywhere, almost simultaneously, followed by its various offshoots: garage rock, hard rock, punk, and grunge. Despite its geographical isolation, the Northwest has always been very hip to American musical trends, often being at the forefront. There's no real explanation for why the Northwest, and Seattle in particular, has created so many great musicians and bands over the decades, but I suspect it may be the combination of an educated and musically savvy population, a high literacy rate, and the sometimes-gloomy weather, which tends to make us hunker down and practice our music and songwriting skills.

The decade of the 1990s has been somewhat mislabeled as the grunge era, when in fact there were so many musical styles emerging at that time, it would be better to describe it as the "alternative decade." The grunge movement, like punk and hip hop before it, came out of a distinctive way of life that mirrored the blue-collar, working class culture of the Northwest. Grunge was about being an authentic human being as well as a musician, and like the blues, grunge was about wearing your work clothes on stage instead of the lace and spandex that was coming out of Los Angeles and all over MTV at the time. Grunge always had more in common with the working man than it ever did with Hollywood. It was a musical slap back, and our philosophy was that music was a form of community after a hard day's work, rather than a slick product of the corporate labels and MTV (although soon enough, we would find ourselves on corporate labels and MTV too).

Grunge was simply a localized extension of a musical ethos that had been building in the Northwest for decades, and by the early 1990s, it hit a nuclear moment. Even our workmen's attire of flannel and denim went from the construction site, to the clubs, and to the fashion houses of New York and Paris almost as fast as the music invaded the airwaves of radio.

I certainly don't claim to know the whole story of grunge, nor would I attempt an exhaustive history on it. I experienced a small slice of it, so my approach is to give my first-hand experience, being as accurate and faithful to the historical details as I possibly can. These stories will perhaps give an overall view of musical life in Seattle at the time, along with some important events that I was witness to. It started with my adolescence in Washington's capital city of Olympia, about an hour south of Seattle.

I was born in the old St. Peters hospital in Olympia in April of 1967, a few months shy of the Summer of Love. I lived the first year of my life in an Airstream trailer and in the tail sections of small airplanes, which my father and grandfather flew around as part of their jobs. This absolutely explains the wanderlust I developed as a young man, something I have never been able to shake off.

I was raised in a loving but strict, hard-working Irish American family that was peppered with musical and poetic talents amongst various relatives. Both sides of my family came from very modest means, but they all valued the importance of hard work, and if possible, a higher education. My father's father, Papa Amos, had been a mechanic for the local Bell telephone company, and although his formal education ended with trade school, he was well-read and loved to quote Socrates, Plato, Aristotle, and the Old Testament. I remember him being a voracious crossword puzzle solver, as he sat in his giant leather armchair after a hard day's work under the hoods of the Bell fleet. My grandmother Marjorie had been born in a hospital tent in a logging camp in the Ozark

Mountains of Arkansas before her family moved to Washington State to work in the forests of the timber-rich Olympic Peninsula. I suppose those genetic links to the American South would also explain a certain love I have always had for that part of the country.

My mother's side of the family were Irish immigrants who had been Midwestern farmers that lived in sod houses literally made of the Earth. That grandfather, Papa Dean, was of Cherokee Indian descent and he started a flying career shortly after his service in WWII, marrying my grandmother at the young age of seventeen. That grandmother, Mary Carol, was the matriarch of the family, and she was proud of the fact that she was a blood descendant of the American president John Adams, which made me a descendent too. She loved to quote writers like Walt Whitman, Mark Twain, and Robert Frost in between her lectures on moral and ethical responsibility. The Irish like to do that, mixing their poetics and moral platitudes, and that explains a lot about my family.

My entire extended family from both sides lived in Olympia, and it was a wonderful way to grow up having both sets of grandparents around. My dad, Brian, started out as a flight instructor with my grandfather's business, but he ended up joining an entirely new profession when he started working in the field of industrial explosives (which created huge debates when I became more of an environmentalist). My mom, Deana, was a homemaker initially and a superb cook, and she maintained two huge gardens on either side of our woodland home, the rows of which we weeded and maintained constantly.

At family gatherings we always played music around an old player piano that my dad had bought at a garage sale. It was from the late 1800s and this was really my first live music experience, a pedal pumped piano that played old-timey music from rolls of perforated paper that directed air from the billows to play the keys. My sister Amy pumped the pedals, I played along on my rickety old drum set (also from a garage sale), my brother Brandon played a trombone, and occasionally someone else would play a guitar or harmonica. Everyone sang along in unison to the words printed on the sheets of the piano roll paper as it rolled by.

During our high school years, I had friends from the jazz ensemble who would come by with their horns to play along with our trusty piano as we scrolled through songs from the ragtime, big band, swing, and show tune eras. We had a stereo and a turntable too, upon which my dad would spin Willie Nelson and other outlaw country artists, but we spent more time around that old player piano than anything else. When I write about it now, it sounds like something my great-grandparents would have done in the 1800s, and likely they did. But this was Olympia, Washington in the late 1970s and 80s, and since the Internet wouldn't exist for another 20 years, a good time at our house was just homemade food, live music, and the company of friends and neighbors who loved to come and sing classic songs at the Martin homestead.

The radio stations back then were still playing most of the popular music of the 60s and 70s on both the AM and FM channels, which was essentially the hits of Motown, Stax, and classic rock—basically music rooted in soul and the blues. New wave music, the later child of punk, was just starting to have success on the newly launched MTV. It was a fascinating and often amusing time to be absorbing music because it was so diverse. My first love was really jazz, largely because of that player piano and also because of a large collection of 78s that my grandparents had given me. It was all big band and swing music, the music of WWII America. It was also the music that we played in our junior high and high school jazz ensembles, and that was my initial love. But then my rock & roll aunt, Mary, gave me my first collection of inherited vinyl, which were classics like The Who's *Tommy*, Elton John's *Goodbye Yellow Brick Road*, some Rolling Stones, Beatles, and Bob Dylan albums, and a few others. The one I played the most was *Elvis' Greatest Hits*, and it was a cassette tape, which I played endlessly until the tape began to warble with magnetic fatigue. Elvis just did it for me.

Those rock albums changed everything and pretty quickly I realized that music was a whole bunch of other things I hadn't even thought about yet. I started to get really excited.

Around the same period of time I got my first job working for a local ranch owner building a new fence line, which involved stretching barbed wire nailed to postholes that we had dug and set by hand. It was hard, sweaty, dusty work, and I was only about 14 at the time, but it really helped to build my work ethic. My next job after that was a full-time job as a busboy at a local hotel called the Tyee Motor Inn. I would go to school in the mornings, and then straight to the Tyee afterwards where I would put in at least eight hours a day, and sometimes more. I liked the job mostly because of the people I worked with, but also because I liked the idea of a place where people came and went, from all over the country and the world.

I earned enough money from the busboy job that I was able to buy my first real professional drum set. It was a used, black Tama kit, made in Japan, and it came with a couple cymbals stands, a set of hi-hats, and a couple of old, tarnished Zildjian cymbals. I'd been playing that small, beat up, garage sale drum set for years, but this Tama kit was the real thing. I set about making a practice space for myself in the hayloft of our barn, and with a very basic turntable and a set of headphones, I would play along to my jazz and rock record collection.

As I got older and continued to buy LPs, my musical tastes expanded to include Led Zeppelin, Rush, and the Police, which were the bands who had the greatest rock drummers. I still loved the jazz because of the freedom and explosiveness in the playing, but rock and new wave started to influence my playing. I found all of it to be truly great music, so the genres were irrelevant. And I've found that by keeping an open mind it has allowed me to discover new forms of music over the course of my life. I think that's kind of what it's all about if you're a musician.

I played in the school bands all through primary, junior high, high school, and eventually college, but it was really my high school band director, Denny Womac, who inspired me to keep playing drums professionally. Mr. Womac had been a Marine, but he was also a superb trumpet and flugelhorn player who inspired his students by telling us funny, anecdotal stories while playing along with us in the jazz ensemble. It was a far more compelling way to teach music as opposed to yelling at us, as one might expect from a Marine. Instead, Mr. Womac inspired us with his kind example, which is of course, the best type of teacher. But he also made us work hard, and taught us to pay attention to the subtle details, which is the secret to excellent musicianship. We learned all the jazz classics, from the big band swing of Count Basie and Duke Ellington, to the bebop of Dizzy Gillespie and Charlie Parker, to the cool jazz of Miles Davis and John Coltrane, and even the fusion works of Chick Corea and Herbie Hancock, which was part of the still-evolving form of jazz at the time.

I also played upright and electric bass for the first two years of my high school jazz career because there was already a drummer seated in the band. I later switched to drums for my junior and senior years, and this is the accidental reason why I understand the art of the rhythm section as deeply as I do—that dual training on both drums and bass, which continued into college. The Tumwater Thunderbird High School

Jazz Ensemble was a very good jazz band indeed. We could sight-read music on the spot and play it very well—well enough that we were hired to play events all around the Northwest at local festivals and town events. In many ways the Thunderbird jazz band was my first real touring band, and I loved it when we went out on the road for a weekend of gigs. We got to eat in restaurants and stay in motel rooms, and I think that's probably when the road bug bit me.

There were also a few very powerful live performances that I saw in those impressionable high school years, the first and most memorable being when my friend and fellow jazz band trumpet player, Jim Lindgren (now a pediatrician), bought tickets for us to see Ray Charles at the Washington State Fair. I'm pretty sure we played a Ray Charles tune in our jazz repertoire, but seeing Ray live was an entirely different experience. Somehow our tickets put us in the front row, right in front of Ray's piano, and it was like getting a private performance from the great master himself. I can still see it in my mind's eye, Ray Charles swaying back and forth on his piano bench as he sang the great Hoagy Carmichael classic, "Georgia on My Mind."

Another great concert I witnessed was during the annual fundraiser for our jazz band, where we would promote a show with a national-level jazz artist and then keep the profits for our touring budget. During my senior year in 1985, we hired the Count Basie Big Band, but a week before the show, the Count took ill and had to cancel. In his stead he sent the great Cab Calloway to sing with his big band, which was actually an even bigger event. Cab was most famous for his role in the movie *The Blues Brothers*, where he sang his hit "Minnie the Moocher," and he sang it again perfectly that night with the Basie Big Band. After the show I got to meet and talk with Cab Calloway, and he was such a kind and elegant gentleman. It was like shaking hands with history.

I went off to college shortly after that, for two years of classical and jazz training at Western Washington University in Bellingham, about three hours north of Olympia. I had both a music and academic scholarship, but I still had to work at my hotel job during the holidays and summer breaks so I could earn a little spending money. I was also itching to see the world, so I signed up for a study abroad program in my sophomore year. During the summer before the trip, I worked two jobs: the late night shift at the hotel, and an early morning shift at the explosives factory where my father was now an executive. It was an intense summer, making explosives by day and clearing tables by night, and I think I only slept about two hours a night, which one can do when you're only 18 and about to fly to Europe for the first time.

By fall quarter of 1986, I was on a flight to Rome, the first foreign city that I had ever visited and the source of all Western civilization. It was perfectly poetic, and after a couple of weeks in Rome, Florence, Venice, and Milan, we drove north to England where our class settled in London. We were in a humanities program that focused on playwriting and theatrical performance, and there I saw dozens of plays and musical performances. One of the concerts that stood out as a life-changing moment was when I saw the legendary Spanish guitarist, Andrés Segovia, perform at the equally legendary Royal Albert Hall. I went with another American student who I had a crush on and who later became my girlfriend for a time, and we sat just a few rows back from the great master himself. Segovia was 93 years old at the time of that concert and he played for a very long time with no microphone on his guitar, all-acoustic, just as it would have been a century earlier. You could have heard a pin drop in the Royal Albert Hall, which held more than 5,000 people and was completely sold out, but it was utterly silent as Segovia played his exquisite guitar. Again, it was like experiencing history.

Seeing and hearing Segovia play his guitar was about the third time I had seen a true master perform his art, and that deeply changed me. I was only 19, but from then onward I had an extremely high bar of what I thought true musical excellence was. It wasn't just about music or fame, it was about looking for excellence in any art form.

A few weeks later our class moved north to Stratford-upon-Avon for the opening of the annual Shakespeare festival. There I saw a young Jeremy Irons in the role of King Leontes in Shakespeare's "The Winter's Tale." Irons is a master actor now, but when I saw him in 1986, he was only 38 and still making his bones. I also saw the force-of-nature actor Anthony Hopkins in the lead role of "Pravda," about a South African newspaper magnate roughly based on the archetype of William Randolph Hearst. Hopkins was 49 at the time, and still hadn't really become the Hollywood star he is today.

These musicians and actors were masters in the making, and you could see from their stage presence that they had an entirely different quality than most performers. Since then, I've come to realize how rare the *right stuff* actually is, especially in the 21st century where cheap fame and celebrity is deemed more important than supreme skill and the desire to master an art. But fake celebrity doesn't last very long, and the real masters eventually have their names inscribed in books, on sheet music, in films, and the recorded mediums. They eventually become immortal.

Seeing masters like Ray Charles, Cab Calloway, Andrés Segovia, Jeremy Irons, and Anthony Hopkins affected me deeply, especially because I wanted to be an artist too. And when one sees true mastery, in any form, it's both humbling and inspiring because it sets a new standard of how good you have to be to be among the best. Later in my musical career I would witness other masters such as Johnny Cash, the Pakistani singer Nusrat Fateh Ali Khan, and the Indian sitar master Ravi Shankar. So when I go out to see a show featuring a young artist who is just starting their career, I always look for the *right stuff* and remind myself that I might be watching history again.

After completing two years of college in sleepy Bellingham, WA, I wanted to move to the big city of Seattle. I got accepted at the University Of Washington and transferred there in the summer of 1987. Call it fate or bad luck, but because of my status as a transfer student, I wasn't able to get any of the classes I needed to stay in the music program. It was as if formal music training was shutting me out, making a decision for me that I hadn't been able to make for myself. Thus, I decided to take a year off to just work and reassess my academic strategy. That year became a 15-year hiatus from academia where music would show me much of the world.

Living in Seattle in 1987 was an exciting time for a 21-year-old musician. I can attest that Seattle was not the hipster-dwelling, tech-driven, micro-brewed, coffee-infused, gentrified city that it has become today. Back in the 1980s and 90s, Seattle was a gritty town where the biggest industries were Boeing, Weyerhaeuser Lumber, and the commercial fishing fleet. Microsoft was just getting started, and I used to get my coffee at the very first Starbucks shop in the Pike Place Market. It wasn't a boomtown by any stretch.

Seattle is a big college town, however, with several universities and community colleges in a relatively small area, so our city has a very educated, literate, music-loving, artistic community that proved to be very supportive of the music that was emerging in the late 1980s.

This was, and still is, the greatest strength of the original Seattleite - our support of the local community, its music, and the creative class in general.

Around the same time, the last glimmering waves of punk were still rippling in cities around the United States, and they too were issuing an amplified call to attention. Just south of Seattle was San Francisco and its label Alternative Tentacles, which gave us the psychedelic experimentations of the Butthole Surfers, as well as the sarcastic punk of the Dead Kennedys. The Los Angeles punk scene had its own label, SST Records based in Long Beach, and they gave us the primal rage of Black Flag, the jazz punk of the Minutemen, the angular pop of the Meat Puppets, the psychedelic rock of Screaming Trees, the wall of noise Sonic Youth, and the deafening roar of Soundgarden.

Then there was Twin/Tone Records in Minneapolis, which was kind of a sister city to Seattle with a like-minded rust belt attitude. Twin/Tone gave us the disheveled beauty of the Replacements, the jagged pop of Soul Asylum, the sonic industrialism of Hüsker Dü, and one of the greatest all-girl bands, Babes In Toyland. Farther east was Chicago and its unique brand of industrial music, which gave us the label Touch and Go and Steve Albini's eardrum-bursting Big Black, the art punk of Scratch Acid, and its later incarnation, The Jesus Lizard.

All the way east in Boston came the indie pop of Galaxie 500, the slacker rock of Dinosaur Jr., and one of the most influential bands of the time, the Pixies, whose sound was a unique blend of punk, pop, and a primordial rage that nodded at grunge before the term had been coined.

Moving south to Washington, D.C. was another vibrant music scene with Dischord Records giving us the hardcore pioneers Minor Threat, and its later incarnation Fugazi. Farther down the east coast was a little scene in Chapel Hill, NC that gave us Superchunk and the extraordinarily successful label they started, Merge Records, which went on to release many important albums of that time. Exactly opposite of Seattle, in the far southeast corner of the country was Athens, GA, one of the earliest indie music scenes in America. Athens gave us Pylon, the B-52s, and the legendary R.E.M., who played house parties in that picturesque college town until their success went global. Peter Buck, the founding guitarist of R.E.M., would later move to Seattle during our own emerging scene, where he befriended me and became a collaborator on multiple albums.

By 1987-88 Seattle was finally reaching its own tipping point, taking its turn in the spotlight of American indie rock. Many of us remember those last couple years of the 1980s as being perhaps the most exciting time of all. But back in 1987, I was a college dropout with no formal training in anything other than music, and even that had been truncated by academic bureaucracy. I found myself working in construction where I worked on houses for $6.00 an hour, and I lived in an unheated warehouse loft in the International District that cost $250 a month. But at least I could practice my drums in my studio loft and live rather cheaply. I didn't really drink and I never used drugs, so my greatest indulgence was taking Kung Fu classes from a Chinese master who had a school in Chinatown, a short walk down the hill from my loft. I would practice Kung Fu in the evenings after work, eat a cheap meal at one of the Vietnamese, Chinese, or Japanese restaurants in the neighborhood, and then walk back home to practice my drums. It was a simple, focused period in my life where I worked hard to hone my drumming skills, and even with no money and no central heat, it was one of the most wonderful times in my life. I loved every hungry, chilly bit of it because I was finally in the heart of Seattle, playing my drums, even if I didn't have a band yet.

I've heard it said that because of the gray, rainy months of Seattle's fall and winter (and sometimes spring and summer), that people tend to stay indoors, read a lot of books, and of course play music. There's certainly a lot of truth in that, but we also spend a fair bit of time in the great outdoors. I grew up that way, and so did many of my musical friends. We connect to the natural beauty of the landscape and it influences our creativity, even if the music we write tends to be dark and loud. Sometimes that's exactly the mood up here. We also spend a great deal of time in our basements, garages, and home studios working out these new musical ideas, and then we bring them forth when they're ready for presentation. Indeed, this musical pattern in Seattle has been happening for about a hundred years now.

It started with the Jackson Street blues and jazz scene in downtown Seattle in the early 1920s and went up through the decades until we had global jazz stars like the singer Ernestine Anderson, the producer Quincy Jones, and the great soul man himself, Ray Charles; the latter two were once roommates in our fair city. By the 1960s garage rock began to emerge, spearheaded by local band The Sonics, a hugely influential band on the early grunge bands. Other Northwest bands like the Kingsmen, Paul Revere & the Raiders, and the Ventures had very high levels of national and international success. Seattle was also the birthplace of Jimi Hendrix, who in the late 1960s moved to London and gave us his own brand of virtuosic, psychedelic rock. The 1970s gave us the beloved Wilson sisters and their band Heart, which blended beautiful vocal harmonies with classic rock songs.

I should also mention that Bruce Lee, the great martial artist and filmmaker, lived in Seattle and attended the University of Washington in the early 1960s before his film career took off. And although his specialty was Kung Fu, there's something very indie rock about Bruce Lee that makes us all proud that he spent time in our city. I think it's because Bruce Lee thought up an original idea, he made his first movies independently like a true punk rocker, and then he took it out to the world and had great success. He was another of those Great Masters, both in his spiritual understanding and in his Kung Fu bad-assery, and that's why we think of Bruce Lee so fondly up here.

The musical explosion that happened around the United States in the late 1980s was the result of a deeply disillusioned Generation X who had grown up in a failing economic system that didn't offer much hope for a young person. As we were growing up in the 1970s, the U.S. was in a period of successive recessions, and by the 1980s we were being spoon-fed the nonsense of trickle-down economics, also known as Reaganomics. We were told that by giving money back to the wealthy, it would trickle down to the common folks and bring the U.S. back into prosperity. Except magic doesn't work in economics, and the wealth stayed at the top, just as it is to this day. All we really had back then was our music.

The rumblings of grunge were just starting to be heard in the clubs and house parties around Seattle and the music had a loud, dark, explosive quality that sounded very different from anything I had heard before. It really was music that mirrored the gray, gritty environment of Seattle at the time, because a city is really just a forest of concrete, brick, and steel with a lot of different people living inside. Grunge reflected that environment, as a mixture of punk, hard rock, and perhaps most importantly, attitude. MTV had only been around for a few years at that point, but I rarely watched TV because I didn't own one, and I rarely watch TV even today. It seems like a big waste of time if you're devoting your life to an active art form. What Seattle did have, and still does, was one of the greatest independent radio stations in the country. KCMU, now known as KEXP, was playing anything and everything that was cool and independent from around the world, and they were also starting to play the music of the local Seattle bands. Many of these bands were also jockeying to be on a local upstart label founded around the same time.

Sub Pop was started in 1987 by Jonathan Poneman and Bruce Pavitt, and was named after an indie music column that Bruce had been writing while he attended the Evergreen State College down in my hometown of Olympia. Sub Pop's earliest releases include vinyl singles, EPs, and LPs from bands like Green River, Mudhoney, Soundgarden, TAD and, most famously, Nirvana. There were also a huge number of bands that were part of the now legendary Sub Pop Singles Club, which offered limited edition 45s from the latest indie bands. The first Sub Pop songs I remember hearing on the airwaves of KCMU were Soundgarden's first single "Hunted Down," and Mudhoney's first single "Touch Me I'm Sick." I was hooked.

If you ordered a Sub Pop single in the years between 1989-90, it very well could have been me who stuffed the 45 into the envelope you received in the mail. That's because I had befriended Sub Pop's house producer Jack Endino, and Sub Pop's director of marketing Daniel House, both of whom played in the proto-grunge band Skin Yard. As a result of these new friendships, I hung out at the Sub Pop offices from time to time and was welcomed as another local musician who was willing to help out. I never made a single dollar working for Sub Pop because they paid us with vinyl, the tender of the day. But it sure was fun to go down to the offices on 1st Avenue in downtown Seattle and help where needed. Bruce would come through the offices and round up all the hangers-on and march us down to the mailroom for the latest round of envelope stuffing. I'd leave with vinyl copies of everything we'd just mailed and it was exciting to be part of something like that, which is probably why I still love doing the press mailings for the label I started many years later. There's just something exciting about sending new music out into the world—you know you're making a difference.

The funny thing is, to this very day, and after all the bands I've been in and albums I've produced, I have never appeared on a single Sub Pop recording. The mailroom was my highest achievement there.

Around 1988, Sub Pop started putting on these little showcases at the Vogue nightclub, just down from the Sub Pop offices on 1st Avenue.

It was a grimy little hole-in-the-wall, but every Tuesday and Wednesday night you could go down to the Vogue and for a $2.00 cover charge you could see a couple of the latest Sub Pop bands, or at least the ones trying to get signed to Sub Pop. I would walk a couple miles from my loft on Jackson Street down to the Vogue, and everyone in the music scene would be there, drinking and smoking and waiting for the bands to begin.

The music was loud, the drums thunderous, and there was a tendency for the guitarists to tune their guitars in a "drop D" tuning, a technique made famous by Soundgarden's Kim Thayil. This gave the guitarists the ability to play chords that were darker and heavier, and actually, quite bluesy. The drummers played heavy and rather simply, sometimes with a tom-tom groove in the beat, a technique that Matt Cameron from Soundgarden, Dan Peters from Mudhoney, and I used in our respective rock bands. The vocalists in these early bands screamed as much as they sang, because grunge was rooted in garage and punk and heavily influenced by early 70s American bands like the Stooges and the MC5—bands with rather famous scream-singers.

At those early Seattle shows the people (and frequently the beer) would be flying around the room as soon as the first song began. This was the beginning of what would become the "mosh pit" and its corollary, "crowd surfing." Of course everyone smoked cigarettes back then, so you usually had a beer in one hand, a cigarette in the other, and you were watching a very cool band who, in a couple of years, might very likely end up on the Billboard charts (although no one knew it at the time).

Between the Vogue and a handful of other clubs around Seattle like the Central Tavern, Squid Row, and new places that seemed to pop up overnight, you could pretty much see all the bands that mattered in Seattle on a weekly basis. I remember seeing one of the first Mudhoney shows at the Vogue, an early TAD show at the Fenix Underground, as well as the awesome and legendary double bill of Soundgarden and Screaming Trees at the Central Tavern. There were countless shows, and it wasn't uncommon to go out and see three or four shows a week. There was no Internet, no smartphones, and most people only had an answering machine. And because there was no Internet, you couldn't prejudge a band based on their Facebook likes or by downloading their album for free. Back then you had to show up, in person, and you had to represent yourself, your band, and support your local music scene. There was almost a code of honor that you had to be at these shows, you had to show that you cared. Often you met your best friends at these shows, your girlfriends, and sometimes your future spouse. It was a very special time to be young, and the music had a special power over us because it happened in real time, with real people.

During those early years, a few of the Sub Pop bands were starting to go out on American tours, and even European tours, such as the now-legendary TAD/Nirvana European tour of 1989, something that was a huge achievement for an indie band at that time. Prior to this, the Seattle bands had only been playing regional clubs up and down the West Coast and occasionally going over to the East Coast, so to play music outside of the country seemed rather exotic, especially when you considered the geographic isolation of the Pacific Northwest.

My very first band was a kind of British-styled punk band that was more in the vein of the Clash and the Damned than what the early grunge bands sounded like. We were called Thin Men (because we were tall and skinny) and it consisted of me on drums, Pat Pederson on bass, and Ben Floresca and Tom Gnoza on dueling guitars and vocal duties. It was a high-energy punk band with good songs but we just couldn't catch a break in grungy Seattle. I mean, we had a following, but we didn't look or sound anything close to grunge. Some would say that's the coolest kind of band to be because we weren't following trends, but the flip side was we had a hard time getting gigs, which is what a band really needs in order to function. We had just released a cassette-only album with the independent label Ensign Records titled, *A Round Hear* (a clever title except that cassettes are rectangular). Still, we couldn't get a gig at the Vogue or the Central because of our "un-grunginess." I remember walking into the office of the Vogue's booking agent to try and get us a gig. I was wearing one of those brand new, crisp Levi's denim trucker jackets, the mainstay of the modern hipster. Except back then it wasn't hip yet, it was just a new denim jacket and it certainly wasn't grungy. The agent just looked me up and down when I handed him our tape and said with a smirk, "Nice denim."

A week later I was wearing a leather jacket that I had bought off the street in the famous leather market of Florence, Italy, when I had been there as a college student in 1986. It was a very Italian cut, with ridiculous zippers that went at an angle across the front of the jacket, and unnecessary shoulder pads sewn inside the jacket. It wasn't grungy at all, but I liked it because it was my souvenir from Italy and it seemed more punk than anything else. One night I was at the Vogue watching a band when Mark Arm of Mudhoney, who I had not met yet but was standing next to me, said mockingly, "Nice shoulder pads." I tried to ignore the slight and I slowly walked to the men's room where I took off the jacket and ripped out the shoulder pads, disposing of them in the garbage can. Knowing Mark Arm now for many years, I told him the story and we both had a good laugh. But back in 1989, I apparently could not find the right jacket.

Later that same year, Thin Men finally recorded a single with Sub Pop producer Jack Endino. Jack became one of my best friends and my first real mentor. He's a man of deep wisdom and great mystical importance to all of the great Seattle bands. But back in 1989, I just wanted Jack to produce Thin Men and make us cool, so we spent one long day and night at his studio, the legendary Reciprocal Studios, where every Sub Pop band had recorded, including Nirvana when they made the *Bleach* album. We emerged with three very good songs, but we never found a label to release them. They remained hidden in Ben Floresca's closet, that is, until we decided to release the best song on the soundtrack to this book, almost 30 years later.

Shortly after we recorded the unreleased songs with Jack, the band started to fracture, we began to bicker, and as a result I decided to leave Thin Men. The band continued on with a new drummer for another couple years, but I found myself bandless. However, Jack invited me to play drums on his new solo album, which he was calling *Endino's Earthworm*, and I happily agreed.

Jack is one of those guys who takes every project he does seriously, no matter the budget. He gives an enormous amount of attention to the details, which I later learned as a producer is where the true greatness of a musician emerges. Jack is like a Zen master of recording, his fingers on the controls, and his boots firmly on the ground. Whether you're an unknown band or a band with some amount of success, he gives you the same effort and dedication. Just being around that kind of energy makes you play better, makes you think about your music in depth, and it kind of sharpens the spear point of the musical statement you want to make. Ask anyone who has ever worked with Jack Endino and you'll get the same story: great effort, impeccable work ethic, and honesty in his assessment of you. You leave his studio with a sense of heightened awareness about music, artistic achievement, and a little bit about the meaning of life. They call him the Godfather of Grunge for a reason— he was the main architect.

And that's when my musical life really started to get interesting.

2. Thin Men "Loneliness Is..."

VERSE 2

DIY: FOUR DUDES, A VAN, AND A SPARE FAN BELT

Skin Yard in Europe, fall 1991. Left to right: Barrett Martin, Ben McMillan, Jack Endino, Pat Pedersen.

"Music is a pure expression of the life force itself. To me, good music is organic, not mathematical. It twitches, it breathes, it can't be reduced to equations, or pinned to a grid like so many dead butterflies. Any production technique that reduces the organic nature of the music is, to me, anti-life."

—Jack Endino

When I first started working with Jack Endino in 1989, he had already produced the first singles and LPs for Soundgarden, Green River, Mudhoney, TAD, and Nirvana, as well as most of the Sub Pop Singles Club. He'd made three albums with his own band Skin Yard, toured most of the U.S. and Canada, and released one solo album. Jack was extremely productive and efficient, as he still is, and in 1989 he was riding the wave of all those productions. He was considered to be one of the most original producers in alternative music at the time, and when he asked me to play drums on his next solo album I was honored. Although he liked my musical instincts, he did not like my drum technique.

I had been playing with a jazz (traditional) grip on my drumsticks since as far back as I could remember, which allows for great speed but not as much in volume. Jack wanted the speed and chops of my playing, but with a much louder delivery. I remember his first words of advice to me over the phone, and it was like a prophet when he first hears the words of his god: "You better learn how to hit harder if you're going to play this kind of music." And so I did. I switched to matched grip and started hitting the drums decidedly harder forever after that. That was the conversation that changed me from a music school drummer into a rock drummer.

We started rehearsing Jack's new songs in the basement of his University District house in north Seattle. It was right across the street from Roosevelt High School, where Duff McKagan of Guns & Roses, and Pearl Jam's Mike McCready, and Stone Gossard went to school together. Jack's solo band was a simple power trio with me on drums, Jack on guitar and vocals, and Coffin Break's Rob Skinner on bass. I'd known Rob since the Thin Men days, we had played some shows together, and thus began a friendship between the three of us.

The new trio was a pretty killer band I have to say, naturally intuitive, powerful, and highly original. We entered Reciprocal Studios once again and recorded what became Jack's second solo album, *Endino's Earthworm*. Jack suggested that we debut our band at the Vogue and play all these new songs, which of course thrilled me to finally play the club that had eluded me for so long. On Wednesday April 25th, 1990, shortly after my 23rd birthday, we made our debut at the Vogue as *Endino's Earthworm*. Rob couldn't make the gig for some reason, so we had Daniel House of Skin Yard subbing on bass. We opened for the crushingly heavy band The Melvins, who were definitely the heaviest band in the Northwest, and possibly the entire world. I count that show as my first real grunge appearance; it was my coming out, my debutante introduction to the larger Seattle music scene.

The most important thing about that show was getting to play with both Jack and Daniel, who were the founders of Skin Yard. That accidental alignment led to an entirely new thing that would emerge in the coming months. But what I also remember from that show, besides the raucous, roaring audience, was a warm and friendly greeting from Dan Peters, the drummer for Mudhoney. Dan is a wonderful drummer, a father, and he's kind of the official mascot of what Seattle grunge really stood for. He is everyone's indie rock hero, and he propelled Mudhoney to global stardom and kept his character intact.

Dan came up to me after the show, and with a beer in one hand and a handshake in the other he said, "I'm Dan Peters from Mudhoney. Nice drumming there mister, glad to meet ya!" That was the moment when I felt like I was really part of a community, something that was substantial and important. And second only to Jack, Dan Peters was one of the first people to recognize my drumming and make an effort to befriend me. We've remained friends ever since, and we even played together as a rhythm section once—I on upright bass and he on drums when we backed up Mark Lanegan opening for Johnny Cash at a couple shows in Seattle and Portland.

Here is a real example of the theory of relativity, and how relative life can be. I was only 23 years old and for me the biggest musical achievement I could think of was playing a show at the Vogue on a Wednesday night. Shortly after that, the road would beckon me and I was more than eager to answer the call. But in that moment I was just happy to be playing a rock show at the center of my musical universe.

A few months later, Jack and Daniel asked me to join Skin Yard, which was one of the most respected bands in Seattle at that time. Originally formed in 1985, they had already made three albums and Matt Cameron, who later became the drummer for Soundgarden and Pearl Jam, had been their first drummer. They had gone through two or three other prominent local drummers before I got the invitation, so I had some big shoes to fill. Jack, Daniel, lead singer Ben McMillan, and I began rehearsing at my loft on Jackson Street where we essentially wrote and arranged the songs that would become the band's fourth album, *1000 Smiling Knuckles.*

We recorded the album in the winter of 1990-91, again at Reciprocal Studios. This time it was a16 track tape machine, instead of the old 8-track machine we had used for the unreleased Thin Men single. It was only the third time I had recorded in that studio, but I was beginning to feel comfortable with setting up my drums and recording an album of a dozen songs. If my memory serves me correctly, we recorded the basic rhythm tracks to *Knuckles* in just two days. Ben would do his vocals after we had done all the drums, bass, and rhythm guitars, and then Jack would sit with the tapes into the wee hours of the night adding guitar solos and his very unique sounds for just the right atmosphere. Then he would begin mixing the songs, giving us cassette tapes of the mixes for our comments, approval, (and sometimes disapproval), until he got it just right. It was a pretty seamless process, and when the album was finally mixed and mastered, we knew we had a very special piece of music on our hands.

1000 Smiling Knuckles was released worldwide on August 6th, 1991 on Cruz Records, which was a new label started by SST Records founder, Greg Ginn. Greg had also been the guitarist for hardcore legends Black Flag, and SST was already a revered record label because of all the amazing albums that they had released. It all felt rather surreal to have my first real album released by such a label and the album was hailed by critics and fans alike as a milestone in Seattle music. It quickly rose to the top of the College Music Journal (CMJ) music chart, which at the time was the most important chart for indie records.

Our booking agent, Ellen Stewart, worked out of the Twin/Tone record label offices in Minneapolis, and she had been booking short little mini-tours for the band throughout 1990 and into 1991. Now she began to book a large tour in support of *Knuckles* that would take Skin Yard all around the U.S. and Canada. The band had a 1973 Dodge Sportsman, the engine of which had blown before I joined the band. The van had been previously owned by a church and was painted school-bus yellow with a black stripe down the side, which only added to the absurd appearance of the thing. The band was convinced it needed to be exorcised.

My brother Brandon and I rebuilt and re-installed the van's engine, and I swear this to be true: when Skin Yard finally went back out on the road to start playing shows again, we put another 50,000 miles on that van over the course of two years of touring between 1990-91. The engine and transmission never failed us, it never leaked oil, and the only break down that ever happened was a thrown fan belt, which I replaced by the side of the road. I attribute most of this good luck to my brother's superb mechanic skills and the fact that he had spent his teenage years rebuilding and restoring classic cars. I also know that every road-worthy indie band usually has a great musician/mechanic, and that's why they arrive, safely, in your town on a regular basis.

It's hard to explain the mysterious pull of the road, traveling fast and light around the country like that. It's literally intoxicating, and anyone who longs for road trips knows exactly what I mean. The idea of leaving your stationary position in life and getting into a rolling, mechanical vehicle that moves you through time and space across the landscapes of the Earth is an experience that, once it hooks you, never really lets you go. I think that's half the reason why we became touring musicians in the first place—the road can be hard, but it changes your soul at an atomic level.

Skin Yard made multiple runs on various legs of our tour and that usually took us through one of two routes: either down the West Coast and across the Deep South, or due east, straight into the American heartland and all the way to the East Coast. Back then, and before smartphones or GPS, our cross-country navigating was done with paper road maps and a Rand McNally Road Atlas. Usually the guy riding shotgun would call out the major changes in the route, when you had to get on a freeway or take a certain exit. By the way, the reason that front passenger seat is called shotgun, is because back in the days of the stagecoaches, the guy riding next to the horseman/driver carried a shotgun to ward off any potential attackers. Given some of the areas we drove through back then, that story made a lot sense.

I loved to drive and I preferred to drink coffee after a show rather than alcohol, so I did most of the driving on that tour. A lot of it was just dead reckoning and kind of knowing where we were and how many miles the odometer read. I've had people tell me many times over the years that I have an internal compass, and I swear it developed from all the roadwork I did back then.

For phone calls we had another method that seems so ancient now. We had to take several rolls of quarters, which we stashed in the glove box, so we could make calls from the various payphones we would find along the way. Now they're virtually nonexistent, and it's kitsch to even have one. We'd call the club we were playing when we were a few hours outside of town, just to get the final directions, and to reassure the promoter that we were indeed on our way to the club. I made these calls frequently, literally from the side of a road in the middle of a cornfield or desert, scribbling out the final directions on a legal notepad I always kept handy. To this day, I still carry yellow legal notepads with me in my backpack. It's the greatest way to organize my creative ideas.

But it was the rolling landscapes of America that always captured my soul.

If we were driving down the Pacific Coast, that meant we'd eventually get to cut across the Mojave Desert east of Los Angeles and drive through vast desert landscapes filled with Joshua trees and Ocotillo cactus. If there had been a thunderstorm, you could smell the natural creosote of the desert after the rain, one of the most extraordinary and unforgettable smells on the natural Earth. We'd then traverse the great Southwest, perhaps stopping at the Grand Canyon for one of the greatest vistas on the planet. The first time I saw it was by the light of a full moon, as we drove south from Utah into northern Arizona. We took the North Rim route, which is the least-traveled road, and the canyon emerged in front of us in the haunting glow of a full moon. We'd then cross into New Mexico, one of the most extraordinarily beautiful places I've ever seen (I'd later live there for a stretch), and then we'd cross over the Rio Grande before traversing the Great Plains of Texas, and then on into the fertile Mississippi Delta where, over the years, I discovered a great truth about how the landscape directly influences the music.

Across the country we continued, through the deep and mystical South, home to some of America's greatest writers and musicians, and I came to understand why they were so brilliant in their use of language. They lived and breathed the landscape and it went straight into their art. At some point we'd start moving up the East Coast, but if we had started our tour using the more northern route, we would have an entirely different landscape experience.

Heading due east out of Seattle, we'd cross the gigantic Rocky Mountains before descending down into the mysterious Badlands of the Dakotas. This was where, back in the late1800s, the great Lakota warrior Crazy Horse climbed Bear Butte for his vision quest on how to defeat the U.S. Cavalry. After those visions, Crazy Horse defeated the Cavalry every single time, on the battlefield and on the moral high ground. He never once lost an engagement, and he later became an inspiration for many soldiers in the American Armed Forces. I've always loved stories like that, about how great people come out of the landscape and go on to change history.

As we continued east, we eventually would reach the Great Lakes, and I realize why so many westward pioneers thought it was the Pacific Ocean when they arrived there, the lakes taking up the entire horizon. After driving through the last of the endless corn and wheat fields that permeate the midwest and near east, we'd finally arrive on the outskirts of New York City, where we'd see that famous skyline starting to emerge on the horizon, poking into the sky above. And when we finally arrived in that iconic city and remembered that we got there on eight cylinders, a lot of coffee, and sheer will, it changes how you think of yourself as a traveler, and as an American.

On that almost two-year North American tour, and despite the critical acclaim of our album, there were shows where only 20 people showed up. Those were usually in the small towns of the central U.S. and the more remote parts of Canada. Other shows, usually in the biggest cities, were sold out with a few hundred people in attendance. But at every show we played, whether for 20 or 200, we played the best show we could.

Most of these gigs were promoted by young college kids about our same age who loved indie rock, punk, and grunge, and that's how we met so many cool and interesting young people along the way, some of whom I'm still friends with to this day. We knew many of them by just their nicknames, guys like "Brubaker" who lived behind razor wire in an unheated warehouse in the roughest part of South Philadelphia, but always greeted us warmly with "Welcome to Philadelphia, boys!" The first time I met Brubaker, there was a huge puddle of blood on the concrete entryway of his building where an intruder had become entangled in the razor wire above, and Brubaker had beat him back to the street with a baseball bat. That was home security in South Philly back then, and I expect, might still be today.

And then there was "Sluggo," who managed to get one of those amazing Victorian houses in San Francisco when they were cheap and always opened his home to us every time we played the Bay Area. Speaking of which, there was one night in San Francisco that I will never forget, and it is of some historical importance.

It was the summer of 1990, a year before *Knuckles* had even been recorded, and Skin Yard was booked to play a show at the I-Beam on Haight Street in San Francisco. The I-Beam was a well-known spot for indie rock and we had arrived a day early for a night off in the city. Somehow Jack had gotten a message from Kurt Cobain and Krist Novoselic of Nirvana, who were also in town, and they wanted to meet up at the I-Beam that same night to see a band. We arrived at the club about the same time Kurt and Krist did and the band they wanted to see was already on stage when we arrived. The band was called Scream, they were from Washington, D.C., and their drummer was a very young Dave Grohl. Dave was absolutely pummeling his drums like a punk rock John Bonham with more enthusiasm than any drummer I had ever seen. I was standing next to Krist and he told me that they were considering Dave for Nirvana. I told Krist, or rather, I yelled into his ear, "Man, you better get that guy in your band before someone else does!"

Back on the road we went, sometimes playing shows just to earn a little gas money. We'd sleep in our sleeping bags on the floors of our friend's apartments, but we'd always go for a hot breakfast in the morning before we'd hit the road again. Every college radio DJ who played our album, or club owner that promoted one of our shows—almost every one of them opened their homes and apartments to us. We were all part of an indie rock society that had an unspoken understanding that what we were doing together was right and true, almost a holy mission. It was certainly the most important single focus in our lives. These folks were some of the finest people I ever met and they would give us their own beds or at least their floors without a second thought. It was like a secret network that was known only to us.

Many years and many tours later, I've driven across the United States and Canada more times than I can count. Some of it was in vans where I was the driver, sometimes it was a tour bus, and other times it was just me and my own car or motorcycle, headed out on the road to some musical destination. I've driven across every state in the union, including Alaska and Hawaii. I've played shows in every major city and most of the smaller ones, and I've met people from every walk of life, from the most religiously conservative, to the most libertine and adventurous. I've eaten countless meals with people I will never see again, had extended conversations that challenged my own beliefs, and I can truly say that the road has changed me more than any other single thing. For the most part, I've found Americans and Canadians to be some of the most polite and good-hearted people on the planet. We come from different states and often very different political beliefs, but we all share the North American continent, a place that is so strikingly beautiful it can still take your breath away.

I highly recommend that everyone take at least one long road trip in your lifetime. Drive across this magnificent land, see the beauty of its landscapes, the national parks, and come to understand the depth and soul of the people. Put aside your political and religious beliefs and go to places you normally wouldn't go, and you'll be amazed and awakened by what you will see and the people you will meet. It'll hook you the moment the rubber meets the road.

Believe it or not, in those 50,000 miles of driving between 1990-91, Skin Yard only missed one show—in Fargo, North Dakota. And the only reason we missed it was because we had to have the U-joints replaced in Wisconsin Dells, a rather bizarre carnival town much like Coney Island but in the middle of Wisconsin. We noticed that the driveline had started to vibrate severely, shaking the van terribly, and if it had dropped into the asphalt, it would have pole-vaulted our van end over end. We had no choice but to stop for repairs and those repairs threw us off by one day of driving and there was just no way we could make it to Fargo in time for the show. I had to make the call to the distraught promoter, who kept saying, "No, no, no, please don't cancel on us!" It was like a felony offense to cancel a show back then; we all worked too hard to allow that. But the reality in this case was that we physically couldn't get there in time and it was better to cancel the show the day before, rather than not show up and leave everyone hanging. It's funny the things you remember and the things you forget in life, but cancelling a show is certainly one of the things I'll never forget. So for all of you in Fargo, North Dakota who bought tickets to that 1991 Skin Yard show, I truly apologize. It really was the U-joints.

Immediately after wrapping up our North American tour in the fall of 1991, Skin Yard finally got an opportunity to tour Europe. It was right on the heels of Nirvana's *Nevermind* album, which had just been released on September 24th, 1991. That album was shaking the music world to its foundation and all of us were somewhat riding the wave of that revolution. Unfortunately Daniel House, Skin Yard's founding bassist, could not do the European tour because of the birth of his son, and I know it was crushing for him not to be able to go, especially since he founded the band with Jack and Ben back in 1985. But having a son was a great blessing for him, and I think he knew that his time on the road was finally over. In his stead, we recruited my old band mate from Thin Men, Pat Pederson, to fill in as our touring bassist.

The crowds that received us in Europe were even more ecstatic than the U.S. audiences we'd been playing to for the previous two years, largely because of the unique European propensity to catch on to American musical trends much faster than Americans do. This pattern still seems true today. When Skin Yard arrived in England in October of 1991, we witnessed that enthusiasm firsthand with our first show at the London Underground, a famous rock club where the Brits had perfected the mosh pit and crowd surfing we would see repeated over and over again during the course of our European jaunt.

Our Dutch tour manager and driver, Tina Van Der Straaten, safely transported us around the European continent like a Wagnerian Valkyrie as she screamed at traffic and hurled our converted delivery truck down the autobahns and highways of Central and Eastern

Europe. Through Holland, Belgium, Germany, and Italy we went, then up through Scandinavia, and finally back to the UK. She would drive and roll cigarettes with one hand, her other hand on the wheel, and all the while telling us stories of her punk rock youth in Holland and her general dislike of Germans. That is, until she married one a few years later.

In Berlin we opened for the brilliant art rock combo "Ween" in an abandoned underground discotheque that would have fit right into one of Werner Herzog's surrealist films. It was just the two of them together, Gene and Dean Ween, with a drum machine in between, and they were the most hilarious, awesome duo that I have ever seen in my life, before or since.

After Berlin, we headed east into the former East Germany, which was now open due to the collapse of the Berlin Wall in 1989. We drove right through the famous Brandenburg Gate, where mile after mile of gray Soviet-era buildings emerged on the horizon like frozen monuments to a Cold War that had finally calcified from the immovable bureaucracy of communism.

We continued south to Rome, the first foreign city I had flown to as a college student back in 1986, and we drove right up to the Roman Coliseum. There we played a sold-out show in a club right across the street from that ancient stadium where gladiators had fought to the death 2,000 years earlier.

Then we headed back north and to the east, over to Ljubljana, Slovenia in the former Yugoslavia, where the Balkan civil war was raging just a few miles to the south in Bosnia, Croatia, and Serbia. Slovenia had sealed its borders and declared itself an independent country and our show was to be the first rock concert held in the new nation. We were opening for another great indie band, No Means No, but it was more of a double bill, where each band played a full headline set. That show was truly incredible because it was staged in a beautiful, medieval church that held about a thousand people. But it was so packed and over-sold-out that at one point I looked up from my drum set to the vaulted ceiling above, and I saw people crawling in through the stained glass windows on the roof of the church, looking down at the surging crowd below.

We ended up staying in beautiful Ljubljana, with its red tile roofs, for several more days since we had some time off on the tour, and the hotel rooms and restaurants were so cheap that we couldn't even spend all the Slovenian money we had earned from the show. This was before the introduction of the Euro, so every show we played in Europe paid us with the currency of that nation. In Slovenia's case, it was a new form of currency that looked very much like Monopoly money, both in size and multi-colored. We made friends with several of the young college students there, had dinner with them every night, and we bought souvenirs for our girlfriends at the local artisan market. When it was finally time for us to start our tour again, we gave each student a large brick of Slovenian money, which made them cry at our generosity. We hugged, said our goodbyes, got back into the van, and headed back out on the road.

Many years later I would meet a young man from Croatia who had moved to Seattle after the Balkan civil war, and he told me of how during that war, he and his friends would climb a hill above their village and listen to a very worn-out bootleg cassette tape that had Pearl Jam's *Ten* album on one side and the Screaming Trees *Sweet Oblivion* album on the other (I would record that Trees album the following year). He told me that he and his friends would climb that hill every day and watch the fighting in the city below, listening to the tape over and over again, imagining the musical revolution that was happening in Seattle, while a very real and bloody war was tearing his country apart. For me, that was one of the most poignant examples of the power of music—that it has the ability to help people mentally survive a war and find hope and possibility in the midst of chaos, destruction, and death.

We drove north into Austria where we had a show opening for Nirvana in Vienna, a somewhat ironic situation since Nirvana had opened a couple shows for Skin Yard back in 1988-89, only two years before they would become the biggest band in the world. That's the Roulette Wheel of music—you never really know what's going to happen until it happens. It was a sold-out club show with about 1,000 people and Skin Yard was opening, with the tongue-in-cheek hipsters Urge Overkill playing in the middle spot, and then Nirvana headlining.

Backstage before the show, Jack and I had the pleasure of being the first Seattleites to tell Kurt, Krist, and Dave that *Nevermind* was exploding across the U.S. Again, this was before the age of cell phones and email, and since Nirvana had been in Europe when *Nevermind* was released, they were somewhat unaware of the furor back in the States. I think the absence of the Internet back then fostered more of a mystique around bands and their music, which has been destroyed by modern social media and instant gratification. But back in October of 1991, we were on the other side of the planet, telling our hometown friends that their album was climbing the Billboard charts and showing no signs of slowing down.

Indeed, *Nevermind* was really just the beginning of a very good, long run of great albums from many Seattle bands, but it was Nirvana who kicked in the door first, and it was incredibly exciting to see it happen in real time.

Our last leg of the tour was a quick run through Scandinavia, which required a ferryboat ride across the North Sea, and then an incredibly scenic train ride across Norway to the arctic city of Bergen on the north coast. That train ride in particular is famous in European travel for its incredible vistas through an ancient forest that fills Norway's interior. When we arrived in Bergen the following day, we played in an enormous cave that had been a munitions dump in WWII until it was converted into the hippest club in Bergen called, the Hulen.

A month after our first show in London, the band finally arrived back in London for a final show before our flight home to Seattle the next day. I don't remember it being a remarkable final gig, probably because we had already debuted in London a month earlier. As we said goodbye to Tina, our fearless tour manager, she handed each of us a one hundred dollar bill, which was our "take-home pay" after paying all the tour expenses and settling all the accounts.

I remember thinking to myself, well, that was one helluva good time. But I'll be back pouring concrete with my construction crew on Monday morning if I'm going to make my rent for the month.

And that is pretty much exactly what happened. Within a few days of my returning to Seattle, my foreman had me on a job site digging out a foundation and filling it in with concrete. I have to be honest and say that it was somewhat disheartening after having just experienced North American and European tours with an emerging indie rock band, playing all the cities of the Western world, both ancient and modern. I was 23 years old, still young and optimistic, but I was pouring concrete in the cold Seattle rain once again.

Although we didn't know it at the time, that European tour would be Skin Yard's last, however we would go on to make one more studio album from the new songs we had been writing and performing on the road. That album, *Inside the Eye*, was released posthumously in 1993 also on Cruz Records. We never played another show, the band broke up, so our final show stands as that unremarkable show in London at the end of our one-and-only European tour in November of 1991.

Like most bands from Seattle, we had been courted off and on by a couple of major labels who were interested in signing us, but we were smart enough to know that signing a new contract when our band was in its twilight years would have been a disastrous mistake. I think Skin Yard was far more savvy and wise, and much of that should be attributed to Jack Endino, who continues to be a remarkable producer to this day. Daniel went on to become a successful computer programmer and a family man, Pat would become a prominent Seattle union leader and start a family himself, and Ben would go on to form another rock band, which I would tour with soon.

Looking back on it 30 years later, I think the best thing that indie rock gave the world is the do-it-yourself movement. DIY is the concept that anyone can come up with an idea, whether it's a band, a film, an art project, a book, and especially a business, and then release it to the world. You do all this without the traditional means of corporate distribution, finances, and elaborate publicity. You just do it because you want to do it, and then you see what happens. That is a truly revolutionary idea, and admittedly, that idea didn't even come from Seattle.

In truth, independent artists had been popping up all over the United States for decades. For example, the great American poet Walt Whitman self-published his most famous book of poetry, *Leaves of Grass*, multiple times in the 1800s. He added new poems, rewriting and editing them with each successive edition, which made Uncle Walt one of America's first true punk rockers. And he's just one of countless examples from my country.

For myself, I had a good first run as a grunge rock drummer and I got to see and play music at a level that I hadn't even imagined a couple years earlier. But I was still working a day job that wasn't the thing I was best at, and I was starting to feel like my first dalliance with professional music was perhaps more of a fluke than anything real or lasting. I was a bit depressed after the demise of Skin Yard, and I wasn't really sure what I wanted do next.

But the universe has a funny way of giving you opportunities when you least expect them, and the next one came through my father, who had recently moved to Australia to work in the mining industry. He invited me to visit.

3. Skin Yard "Inside the Eye"

VERSE 3

AUSTRALIA, NEW ZEALAND: SONGLINES AND SEATRAILS

Rainbow Serpent songline painting, Ramindjeri tribe, South Australia

"We are all visitors to this time, this place. We are just passing through. Our purpose here is to observe, to learn, to grow, to love...and then we return home."

—Aboriginal Elder

When I first arrived in Australia in the winter of 1991, I was twenty-four and my travel experience had largely been limited to playing shows in the big cities of the United States, Canada, and Europe. This would be the first of several trips that I would make to both Australia and New Zealand over the ensuing years, and I would also do two full tours of Australia with my future bands, Screaming Trees and Walking Papers. The early 1990s was also right about the time world music was just starting to become popular, largely because of the advent of the CD. Australia was my first real dive into the deep ocean of world music, and it was a trip that would radically change the way I thought about music and how it shapes our relationship to the landscapes in which we live.

The main reason for my first trip down under was to visit my parents who had recently moved to Sydney for my father's work in the mining industry. After his early years as a flight instructor, my dad had made a radical career change into the highly specialized world of industrial explosives. It's a very dangerous industry, but if you want to build a straight road, an airport runway, or open a mine so that minerals can be extracted, you'll need explosives to clear the way.

My dad had recently gotten a promotion to be the Chief Operating Officer of a large Norwegian-Australian joint venture, and that meant a huge new responsibility in the Australian and South Pacific markets. He and my mom packed up and moved from sleepy Olympia to cosmopolitan Sydney where the company was based. Over the years, my dad was involved with mining and construction projects in a variety of countries. If you ever flew into the famous floating airport in Hong Kong, my dad worked on the runways in the ocean. He always had incredible stories, sort of Indiana Jones-style, and they ranged from being chased through an Alaskan hotel by an ax-wielding logger; to being caught in a blowgun war between two opposing tribes in Papua New Guinea; to being trapped in a mining camp in Borneo that was invaded by a sea of cobras who were fleeing a forest fire. I mean, you can't make that kind of stuff up, and perhaps to a certain degree, those stories inspired my taste for adventure (although I've always tried to limit mine to ones that didn't involve snakes).

In stark contrast to my dad's rather rough trade, my mom, the animal lover, worked for the World Wildlife Fund as a dispatcher for wounded and distressed animals that needed rescuing. Creatures like kangaroos, koalas, wallabies, and even snakes that frequently found refuge in swimming pools after a brush fire—these were my mother's specialty. She had already raised us three kids by that time (wild creatures, all three of us), so my parents' new life in Australia was quite an adventure by comparison.

As much as I respected my dad's extremely dangerous work and the men who worked in the mines and construction projects, we had many arguments over the years about the destructive aspects of the industry. I would argue about the damage being done to the environment, as well as the violations to the rights of the indigenous people. This is such a common argument between the older and younger generations that it has become a stereotype, which doesn't mean it isn't valid, but both sides need to listen to each other.

My father would argue for the necessity of mining and the need for raw materials to build our ever-expanding civilization. It's true, we need raw materials to build modern infrastructure, like airports and airplanes, which might be the most important invention that connected our world before the Internet. And for that matter, the Internet, your computer, and your cell phone require a lot of very special minerals called "rare earths," all of which come directly from mining, and mostly from Australia, Asia, and Africa. I also knew that indigenous people had been mining the Earth for metals and precious stones for thousands of years, albeit on a much smaller, and far less invasive scale. The argument is really a matter of perspective: We need raw materials to build new roads, cars, airplanes, ships, trains, bridges, buildings and, as my father loved to jibe me with, "The cymbals for your drums!"

Well, he had me there. But I also think he started thinking about our planet and human rights a lot more. For example, when I suggested that his company boycott Shell Oil until apartheid was ended in South Africa, he researched Shell and issued a company order to stop using all Shell products until apartheid was ended. In his eyes, basic morality should always come before profit. Later when I was visiting the company office, a rough looking blaster who worked for my dad said to me, "I don't really agree with you, but I think you're probably right." And we shook hands with respect, which is what real men do.

I use mining as an example here, because it illustrates the delicate balance we must find if we are to become an advanced species without destroying ourselves in the process. When I taught this dilemma in my university class, I had my students watch Werner Herzog's movie *Where the Green Ants Dream*, which pits a tribe of Aboriginal people against an Australian blasting company, which could very easily have been my dad's crew. The question is, what is the balance between extracting resources from the Earth, and destroying it? When do we cross the threshold and do more harm than good, destroying the land and ourselves? In my opinion, I believe we have to start moving away from burning fossil fuels at this point in history, especially when the gasses from carbon emissions are melting the ice caps and destroying the atmosphere. We need renewable energies, not 19th century crude oil. Scientists say we have crossed the threshold of irreversible destruction in many places on our planet, however we've also seen from the river and lake restoration projects around the world that the Earth can heal quickly once we stop pumping toxins into the air and water.

One thing is for certain: We are at a critical threshold in human history where we must become self-aware of our relationship to the land and waters, and we must change our behaviors or there will be some very bad results. As we are seeing from the state of the world today, we are rarely led by great leaders anymore. They don't seem to exist, or they are not allowed to rise through the ranks. There is corruption, greed, and arrogance in their character, and a sinister disregard for human beings who don't have the same skin color. These are the worst kind of men. We have neglected our forests, our oceans, our fresh waters, the animal kingdom, and now worst of all, our own people. There is a reckoning coming, and I think we can all feel that.

These same conversations are happening right now in the indigenous nations of the world who have seen this coming since colonialization, 500 years ago. I've been invited to some of those gatherings, mostly in North and South America, and much of the debate in the Southern Hemisphere is being lead by the indigenous people of Australia and New Zealand, the Aboriginals and Maoris, and this story is about what I learned from those cultures.

I think the natural power that resides in the Australian landscape has much to do with why its people are so strong. Once you see the landscapes, you will never forget them. I've been in all of the territories, and visited most of the great national parks. There are places in Australia that are just beyond all verbal description—they look like alien planetary landscapes. And the Great Barrier Reef, which is sadly dying from warming waters and industrial pollution coming down from South East Asia, is another problem entirely. I can only imagine what it might have been like 100,000 years ago when the first Aboriginals arrived here.

These First Peoples were coming down from Southeast Asia, Indonesia, and the islands off the north coast of Australia. During the last ice age, the ocean level was much lower and an archipelago of many small islands emerged that allowed people to "island hop" all the way down to the Australian continent. That was at least 40,000 years ago, but some anthropologists place it closer to 100,000 years ago. They were quite happy there until the British came along in the late 18th century.

Linguists have calculated that there were perhaps as many as 500 different Aboriginal languages spoken at the time of British contact, but by the late 20th century, there were only about 100 languages left. It's possible that those remaining languages will also be destroyed since English, the language of capitalism, has a propensity for destroying languages. This terrible pattern has led to the loss of thousands of indigenous languages around the world, and with that extinction comes the subsequent loss of environmental and cultural wisdom that was contained in those languages.

The soil of Australia is naturally geologically red, but it was made redder by the genocidal acts of the British and the slaughter of Aboriginal people committed during the colonial era. Using techniques that were similar to the United States government in its war against the American Indian, the British did a variety of horrible things, ranging from poisoning bread flour, to issuing blankets infected with smallpox, a favorite method of the U.S. Cavalry. There was also the infamous "Black Line" of Tasmania where British troops shot every Aboriginal man, woman, and child they encountered as they marched across the island. As a result, there are no more living indigenous Tasmanians, and virtually none of these genocides were ever brought to justice.

Up until 1967, Aboriginal people were not even counted in the Australian census, and the first anti-discrimination laws weren't even passed until 1975. The Native Title Act of 1993 slowly began to return Aboriginal lands to their rightful owners, a process that continues to this day. As parts of their sacred land is slowly returned, an awakening pride is emerging in their culture, and there is a special focus on conservation. And that is because these people have learned that by protecting their environment, it creates both cultural pride and broad economic possibility. This is a worldview that all of us should consider, especially as globalism begins to falter.

Much of this renewed respect for Aboriginal culture is centered around their beautiful cosmology and creation stories known as The Dreaming, which has an amazing musical corollary known as the *songlines*. The Dreaming is a series of creation stories that can best be described as a period in the ancient, historical past when large animals and anthropomorphic proto-humans emerged out of the Earth to create the living landscape. These mythic beings shaped, carved, and sculpted the land in such a way that The Dreaming stories have become the sacred equivalent to the Christian Bible, the Jewish Torah, or the Hindu Vedas.

Out of The Dreaming came the songlines, and these songs contain lengthy verses that describe the various geographical features of the landscape, as well as the important myths, teaching stories, and morality lessons that took place within the landscape. These songs were preserved by the tribal elders, who inherited the responsibility of being both the caretakers of the land, and the guardians of the ceremonies and initiations of their people. The songline tradition serves as a way to musically communicate the sacred relationship between the land and its people. Some of these songlines can take days and even weeks to sing to their conclusion during a long walkabout on the land, and some songs go back many generations, perhaps hundreds or even thousands of years. They are taught aurally (by ear and memory) to each successive generation of singers, which preserves the integrity of songline without variance or deviation. In other words, it's a musical way of conceptualizing in rhythm, melody, and stories the direct link between man and the land he was born into.

As a great example of modern, enlightened thinking in the Australian government, some regional courts have even come to recognize these songlines as the equivalent of deed and title to a piece of land. It's remarkable how that small shift in thinking has transformed Australia into becoming a protector of Aboriginal traditions, instead of a destroyer of them. Again, it's a model the rest of the world could learn from.

I've found similar beliefs amongst indigenous people around the world, and some of the stories in this book follow this theme. For example, in West Africa, the storytelling Griots are always using the beauty of the landscape as a background for their historical tales. The Shipibo of the Upper Peruvian Amazon use their sacred curing songs as a way to express life and the important teachings of the Amazon rainforest. And when I spent time in the Mississippi Delta, I found the words in the delta blues to be embedded with rich and often humorous metaphors of life borne from that hypnotic landscape. Almost everywhere you look around the world, you will find that music is localized in the place of its origin, whether it's a folk song about the Hudson River, life in the Andes Mountains, or a Detroit punk band singing about the city in which they came of age. Everywhere we find music, there is a story, and the first and oldest examples of this are in the Aboriginal songlines.

I heard my first songline on a trip I took with my dad out to the Red Center in Australia's Northern Territory, near the town of Alice Springs in the dead center of the continent. We were going to see the gigantic rock formations known as *Uluru* and *Kata Tjuta,* which you've seen on every postcard and TV commercial from the Australian tourist commission. These rock formations are two of the most sacred places in all of Aboriginal cosmology, because in The Dreaming, a series of epic events took place here.

With Uluru and Kata Tjuta looming on opposites ends of the horizon, we listened as an elderly man from the local Pitjantjatjara tribe told us stories that took place around the great rocks. Shortly before sunset, he built a small bonfire on the top of a hill and began to sing a songline about his ancestor's land. He was very much as I would have imagined a wise man to be—gentle and kind, and he sang with the most beautiful voice in his native language. In the fading light and out of the corner of my eye, I saw a pack of wild dingos, the ferocious desert dogs, trotting stealthily through the scrub brush a hundred yards below us. The man saw my eyes following the dingos, and he winked back at me in silent understanding.

The fire now burned brightly as the sun began to set, and in that moment I saw the landscape change and become this timeless thing, as if I was looking at a landscape from a million years ago. From that moment onward, I started to think very differently about what music meant, and how it was so deeply connected to the landscape.

We didn't climb Uluru on that trip, we simply walked around its circumference in amazement at the unbelievable immensity of the sacred rock. We did the same at Kata Tjuta a few miles away, walking around the giant rocks in awe. On a subsequent trip, I did climb to the top of Uluru, and I must admit, it was a rather frightening climb. People used to fall off and die every year, and now only Aboriginal people are allowed to climb it, which I think is the right way for it to be. But when I had the honor of standing on the top of the largest sacred rock in Australia, I saw that it had several large billabongs (water holes) surrounded by lush green trees, plants, and chattering birds, all of it existing in the mysterious, otherworldly environment on the roof of the world. I sat there for a very long time, looking out over the vast desert a thousand feet below. I could feel the magic of this most extraordinary place, and I could faintly hear the land humming with me in a very quiet, but insistent way.

Within a few days of our return from the red center, I bought several books on Aboriginal myths and teaching stories, which are listed in the bibliography in the back of this book. I highly recommend all of these books if you like mythology. I selected a few of the most important myths to tell here so you can get an idea of the beauty and wisdom of the Aboriginal people.

The concept of a Creator or Great Spirit is a common belief in Australia, and one with as many names as there are languages. The

Creator is mysterious and unseen, yet at the same time all-seeing. Beautifully, it can only be communicated with through sound. It has many names, such as Baiame, Bunjil the Eagle Hawk, and Dhurramulan, whose name is also synonymous with the voice of the bullroarer. The bullroarer is found all over the world in almost all Paleolithic cultures and the oldest one discovered so far is from an archeological dig in the Ukraine dating to about 17,000 BC. It consists of a single piece of wood shaped like an airplane wing and fastened with a leather thong at one end. It is swung around the head in rapid circles like a lasso, and it emits a low rumbling sound with cycling, rhythmic pulses that evoke a low-pitched, otherworldly voice. This sound - the "voice of the Creator" - is interpreted by the Wireenuns, the wise medicine men, who consult the voice whenever an important decision needs to be made.

Many of the creation stories from around Australia tell the story of Wanambi, an all-powerful and sometimes dangerous rainbow serpent who lives within the billabongs. Wanambi is one of the main creation deities, and its undulating movements across the Australian landscape carved out the riverbeds and lakes, which later filled with water. In a different story, the rivers and lakes were made when the birds of the forest tried to kill the snake people by setting fire to the forest. The snakes slithered away ahead of the oncoming fire and simultaneously created the rivers and lakes, which were subsequently filled with the tears of the Creator, who was saddened that its children were trying to kill one another.

In another Dreaming story, the creator Jambuwal makes thunder and rain when it walks upon the water, and the ancestor whale, Wuimir, creates rain clouds when it sprays water from his blowhole into the sky. One of my favorite stories, which made me snort with a chuckle, is how salt water was created. Originally all water was fresh water, that is, until the sea turtle ancestor, Inibungei, was speared by a careless fisherman, which caused the angry Inibungei to pee into the water, salinating the oceans forever.

The element of fire plays a hugely important role in many of these myths. It's the element that allows us to cook food, forge iron for tools, weapons, and technology, and perhaps most importantly, to keep us warm. In one Dreaming story, fire was given to the earliest humans by Eagle Hawk, the creation deity who appears as Venus in the morning sky. Eagle Hawk brought the fire from the sky in the form of lightning, which also appears as battle axes thrown by the great Aboriginal warrior, Namarrkon.

In another version of this story, fire came from a crocodile-shaman who selfishly kept the sacred fire sticks hidden under water. The crocodile, known as the Whowie, was infamous for devouring careless men and women who wandered into its waterholes without reciting the proper prayers. Fortunately, the Rainbow Bird tricked Whowie into revealing its underwater hiding place and the Rainbow Bird was able to disperse fire to humanity so they could warm themselves again. This was probably also a teaching story to warn people about the estuarine crocodile, which can grow upwards of 20 feet in length in the northern territories of Australia, and still occasionally "take" a careless swimmer.

Like many European folk tales, the stories of The Dreaming also have a darker side. They tell of how the soil became red from the blood spilled during the combat of ancestral tribes, such as the story of the Pitinjara people of Uluru. There, an epic battle between two clans took place between the Kuniya carpet snake clan and the Liru poisonous snake clan. In this battle, the Liru leader, Kulikudgeri, was killed by the mother of a carpet snake warrior, and Kulikudgeri's blood stained the soil with the reddish color it has today.

When a person died, it was believed that their spirit passed between the two Magellanic Clouds, known as the Kungara Brothers. If the person had been a good and generous person in life, they could reside with their ancestors in the large cloud of the Older Brother. If, however, they were judged to have led an ignoble and selfish life, then their spirit would be eaten by the Younger Brother in the smaller cloud.

The three stars in the belt of Orion are believed to be three ancestor fishermen who were thrust into the sky by a giant waterspout. And the seven stars in the Pleiades are seven beautiful sisters who grew tired of being over-controlled by their husbands, and who fled up to the stars to live in peace. In one of the most beautiful stories, the stars of the Milky Way are believed to be the campfires of the ancestors, their fires blazing in the night as a warm reminder of their watchful presence throughout the ages.

Aboriginal people generally think of the sun as being feminine, and the moon as being masculine. This is because the sun, like a mother, is life-giving and life-affirming. The moon, on the other hand, is associated with coolness, masculine power, initiation ceremonies, the tides, seasonal changes, and death. An eclipse between the two is seen as their sexual union. When boys are being initiated into men, white clay is often smeared on their bodies, the clay representing the power of the moon. This symbolizes a liminal death (the death of one's status in the tribe) and their rebirth into a new status of initiated men. During these initiations, sacred designs are painted on the body, which are attributed to the great ancestor Marwai, the first painter who taught people how to use natural ochre to paint the sacred designs.

Just like the singing of a songline, painting a songline is another way to reaffirm the sacred stories of The Dreaming. A songline must be periodically sung to reaffirm the landscape, and so must sacred paintings be made for the animals, fish, insects, trees, and plants who need to be reenergized in order to reproduce and flourish in The Dreaming of continued reality.

There are stories about how humans first learned to find food, how to fish, and how to make hunting weapons, and there are songs about the gathering, harvesting, and sharing of food. One of the most fascinating and utterly beautiful aspects of Aboriginal culture is the way food and natural resources are shared. For example, if the land you are born into has fishing rights, a hunting ground, a forest, water, or some other resource that's needed in the greater community—then you are the natural born caretaker of that resource. Ironically, you as the caretaker are not its owner—everyone else is, but you still have a sacred responsibility to take care of your patch of paradise. Conversely, you also have a right to use everyone else's resources, which they are obligated to share with you. Thus, the shared obligation is to take care of each other's resources, making sure they are healthy, maintained, and free of any environmental pollution, so that everyone in the community can benefit from them.

In addition to the honoring of food and natural resources, there was one other thing that was held as the highest, most important thing in Aboriginal society: a reverence for the elderly, wise men and women of the tribe. In Aboriginal culture, as a person advances in age they are initiated into higher and higher levels of knowledge and wisdom, so that only the oldest people carry the most sacred knowledge. These people are not forgotten or cast aside as they are in Western society, but are instead revered for their deep knowledge of the life experience. Materialism is not particularly valued in Aboriginal culture because it is transient and disposable, and the youth are often reckless, immature, and shortsighted. But real wisdom - the thing that is only attainable through deep experience, struggle and loss, and the understanding of life's deep processes—that is the prize most highly valued in a human being.

Can you imagine how different our world would be if we followed these simple, basic ways in our own communities? If we had to be responsible for our resources, to keep them clean and renewable, and share them rather than exploit them? What could we learn if we truly valued the life experience of our elders instead of focusing on youth and beauty, the most transient of things? We'd be living in a very, very different world indeed, and a much better one I would argue.

NEW ZEALAND

After those first few weeks of utter amazement and transformation in Australia, I flew across the Tasman Sea to New Zealand. It's only about three hours east of Sydney, and it was easy for me to make a stop over on my way home.

Like Australia, New Zealand was colonized by the British in the early part of the 1800s, but when they realized that the indigenous Maori were extremely fierce warriors and much stronger than any the British had previously encountered, they realized they had to negotiate rather than conquer. They established the Treaty Of Waitangi in 1840 to preserve Maori culture, but this was really a thinly veiled guise to control the Maori under British rule. Predictably, the same European diseases of smallpox and tuberculosis, which had decimated the Australian Aboriginal and the American Indian, also caused a large decline in the Maori population. As a result, the previously allocated indigenous land from the Treaty Of Waitangi was surreptitiously taken back as "British-owned land." Over time, however, and especially with the momentum of indigenous rights movements around the world in the 1970s, the Maori began to make strides in the reclamation of their lands and culture.

Like the Aboriginal, the Maori are amazingly sophisticated in how they utilize their lands and resources. For example, the fishing rights in a particular aquatic area might be granted to one extended family, or the right to hunt in a certain forest might be granted to a different extended family. In this way, Maori land use rights were determined by a family's historical claim to a certain aspect of the water, land, or forest, and not by the European concept of a border. These land use rights were handed down generation to generation within the family, and as long as each new generation continued to exercise the land use, it was usually renewed in perpetuity. The Maori use of landmarks, both geographical and within the natural flora and fauna of the landscape, is quite similar to the Aboriginal description of their own landscapes through The Dreaming stories and songlines.

In addition to their deep understanding of the land and its resources, the Maori are famous for their memories, especially when it comes to the genealogical history of their families, known as the *Whakapapa*. This is one of the most amazing feats of the human mind known to man and in this tradition, a Whakapapa lineage is recited by memory back to the original Polynesian discoverers of New Zealand, a thousand years ago, family by family, name by name. These ancient mariners rode the seatrails of ocean currents across the Pacific Ocean, and over the course of many centuries succeeded in populating all of the Polynesian islands, from Easter Island to Fiji and Tahiti, and eventually New Zealand, as well.

The discovery and colonization of New Zealand is an incredible, epic story in and of itself. It is a story of deep intuition, great courage, and shear physical endurance. In the stories, it is said that the people of Waitangi Ki Roto (Easter Island) came west across the Pacific Ocean on the seatrails, which are giant ocean currents that run fast and deep in all directions across the Pacific. These currents still exist today, but they can be extremely treacherous if not navigated correctly, which could send an entire boat of people off in the wrong direction, missing the intended islands and being lost at sea forever. The giant ocean-going canoes that were used for these journeys were called *wakas* and they were navigated by the most important people on the journey, the *Tohungas*.

The Tohungas were the equivalent of a Hawaiian *Kahuna* or an American Indian shaman or medicine person. They carried the stories of their people, which included their family lineages, their sacred songs, and an unmatched understanding of the Pacific Ocean and its currents and weather patterns.

The Tohungas also had songs that followed the seatrails in a way very similar to the Australian songlines. They sang out the direction of the currents, the stars, the sun and moon, the weather, and even the dozens of different wave forms, which change in shape depending on the sea and their proximity to the various islands. All of this navigational wisdom, as well as the appropriate songs, had to be memorized and recited in the proper sequence to ensure a safe passage across the Pacific. These incredible voyages had several families traveling together as they populated the islands, up to a hundred men, women, and children in a single, giant waka.

The making of a waka was a process that could take as long as a year, from the time the tree was cut down, to the time the waka was ready to launch. Made from giant kauri trees, an enormous tree that can be traced back to the Jurassic period, the cutting down of the tree was done with great ceremony so as to imbue spiritual power into the waka. Again the Tohunga would lead the ceremony with sacred songs, thanking the spirit of the tree for giving its life to carry the children of future generations. Before its launch, the waka would be given the name of the sea trail it would follow across the ocean, and this name would be carved into its prow to ensure success.

It was not uncommon for two wakas to be made at the same time, and then subsequently lashed together with a platform, a mast, and a sail in the middle, thus creating a very stable catamaran. A double waka like this would have two names, one for each canoe, and it could carry upwards of two hundred people, which is about the same number as many modern airliners. On these journeys, seeds, plants, and tubers were taken along to help plant the gardens of the next colony, and this included the kumara, or sweet potato that the Polynesians found in South America, which they had discovered hundreds of years before the Spanish ever set foot on its eastern shores in the 16th century.

I ask you to imagine all of this: the unbelievable courage and fortitude of the Polynesian people who traversed the Pacific Ocean with nothing more than a large wooden canoe, small provisions to feed their families, their sacred songs, and the immense memories of the Tohungas, which countless generations had cultivated to a level or mastery we can barely comprehend. These were absolutely fearless people and very musical ones as well.

Over hundreds of years of island hopping and colonizing, the Maori finally settled New Zealand about 1,000 years ago. The country itself is made up of two large islands, the north island being called *Whai Repo*, after the sacred stingray whose shape the island resembles. The southern and largest of the two island is known as *Aotea Roa*, which means land of the long white cloud, a reference to the mountain range and perpetual layer of clouds that stretches the length of the island. In this beautiful tradition of personifying the land itself, the Earth Mother is referred to as *Papatuanuku,* the Sky Father is known as *Ranginui,* and together they have several sons, each of whom rules a different natural domain on Earth.

During my half dozen visits to New Zealand throughout the 1990s and 2000s, I would often rent a car and drive around the North Island to see the gorgeous landscapes, soak in hot springs, and visit the Maori *Maraes* (sacred community centers) that were open for public visitation. Maraes are exquisitely beautiful places, and this is sacred ground where the indigenous beliefs are integrated into the family, the community, and the Maori way of life. It's a living embodiment of Maori culture, where the ancestors reside within the very architecture of the buildings.

When you approach a Marae, there is an elaborate ritual that takes place where the visitors are cleansed of any negative *tapu* (energy) that they might be carrying, and it goes like this: As the visitors approach the Marae, an elderly matriarch known as a *Kuia* gives a crying shout called the *Karanga.* In some cases, a warrior may run down the entrance way and challenge the visitor with his physical presence. Next, formal speeches of welcome are done at a safe distance, there is an honoring of the ancestors, and the visitors may finally enter.

The Marae itself contains several community buildings, which are built around a central courtyard in the sacred area of the village. The largest of these buildings is the Whare Nui, the ancestor's house, and this serves as both a ceremonial center and as a meetinghouse. It is built with absolute precision, extreme attention to detail, and decorated with the most incredible woodcarvings that are unrivaled in the world. These exquisite woodcarvings carry the *mana* (divine presence) of the ancestors, as is revealed in the architecture itself.

The ridgepole of the house is symbolic of the ancestors' strong spines; it upholds the lineage of the people for current and future generations. The ancestors' ribs are represented in the elaborately carved rafters, and the various wall panels depict significant historical events from the past. Carved statues of warriors guard the buildings and are placed in prominent places, usually on each side of a doorway, and this is also a common practice throughout New Zealand households (and my own), where a Maori warrior statue stands guards near the front door.

When meetings are held within this building, a circular nature of conversation is encouraged, where everyone's opinion is weighed and considered. It would be considered rude to come to a conclusion right away, until everyone has had a chance to speak and a consensus is reached. It is a way of honoring everyone's point of view.

Unfortunately, in our 500 years of New World conquest, we've taken a terribly destructive approach to the way we view the land and the indigenous people, whose wisdom is priceless and stretches back for many thousands of years. In the Western World, we tend to think of the Earth as an unlimited resource for our various appetites, instead of seeing that these are limited and finite resources that we need to protect for future generations. This malformed way of thinking began with the violent horrors of the Spanish conquistadors who were sanctioned by the church, and it continues to this day in the form of global capitalism and corporate extraction. For some reason, the Western mind has developed a delusional birthright that it is acceptable to pillage the land, turning pristine into polluted, sacred into profane, as we try to wring the last great resources from the Earth.

I would return to Australia and New Zealand several more times over the ensuing 20 years, both to visit my family, and to play music in those cities. But that first trip in the late fall of 1991 changed me forever, and in a very real way, it's why I wrote this book. To see such beautiful and dramatic landscapes and to hear songs that were connected to those landscapes—that was something I had never experienced before.

When I returned to Seattle in the winter of late 1991, I went back with a mission to play music again. I still wanted to play rock & roll, but it had to have real meaning with real stories behind the songs. And man, did I find it.

4. Australian Aboriginal Bullroarers

VERSE 4

GO MAJOR: BOURBON AND BRAWLING WITH THE TREES

Screaming Trees on the MTV Alternative Nation Tour, summer 1993

"Our scene was a wonderful confluence of the Baby Boomers and Generation X; a traversing of the chasm between heavy metal and punk rock; an experience of the transition from analog to digital recording formats; and a dynamic exploration of the conundrum, 'would you like paper, or plastic?"

—Kim Thayil

To tell the full story of the Screaming Trees would entail writing an entire book on the band, and that is not something I am prepared or want to do. Nor do I think I am the best-qualified person for such an undertaking. However, I did spend the better part of a decade in that seminal Seattle band, and there are a few good stories worth telling. I'll just start at the beginning, when I first met the band.

As a musician, it's pretty hard to forget the first time I saw the Screaming Trees. It was in 1989, when they played a show at Western Washington University in Bellingham, WA. The Trees were already a well-known Northwest band, having formed in 1985 and releasing a handful of critically acclaimed indie rock albums on the legendary SST label. My first rock band, Thin Men, was picked to be the opener for the WWU show, and we did our punk rock best against the rising tide of what was fast becoming known around the world as "grunge". When the Trees took the stage that night, I was awed at the sight of the Conner brothers, Van and Gary Lee, as they bookended the tall stoic figure of Mark Lanegan, all of them propelled by the bombastic drumming of Mark Pickerel as the Trees threw down lightning bolts of sonic fury.

By late 1991, Skin Yard had called it quits after almost two years on the road, and I had just returned from my first trip to Australia. I'd only been back at my warehouse loft for two weeks when I got a call from Van Conner asking me to audition for the Trees.

It was December of 1991 and the audition was at a place called the Olympic Foundry in south Seattle. It was a cold, grimy place where they forged iron manhole covers, and still do to this day, but the owner of the foundry also loved rock & roll, so he made some rooms available for local bands to rehearse. My audition was essentially a jam session with Van on bass and his brother Gary Lee on guitar, and the three of us had a fun, exciting time working on new songs that were still in their infancy. We played early versions of "Shadow of the Season," "Dollar Bill," "Julie Paradise," and "Nearly Lost You," as well as several other skeletal ideas that later evolved into songs. Our musical chemistry was immediate and the next day Van called to offer me the gig, which I happily accepted.

We were about to start regular rehearsals at the foundry until one day when Van visited me at my loft and decided on the spot that he wanted to move the band's backline into my studio and start rehearsing there instead. I think this was largely because I had a kitchen, a bathroom, a refrigerator for beer, and a coffee pot for life's most important beverage. I've said more than a few times over the years that a drummer can always find a gig if they have a great rehearsal space, because the bands will generally flock to them. In my case, that loft on Jackson Street had been the perfect rehearsal space for Thin Men, Skin Yard, and now the Screaming Trees as we refined our new songs.

I was back to work at my construction job during the day, pouring foundations and framing houses, but at quitting time I went straight home, showered, and got ready for the next batch of Trees songs we'd be working on that evening. The rehearsals at the loft had a fiery, energetic quality to them, which I think was partly due to my influence as a new drummer, but also because the band had exceptionally good songs that were really starting to take shape. We continued to rehearse diligently for another month, as Mark Lanegan added his evolving lyrics to the mix. We would methodically go through the songs, arranging and perfecting them as we went, and taking time to talk about our individual musical influences and the directions we wanted to take when it came time to finally record the album. We all had different musical tastes: I was rooted in jazz and punk, Van loved hard rock and metal, Gary Lee was an aficionado of classic psychedelia, and Mark loved the blues and classic rock. It all came from the same musical source really, but the one thing we all had in common was the ability to recognize a great song. Recognizing a great song as a stand-alone entity—that was the hidden secret of the Screaming Trees.

Sometime after the new year of 1992 we had a meeting with our A&R from Epic Records, Bob Pfeifer. He flew to Seattle to observe us as we recorded demos of all the new songs in a whirlwind one-day session at Seattle's Avast Studios with our chosen producer, Don Fleming. Don was connected to Sonic Youth and had produced several bands in the growing alternative rock movement including the acclaimed Scottish band, Teenage Fanclub. The day after the session Bob sat us down and told us that because the Trees' previous album *Uncle Anesthesia* hadn't sold well (even though it is a great album), and because bands like Nirvana and Pearl Jam were now selling albums by the millions, we were really in a make-or-break situation. In other words, if we didn't make one hell of a great album that got serious attention and sold well, we would likely be dropped from the label and that would be the end of our major label recording career.

This was to be the first major label album I had ever played on, and it was now looking like it could also be my last. Thus, I joined the Screaming Trees with the odds of an underdog, a metaphor I've always kept close to my heart and which very aptly applied to that band. When the underdog has the odds stacked against him, he has to work twice as hard to overcome those odds. Everyone is betting against him, yet they're also secretly hoping he'll win, and that is the great paradox of the underdog.

About a month later we got the official green light from Epic that our demos and recording budget had been approved, so we packed up our gear and had everything shipped to New York in wooden crates, because the band couldn't afford proper road cases at that time. I put my personal belongings in storage, gave up my lease on the Jackson Street loft that had served me and my bands so well, and I said goodbye to the space where so many great songs had been written. It was now February of 1992 and I was 24 years old, half the age I am as I write this. It was the end of the early grunge era, but it was also the beginning of an entirely new era for the Screaming Trees.

We flew to New York and checked into the elegantly dilapidated Gramercy Park Hotel. The next morning we converged on the studio Don Fleming had picked out for us called Baby Monsters, which was located on 14th Street in the Chelsea neighborhood of Manhattan. The studio was rustic, as warehouse studios tend to be, but it also had many vintage guitars and amps, and enough space to get a good, cracking drum sound. We were also fortunate to have the engineer John Agnello, who, like Don, had worked on some classic alternative albums. So we set to work unpacking the wooden shipping crates, getting our gear set up, and dialing in the sounds that would become the bedrock of the album.

By the second day we were cutting the first basic tracks and the sessions were "hot", as they say, very focused and inspired, with a sense of urgency and intensity that permeated the room. We'd work for many hours throughout the day and late into the night, and around 12 a.m. we'd start breaking off into groups to catch taxis back to the hotel.

At that time, the Gramercy Park Hotel was not the glamorous hotel it is today. It had been a swanky place back in the 1920s, but by the 1990s it was a rather grim and rundown affair. Van Conner and I roomed together and we often joked that we might catch Legionnaires' disease as we languished in our dark, steam-heated room. Thus, we rarely spent any time in there except to sleep, choosing instead to walk the streets of Manhattan every chance we got.

Conveniently, the Gramercy's best feature was its downstairs bar, which was a famous watering hole for every rock musician who was passing through New York on tour. Everyone made a stop at the hotel bar, it was a destination, and every night Van Conner and I would return from our evening walk to have a nightcap before retiring to our room of gloom. Almost every night we'd run into someone or some band that we had known from our previous time on the road, and this would lead to a long night of highly animated and exaggerated storytelling and bragging.

I remember a lot of laughing in that bar, the clinking of glasses, and a room so thick with cigarette smoke that it seemed more like a cowboy saloon out of the Wild West than a hipster bar in Manhattan. And when I look back at the month we spent recording our album in New York, I mostly remember the inside of Baby Monsters Studio, the Gramercy Hotel bar, and the pizza joint across the street, on whose slices we survived with our very shallow pockets.

Spending time walking the streets and sitting inside smoky bars was actually part of the recording process for us—we took in the energy of New York and we channeled it into our songs. But perhaps the most important facet in the making of our album was the philosophy we took as we approached each song. We believed that it was our highest goal to serve the song first, whatever that meant, and whatever the song needed. Usually that meant simplifying our parts and playing with more feeling and emotion, rather than a technically perfect performance. I remember that Don didn't want me to use a click track for any of the songs, and instead he had the band follow my natural tempos as they ebbed and flowed. This made the music come alive, and you can hear that feeling in the songs—waiting, breathing, and then accelerating like a sprinter at the starting gun.

We recorded the rhythm tracks live as a band with Mark singing only a scratch vocal part, which he would later re-sing after we had picked the final takes. We usually got the basic track within the first three to four takes because we were so well rehearsed. Sometimes it was even the first or second take that had the magic that we were trying to capture. We'd often keep a take even if there was a slight mistake in the performance, and that's because we were recording onto 2" magnetic tape. With tape, you have to make a decision after each performance whether you got "the take" or close to it, and if it wasn't, you took a chance that you would lose the magic when you recorded over it. A great basic track, even with a little mistake or flaw, always has more life and character than a technically perfect performance with no soul. And that's because a great song represents life itself, full of all our mistakes and flaws. They say that David Bowie would seize upon a mistake in a basic track, and then use that mistake to create a new part of the song that he hadn't thought of before. That is true genius, true soul. And as every Screaming Trees fan knows, the Trees were all about the soul of the song, and that became our mantra: does the song have soul or not?

After the basic tracks were picked and finalized, Lee would do a few guitar overdubs—but not too many. Usually he's just do a second rhythm guitar and maybe an acoustic guitar, a lead, or a solo. I would record some simple hand percussion like tambourine or shaker, and then Mark would sing his final vocal performance after drinking a small amount of whiskey that Don Fleming would serve in measured doses. Don's theory was that whiskey warmed the vocal cords and put a little hair in the voice. As a result, Mark's vocal performances on *Sweet Oblivion* are arguably some of the best in his long and varied career. I think that, combined with the band's ferociously tight musical delivery, is what gave our album its classic, timeless quality.

As we were finishing the last few overdubs on the album, the final mixes started coming back from Andy Wallace's studio across town. Andy had just mixed Nirvana's *Nevermind*, Jeff Buckley's *Grace*, and a slew of other brilliant albums that had been hugely successful in the previous year. Andy definitely had the golden ear, and when we heard his first mix for the song "No One Knows," we knew right away that we had a very special album on our hands. Andy mixed about one song per day over the next two weeks, including all the B-sides from the album, and they were immediately sent over to Epic Record's Manhattan office for final approval. When word came back that the label was very excited, the band was relieved, and it seemed like the hangman would not be getting his silver coin after all.

A few weeks later, Van Conner and I returned to New York to master the album with Howie Weinberg, who liked to master his albums at full volume. That methodology suited our music very well, and I'll never forget how good our album sounded that one fine day we rocked out with Howie in his mastering suite.

We gave our album the title *Sweet Oblivion*, which was taken from a line in the opening track "Shadow of the Season," in which Mark sings, "Ah sweet oblivion feels alright!" I think it was also because we had been living that lifestyle for the last few months as we shuttled back and forth between Seattle and New York, and it was a theme deeply embedded in the songs themselves.

It was now the spring of 1992 and Epic decided upon a September release date, which gave them a few months to set up the album properly. It also gave them the opportunity to release the album's first single, "Nearly Lost You," on the soundtrack for the movie *Singles*, a film that featured twenty-somethings looking for love and musical fame in early '90s Seattle. The film was a minor hit, but the soundtrack was a huge success because all the major bands from Seattle were on it. "Nearly Lost You" helped propel the album to platinum status, and that song turned out to be our first and biggest hit, cracking the top 10 of the rock charts. Even president-elect Bill Clinton used the bridge of "Nearly Lost You" as the soundtrack for his inaugural entrance onto the global stage. At one point, on a commercial flight out of Seattle, the flight attendant announced over the intercom that the Screaming Trees were on board and everyone on the plane (in coach, anyway) cheered wildly. It was a surreal moment in time to say the least, and we subsequently hit the road for two straight years of touring around the world.

When I listen to Sweet O' today, I hear the rise and fall of the tempos, the ferociousness of the musical delivery, and the emotional tension and release of the songs. Mark's vocals howl and roar with the wisdom of a man much older than the 26 years he had racked up at the time we made the album. He tells stories that are both majestic and spiritual, as well as haunting and ephemeral. Gary Lee's guitar work is highly original and inspiring, even brilliant in places. And the rhythm section work of Van Conner's bass and my drumming makes the band swing like a battleship, which in many ways, it kind of was.

Mostly though, I hear the sound of New York City on that album. I hear the creak and groan of the metropolis, the clinking of glasses in smoky dive bars, the shouts of streetwalkers and hustlers, and the kinetic energy of a city bursting with so much energy that it almost pulls you down the sidewalk. That record is imbued with the soul of New York City itself.

Now in the early 21st century, most albums are recorded digitally, with click tracks or programmed drum machines, so the rhythmic feel is linear, extremely sterile, and utterly lacks swing. I tend to think that a great album, like a human being, should be a living and breathing thing. The body inhales and expands, and then it exhales and contracts. So too should the feel of a song move like a human body. It is life, after all. This is also why when we hear a real band, whether its rock, blues, jazz or otherwise—we all feel it in a much different way. Live music reminds us of our earliest origins, our shared humanity, back in the ancient past when music kept us warm and secure around the embers of a collective fire.

That was the power of the Screaming Trees when we made *Sweet Oblivion* in the New York winter of 1992. We conjured the internal fire and captured it on magnetic tape, in real time, with swing and soul. It's an album about love, hope, and the possibility of the future, with a fearless abandon that says, *I will go for it all, right here, right now, because I have nothing else to lose and everything to gain.* We were the underdogs, we were the champions of the people, and that's why we are still in their hearts.

As Epic Records continued to work the "Nearly Lost You" single and set up the release of *Sweet Oblivion*, the band made plans to go to Europe in the summer of 1992. Our strategy was to play some club shows and practice playing these new songs in the safe environs of Europe, before the record was released and more attention would be focused on the band. That was, and still is, a common practice for bands today, where they tour in Europe before the release of a new album, and then hit the ground running when they return to the US.

By all accounts, 1992 was just about the most powerful year of music that had happened for many, many years. So many great records were released between 1991 and 1992, and it seemed to climax in the summer and autumn of 1992. Artists like Soundgarden, Alice In Chains, Nirvana, Pearl Jam, R.E.M., Sonic Youth, Nick Cave And The Bad Seeds, Mudhoney, Rage Against The Machine, Smashing Pumpkins, the Beastie Boys—the list goes on and on and on of bands who had breakthrough albums during those two powerful years. It was really a powder keg that ignited alternative rock for all the years to come, and the summer of 1992 was when it reached a critical mass.

In June of 1992, the Trees flew from Seattle to London, an eight-hour straight shot across the Arctic Circle. We started with some small club shows around the UK, including a sold out show at the same Camden Underworld in London where Skin Yard had played the year before. Then we moved down to the continent, zipping around Europe in a rented Peugeot sedan and a converted milk truck for our gear, driven by our first employee, Martin Feveyear. Martin had just been divorced and was escaping his miserable life in the claustrophobic town of Ipswich, England. He was in a terrible condition when we met him, but he perked right up as he contemplated the next chapter of his life with our rowdy band. As the years went by, Martin went on to become our chief sound engineer, and eventually a full-time Seattleite with an American family and his own recording studio, where the Trees would eventually record. But in the summer of 1992, it was all of us driving around Europe in a milk truck that seemed to be rattling off its frame.

Our manager, Kim White, had rented the Peugeot on her credit card, since none of us even had one of those yet. I was the designated driver because I absolutely loved to drive, especially on the German autobahns. The entire tour was quite fun as we played everything from Italian castles, to open fields in thunderstorms, to over-sold nightclubs with screaming fans. We drank a lot, smoked countless European cigarettes, and ate rather excellent food at restaurants and numerous *auto-grills*, which are a much fancier version of the American truck stop.

We also had two invitations to open for Nirvana, who were by now riding the full wave of hysteria that their album *Nevermind* had unleashed. The first show we played with them was at the massive Roskilde Festival in Denmark. At this festival we ended up having to play after Nirvana, which is very much like being on the cleanup crew after the Super Bowl. Nirvana had become so huge since the release of *Nevermind* a year earlier that playing after them was about the biggest letdown a crowd could expect. Nirvana played in front of almost 100,000 people, and by the time the Trees took the stage it was probably down to a paltry 50,000 seemingly uninterested Danes.

To shorten the story a bit, we all had a little too much to drink before our set. Our friend Mike McCready of Pearl Jam, who had played earlier that day, was drinking with us and we were all having a pretty good time, but it was really due to the anxiety of having to play after Nirvana. We started our set with the powerful opening song "Change Has Come," but Mark's vocal monitor wasn't working properly. He ended up pushing his monitor off the edge of the stage, which crushed a very expensive television camera down below, and very nearly its operator. It wasn't "rock & roll" and it wasn't cool by any stretch of the imagination, and it turned our stage into an absolute catastrophe, with security rushing us and the Trees fending them off by swinging guitars and cymbal stands. Our show ended during that first song-calamity.

We eventually tussled our way back the musician's area and barricaded ourselves in the dressing room where Mike McCready was happily waiting. Mike loved that kind of chaos back then, and I suppose we all did. A couple years later I'd be in a band with Mike called Mad Season as we tried to get sober, but at that moment at the Roskilde Festival in Denmark, it was sheer drunken buffoonery from the Screaming Trees. The promoter was furious with us, but he also said it was the greatest thing he had seen since he watched The Who destroy their backline two decades earlier. I think I would have rather seen The Who to be perfectly honest.

The destruction of the television camera cost us our guarantee, which was many thousands of dollars that would have underwritten the cost of our shoestring budget. Now the tour was going to lose money, which meant the band members wouldn't make any money either. And at these festivals, word gets around fast as to which bands are cool and which bands are troublemakers. Our reputation was not good and this was also my first experience with the self-destructive aspect of rock & roll, something I would witness time and time again thereafter.

We returned to the United States shortly after the Roskilde debacle, but we flew right back to England a month later to play the famed Reading Festival, the great showcase for emerging alternative bands. Nirvana was headlining the third and final day of the festival and Kurt Cobain had personally picked his opening bands. It was generally considered to be the "Seattle day" and the lineup included (in this running order): The Melvins, Screaming Trees, Pavement, The Beastie Boys, L7, Teenage Fan Club, Mudhoney, Nick Cave & The Bad Seeds, and finally, Nirvana. All of those bands had had major breakthrough albums during those magical years of 1991-92 and to have them all on one stage, on one day, was pretty spectacular. It was THE lineup of all the festival line-ups that summer, and Kurt was basically showing the world who his favorite bands were.

I remember that every band played extremely well that day, the audience was ecstatic, and there were none of the major technical problems that can frequently plague these kinds of massive festivals. It was all pretty flawless. When Nirvana came out to do their set, Kurt famously emerged from their dressing room in a white hospital gown, seated in a wheelchair. He was making a joke of his rumored health problems, but when Nirvana finally walked out (and Kurt rolled) onto the stage, they unleashed an absolutely transcendental performance, which was one of the greatest musical events I have ever seen in my life. I watched from behind the monitor desk on Kurt's side of the stage as the band exploded with one great song after another. They were unstoppable, delivering the songs that would become the anthems of a generation, and they ended with the most elegant destruction of their backline that I have ever seen. The Who would have been proud.

That show is memorialized on DVD and you should watch it, because that is exactly how a rock band should play at its peak. I was fortunate enough to stand there and watch what was likely the best live band in the world at that time, and to think that just a couple of years earlier I had been standing there with Kurt and Krist when they were checking out Dave Grohl in San Francisco. It's amazing how fast things can happen when the moment is right.

That summer of 1992, the European tour, and the festivals we played all happened before the official release date of *Sweet Oblivion*. It was only about a week after we got back to Seattle from the Reading Festival that the album was officially released on September 8th, 1992. *Rolling Stone* gave the album a 4-star review, and all the other music publications gave it similarly high marks. The album was a critical success, but would it be a commercial success? Only touring would determine that factor.

Over the next two years the Trees would tour non-stop, hopping back and forth across the Atlantic and Pacific Oceans to play shows across North America, the UK, Europe, and even Australia. We hired our first real crew, which included guitar tech and stage manager Danny Baird, drum tech and "Lanegan assistant" John Hicks, front of house engineer Martin Feveyear, and tour manager Rod Doak. There were a few other roadies who rotated in here and there, but the aforementioned guys were with us for most of the 1990s.

Our first American tour in the fall of 1992 took us across the U.S. and Canada with the incredibly cool New York band, Luna, opening for us. We had a marvelous time playing with those lads and I remain friends with them to this day.

Then in February of 1993, we started a grueling European tour opening for Alice In Chains. Alice's masterpiece album, *Dirt*, had just come out and with the success of our mutual albums, the shows were all sold out well in advance. The tour took us to almost every country in Europe, but it was under such a brutal tour schedule that we virtually lived inside our tour buses and saw very little of anything except the inside of venues. The tour was so successful however that it was extended back to North America and continued well into the summer, hitting almost every major US and Canadian city. We became like blood brothers with the Alice boys, in a way that only a tour like that can create. It was also the beginning of my friendship with Alice's singer, Layne Staley, one of the greatest singers of my generation.

Later that summer of 1993 we opened for our Minneapolis brethren, Soul Asylum, and the hippy jam band, Spin Doctors, both of whom had major hits on the radio at that time. The tour, sponsored by MTV and dubbed the "Alternative Nation Tour" was also sold out, and we played even bigger venues, the giant outdoor amphitheaters that every major city has, some of them upwards of 30,000 capacity.

In between all this mad dashing about, we managed to play the late night TV shows like *Late Night with David Letterman, The Tonight Show with Jay Leno,* and a few other smaller shows. It all became a blur after a while, but *Sweet Oblivion* did sell more than 350,000 copies, which although not a staggering number, was a giant leap for the Screaming Trees.

Oh, and those brawls we were so famous for—yes, there were a few, and none of them were anything to be proud of. There was the one where Mark and I got jumped by about five or six Jersey boys outside of the Stone Pony in Asbury Park, New Jersey, the night before we were supposed to play on Letterman's show. We fended them off quite well actually, it was pretty much a draw, but Mark got a real shiner of a black eye that he sported on Letterman the next day. I separated my shoulder in the fight, so the great Steve Ferrone drummed in my stead. You can still watch the performance on YouTube, its pretty great, and Mark's shiner is quite obvious.

I returned to playing a few days later and the tour continued. But then there was a scuffle at a nightclub in Florida where Mark got his nose broken, which is a terrible injury for any singer. I think we had to cancel a couple shows after that one. Then there was a particularly nasty brawl involving several people at a bar in Montreal, which involved broken bottles, and some brutal fisticuffs. We all came away bruised and cut from that one. There were a few other minor skirmishes, but in all of these events, the bouncers intervened before anyone got too badly hurt, because in truth, the way the Screaming Trees looked for trouble, somebody could have easily left in a hearse.

The funny thing about it all is that the fans were never violent. The great people we met out there during those years were as varied as the world's population, and they seemed to get along just fine. I never saw anyone fight at our shows, it was only the band that seemed to find that dark energy. I remember a show where I was literally talking to some Hell's Angels and a couple college professors, all of us in a circle, and the Angels and the professors were laughing and drinking beer together and really having a great time. That's how diverse our following was—from hard-core bikers, to hard-core intellectuals.

We even had a wedding proposal at a show one night, where Van was asked to propose on behalf of the groom, to his girlfriend in the audience. It was a sold out show and halfway through the set Van called out the girl's name, found her in the audience, and asked her if she would marry Mr. so-and-so. When she screamed out "Yeeeessss!" the whole place erupted in the greatest feel-goods you ever felt in your life.

The Trees would attempt to record a follow-up to *Sweet Oblivion* in 1994 with the same production team of Don Fleming and John Angello. This time we chose Seattle's Bad Animals Studios so we could be closer to our families. Unfortunately the recordings sounded flat and fairly lifeless, the result of a band that had burned itself out on the road without taking any time to rest and prepare for a new album. There was also the growing heroin addiction of our singer, Mark Lanegan, which had resulted in stunted live shows and an increasingly erratic reputation for the band. Spirits were low when the 1994 album was finally aborted, and we all retreated to our homes to rest and contemplate our trajectory, which was now in a downward spiral.

The Trees would eventually rally back in 1995 to do a short tour of Australia, hitting the five major cities on the Big Day Out Festival. And we would eventually make two more studio albums—1996's *Dust* (produced by George Drakoulias) and 1999's *Last Words* (produced by me and posthumously released in 2011). In support of the *Dust* album, we played every single date on the touring version of the 1996 Lollapalooza, opening for The Ramones, Soundgarden, and Metallica. Later that fall, there was a brief tour opening for Oasis and the Manic Street Preachers on the American East Coast, and there was a relatively short European headlining tour in 1997. A few select American dates straggled into 1998 until the tour, and the band, ground to an undramatic halt.

To be fair, *Dust* was a truly great album and George Drakoulias did a magnificent job producing it. Again, it got 4-star reviews around the world, and some critics named *Dust* record of the year, declaring that our godhead was imminent. But when the Trees made the decision to leave the smaller, headlining position and become an opening band for larger but ill-suited tours—that was when we made our fatal mistake.

Instead of growing our base and evolving our headline show, we naively (or perhaps lazily) thought we could just play 40-minute opening sets and the world would be delivered to us. It wasn't.

I remember those last few years of the 1990s feeling more like drudgery and boredom, as if we were working a day job and not doing the very thing we loved the most. Everything we did seemed like sailing against the wind, and the shows got shorter, yet exponentially harder to pull off properly. I began to realize that the soul of the band had been broken, slowly but assuredly, and it had never really healed. With the increasing use of heroin by our singer, and alcohol by the rest of us, the band was ultimately destroyed by the worst drug of them all—ego.

It was early in the winter of 1997, and although the Trees would still be a band for a couple more years, I found myself with increasing amounts of spare time. Not being one to waste time when I had it, I found two new musical projects to pour myself into—Mad Season with Mike McCready and Layne Staley, and Tuatara, an instrumental band I formed with Peter Buck of R.E.M., Justin Harwood of Luna, and saxophonist Skerik. I also made a conscious decision to start traveling on my own a lot more, and to learn as much as I could about the musical world that existed outside the narrow parameters of major label rock & roll.

Maybe it was because I regretted not finishing my music education in college, or maybe it was because I just loved to travel. Perhaps it was both. In any case, I wanted to be alone and on the musical road again, with a backpack and a field-recorder in my hand. I had made contact with a distant cousin during the holidays of 1996 and learned that she owned a farm in the small Central American country of Belize. So in early January of 1997, I loaded up the backpack and caught a flight to Belize City on the Caribbean Sea.

5. Screaming Trees "Ash Gray Sunday"

VERSE 5

BELIZE: ANCESTORS IN THE NEW WORLD

Barrett and Garifuna drum master Joel Coleman, Hopkins Village, Belize 1997

"The land is like your mother. You don't sell her, nor do you rent her. In her we are born, and toward her we are returned at the end of our existence."

—Celeo Alvarez Casildo, Garifuna leader

After the abbreviated world tour for the Screaming Trees *Dust* album, I still had a little bit of money saved up. I had just bought my first house, but it also needed a bit of a remodel. I hired the very same construction company that had employed me for so many years and I even pitched in and worked beside my old workmates as we made the house into a home. A couple of the construction guys were veterans who had served in the first Gulf War during the same period of time that I had been out on the road with my first bands. It felt good to work beside them doing something positive and constructive together, and we talked about how we had seen the world in different ways.

By the time the work on my house was finished, winter had set in and the gray gloom of the Pacific Northwest had returned. Things looked grim for the Screaming Trees and my gut instinct told me that the band wasn't going to last much longer after the latest round of touring and the personal self-destruction that had set in with our singer. We had a few more sporadic shows coming up but I knew we were probably done as a band and it only remained to be seen how things would formally play out. I pondered what to do next, especially with the enormous amount of time I had in the foreseeable future, which was now devoid of tour dates or recording sessions. I knew I would start another band eventually but that wasn't in the forefront of my mind. What I really needed was a vacation with some musical inspiration, much like that first trip I took to Australia and New Zealand back in 1991.

Over the holidays between 1996-97, my mom had gotten back in touch with a distant cousin of mine who lived on a farm in Belize, down in Central America. She owned a soybean plantation in Belmopan, the capital of Belize, where Mayan ruins were scattered across the landscape in abundance. It was a perfect winter escape for the amateur anthropologist inside of me, so I invited myself down to visit and she graciously accepted.

Central America and the greater Caribbean is one of the most fascinating and beautiful regions on Earth. From an historical perspective, it's the first place that many brutal collisions between European, Indigenous, and African peoples occurred, yet some incredible new cultures and spiritual understandings emerged as a result of that collision. Belize is one of those places, right smack in the middle of it all, where the extraordinary *Garifuna* culture emerged.

The Spanish were the first to colonize the Caribbean and Central America, as well as most of South America (the Portuguese took Brazil). They were soon followed by French, Dutch, and English colonists, and from the ensuing global trade came the emergence of the coffee, tobacco, and sugar cash crops. This was essentially the first "drug trade" in Europe, because when these three drugs entered the European economy, it set off an economic cycle of extreme wealth, extreme greed, and the horrors of the slave trade.

The Spanish had been bringing slaves from the shores of West Africa to the islands of the Caribbean since 1502, the year the first African slave was documented. With the explosion of the cash crops and the gold and silver that was being looted from the Aztec and Inca Empires, Spain's wealth grew obscenely large. From that wealth they built the gigantic Spanish Armada, and stories abounded about the decadence of New World Spanish cities, where the wealthiest women wore their dresses only once, and gold and silver jewelry was tossed in the streets after an evening of revelry. The French, Dutch, and English were no less guilty of this excess, all of which was created upon the backs of indigenous and African slaves.

The British would eventually end slavery first, in 1834, with the French following in 1848, and the U.S. (through civil war) finally ending slavery in 1863. But slavery would remain in the Spanish territories until 1886 and in Portuguese Brazil until 1888. The island of Haiti, a small French colony in the Caribbean, threw off slavery permanently with its own successful slave rebellion in 1791. Legend has it that the rebellion started with a Voodoo ceremony, Voodoo being a syncretic mixture of Catholicism and the indigenous beliefs of the Dahomean people who had been taken there from West Africa. The Haitian rebellion was successful, they ejected their French masters, and by 1804 they had became the first truly independent nation in the Caribbean. And to think that it started with drumming, dancing, and the invocation of the African Saints known as the Orishas—I just love that kind of history.

I arrived in Belize City in January of 1997 and I found the weather to be a perfect balance of sunshine and natural warmth. The country was originally called British Honduras, and according to Mayan archeologists, Belize was also the geographic center of the ancient Mayan Empire. But Belize doesn't get the excavation funding that Mexico gets, so most of the gigantic Mayan ruins in Belize still lay hidden beneath centuries of soil accumulation and a thick jungle canopy.

British Honduras was renamed Belize in 1973, and in 1981 it received its full independence. The national language is English, however a variety of other languages are also spoken there, including Spanish near the Guatemalan and Mexican borders, various Mayan dialects throughout the country's interior, and Garifuna, the language of the Afro-Caribbean people who would soon captivate my heart.

After clearing customs and renting an American Jeep, I loaded my bags and immediately headed south down the Hummingbird Highway to my cousin's ranch in the heart of the country. After a few hours of driving down the narrow highway, where the jungle creeps right up to the road's edge, I found myself at The Banana Ranch, a name my cousin aptly gave to honor all the banana trees that grew abundantly around her farm. She greeted me warmly and gave me a brief tour of the fields and the surrounding jungle before we joined the farm hands for evening supper. I then settled into one of the ranch bungalows for my first evening in the gloriously noisy Belizean rainforest.

The thing about rainforests is that they are not quiet, serene places, although at certain times they can be. They are quieter during the hottest part of the day and very late at night, but during the day and especially at sunrise and sunset, they reverberate with an incredibly loud cacophony of buzzing insects, screeching birds, and howling monkeys that sound more like a sawmill than a forest. In my journal, I wrote that I had one of the best nights of rest in my life, lulled to sleep by that relentlessly hypnotic animal-insect orchestra, the memory of which lies deep within our primordial DNA.

The next morning after strong coffee and breakfast, my cousin showed me photographs from our mutual family tree, because her family also shared my grandmother's family name, Adams. One of them was a remarkable photo taken in the early 1900s that showed an entire family of our mutual ancestors—an Irishman and his full-blooded Cherokee wife, with their seven half Irish, half Cherokee sons. That's right, seven sons, and all of them were musicians. The Irishman had married his Cherokee maiden shortly after his arrival in Oklahoma territory, finding the common bond between displaced peoples, which united them and their similar histories. The indigenous Cherokee had been forcibly removed by the U.S. Army from their Southeastern origins, and marched to Oklahoma territory on the Trail Of Tears in 1838. The Irish had been forced to leave Ireland in the mid-1800s, mostly as a result of famine and brutal economic conditions, and they immigrated by the shipload to the United States. These two extremely tough people found each other in the aftermath of those hardships, fell in love, had seven sons, and one of them became my great-grandfather—a half Irish, half Cherokee musician.

According to family lore, this mixed-race family played at all the dances, weddings, parties, and funerals in their little corner of the Cherokee reservation. I'd never seen this particular photo before, but there was my great-grandfather, a musician like me, his strong, handsome face staring at me through the sepia tone of a century past.

I remember thinking at the time what a great tragedy it is that so many of us do not really know our family lineages, like the Maori and their Whakapapa. Most of us Americans are mongrels of many different races, and in a way that's what makes us strong, like the mixing of metals to make a stronger alloy. But we've also been cut off from our cultural past, our lives compartmentalized into a digitized world of office cubicles and social media, where we sift through meaningless, soulless data on square screens. We often forget the most important thing a human being has to offer—the wisdom gained from those who lived before us. I find it sad how quickly we forget our elders, considering them useless, when they contain the deepest knowledge and wisdom.

That evening I sat and talked with my cousin as the rainforest came alive again at sunset and we chatted late into the night. She described the many cultural things I might find of interest in Belize and she mentioned the local Garifuna people who lived in the southern half of Belize and down into northern Honduras. The Garifuna were famous for their drumming, as well as for their unique form of ancestral worship, which traced its lineage back to West Africa. So, after a couple of days hanging out at the Banana Ranch and getting up to speed on the history of my family, and Belize in general, I decided it was time to continue my journey south to try and meet some of these famous Garifuna drummers.

The Garifuna, like most of the New World peoples, are a mixture of different races that came into contact during the colonialization of the Americas. They're a combination of escaped and freed African slaves who intermarried with the indigenous Carib and Arawak Indians, and sometimes with Europeans as well. They were originally destined for the French-controlled island of Saint Vincent, but through a series of inter-island wars, slave revolts, and shipwrecks, they found themselves moving west to the Central American mainland.

It all started in 1763 when the British declared war on France and attempted to seize control of all the Caribbean islands under French possession, starting with naval attacks on the islands of Martinique, Saint Vincent, and the Grenadines. The ancestors of the Garifuna, known as the "Black Caribs," owned farms on these islands and they united with the French colonists to repel the British invaders. These ongoing skirmishes lasted for over 30 years, until finally in 1796 a massive British Armada finally extracted the surrender of the French colonists and their Black Carib allies.

Almost immediately the British began to seize Carib-owned farms and they did what most colonists did at that time—they divided the natives by their skin color. Those with the darker skin, approximately 4,000 of them, were sent to the island of Baliceaux, where more than half died of starvation and disease under the appalling conditions in which they were held.

Over the course of the next year, the island changed hands back and forth as the French and British occupiers battled each other, which led to yet another revolt by the natives. The British, realizing that these people would never be conquered, responded by loading all of the remaining Black Caribs onto ships, sending them to the even more remote Roatán Island, off the coast of Honduras. During this entire period, the changing mix of Afro-Indian people began to be called the Garifuna, and a distinctly new identity began to emerge.

Roatán Island is now revered as the official landing spot of the first group of Garifuna, who arrived on April 12, 1797, the official day of Garifuna Independence. As the years passed, the Garifuna began to cross the short distance to the mainland, populating the Central American coastline and establishing fishing villages along the coasts of Honduras, Nicaragua, Guatemala, and Belize. According to legend, during the difficult passage to Roatán Island, the Garifuna kept cassava plants inside their clothes, the roots staying alive from the sweat of their bodies. When they arrived on Roatán, they planted these cassava shoots where it grew abundantly, providing the main staple of their diet. Thus, every April in Belize, the locals re-enact their victorious arrival by riding their fishing boats from the surf onto the shore and waving palm fronds to symbolize the cassava that sustained their ancestors during their difficult exodus.

There are other stories in Garifuna lore about shipwrecks and groundings off the coast of Central America, where the gods intervened and the Africans would escape their bondage, swimming or rowing to shore and to freedom. Belize has the largest oceanic reef in the Western Hemisphere, second only to Australia's Great Barrier Reef, and shipwrecks were quite common in this area. Thus, it's very likely that some Africans were freed by the occasional shipwreck (and I'd also like to think that a few mutinies occurred as well).

In the ensuing 200 years, the Garifuna have created a living culture that subsists on a combination of fishing and farming, as well as tourism, folk art, and music. It's estimated that there are about 60 Garifuna communities along the Central American coastline, and there are now sizeable Garifuna communities in New Orleans, Chicago, Los Angeles, New York, and even Great Britain. Although the population is difficult to pin down, there are estimated to be around 500,000 Garifuna living worldwide who are descended from those few thousand sturdy survivors.

In April of 1997, shortly after I visited Belize, the Garifuna celebrated their 200th anniversary of independence, and in 2001 the Garifuna were officially listed as a World Heritage Culture by the United Nations. After more than 200 years of exile, oceanic wanderings, and island hardship, the Garifuna were finally recognized by the UN as a people worthy of special distinction. Then in 2007, the late producer Andy Palacio and his Garifuna Collective put the global spotlight on Garifuna music when they stormed the world with their amazing album, *Wátina*, and spirited live performances. That album alone created a huge boom in musical tourism for the Belizean Garifuna. They say that the land is enchanted here, and as a visitor, I can definitely say there is a spirit in the soil that captivates you, for sure.

As I continued my journey south down the Hummingbird Highway, I contemplated what it might be like to be from another country, another continent even, and then to be shipwrecked and stranded on the beaches that were now emerging as I neared the coastline. I thought about what it might be like during that first night alone, with no idea where you were, what you would eat? What direction would your life take in the ensuing days and weeks? How would you survive in this foreign landscape?

I was now nearing the port city of Dangriga, an early Garifuna settlement in the Stann Creek District of southern Belize. I had been driving slowly, contemplatively, for a few hours as the highway disintegrated into a dirt road, where jungle meets the ocean. I arrived in the late evening, surprised at how dark and dimly lit the town was, and it gave me the illusion that I could have been arriving at a colonial port city 200 years ago, barely lit by street lamps, with shadowy figures moving about in the dark streets and alleyways. It was a little spooky to be honest, which excited my senses even more.

I checked into a small motel, a run-down affair that had previously been a British Army barracks several decades earlier. My room smelled of mildew and saltwater, that classic Caribbean smell, but it was clean and stark, a simple and easy place to be based for the time. The next morning I walked into town, as I prefer to walk as much as possible when visiting a place. It helps to feel the energy of the land through my feet, and I can sometimes even feel rhythms—or "paces", as I call them—coming up from the Earth. I inquired at a couple of the bars and cafes along the main road as to where I might find some live Garifuna music. Was there a music scene in Dangriga, and if so, where could I find it? I was told that indeed, there was a Garifuna form of music called *Punta*, which was a popular dance, propelled by the driving rhythms of the Garifuna drummers and a hip-thrusting dance style. There would be some dancing later that night if I wanted to return, which of course I did.

The word Punta itself is probably a linguistical drift from the African Mande word *Bunda*, which means buttocks. It's also the name of a fertility dance which highlights the gyrating movements of the pelvis. As soon as I saw the Punta danced in Dangriga, I saw its sexually charged style, the hips moving in unison to the drums, the sweat pouring from the drummers and dancers alike. I would learn more about the roots of African drum and dance culture in West Africa the following year, but here on my first trip to Belize, this New World rhythm was shaking its hips right in front of me and I liked it! From that night onward I thought about drumming very differently, that it should move people instead of numbing them, as Western pop music has a tendency to do. After that first hot night in Dangriga, drumming for me was all about making people dance, and that became my new prime directive.

As I navigated the nightlife of Dangriga, I started hearing about some religious drummers whose primary focus was playing the sacred rhythms of the Garifuna religion, as opposed to its more secular dance styles, which I had just witnessed. These religious drummers work with spirit mediums who are induced by the sacred rhythms into an ecstatic trance, during which deceased ancestors are able to communicate through the mediums. This is similar to other Afro-Caribbean religions such as Haitian Voodoo, Cuban Santeria, and Brazilian Candomblé. The general concept is that the drumming and singing of the sacred songs creates a "pathway" by which the ancestral spirits can come down from the heavens and "ride" the body of the medium, possessing it and speaking through their voice. In this tradition, the ancestral spirits are being summoned to answer questions regarding the spiritual and physical health of the individuals and their community, their interpersonal relationships, land, agriculture, and business. It's a spiritual, pragmatic way to reaffirm and reinforce the health of the people and their community, using the traditional wisdom of their ancestors.

Although the Garifuna religion uses an African-style system of trance possession, it also holds many beliefs around shamanism, which are deeply embedded throughout the indigenous world. Shamanism, and its foundation in animism, is something I've been studying for many years now, and it is the oldest belief system on the planet. Every culture on Earth has practiced shamanism at some point in their history, and many still do today. The basic belief is that everything on this Earth—every object in existence, whether it be a stone, a river, a tree, a bird, a bear, the elements of earth, fire, water, wind—whatever natural thing you can give a name to, that object has a certain kind of spiritual power. By spirit, I mean a molecular intelligence, and sometimes a spiritual intelligence as well. A shaman (which is originally a Siberian word but is now a universal term) is a person who can access the intelligence of a spirit. He or she receives this information in a certain mental state, and this can be achieved through drumming, dancing, singing, or a combination of all three.

Drumming is the most common method found around the world to help create a shamanic experience, and the technique itself is really quite simple. One of the theories that has been tested and proven is that drumming and continuous rhythm at a tempo close to the human heartbeat (about 60 BPMs) helps to synchronize the hemispheres of the brain, thus creating a deep, focused state in the visual cortex of the mind. This focused, visual state allows the shaman to mentally travel and gain information from the spirit world.

In the indigenous world, shamanism is a system for understanding the spirits of all things, and then using that knowledge to heal their people and their communities. Sometimes this healing is a physical one, complete with herbal remedies. Other times the shaman might have a vision that explains a complicated situation and how it can be remedied in the social realm. In my own experience, I've witnessed shamans helping people with emotional and spiritual problems, I've watched them prepare a person for surgery, and I once saw a shaman in the Peruvian Amazon heal a man's broken back, so that in just a couple of weeks' time the man's spine was back in perfect alignment. Shamanism is really just a pre-scientific way of understanding the natural universe, and its closest modern parallel would be the quantum physicists who can see the spiritual dance of atomic structure. Shamans seem to understand that dance at an intuitive level, they know how to use it for good, and amazingly, they still continue to incarnate in modern cultures around the world.

As a drummer, the idea of rhythm and song being a vehicle for spiritual evolution and communication has long been a focus of my life. Having played for decades now, I can feel the effects of rhythm and music on my own mind and body. And even though a live performance is more entertainment than religion, many will often refer to their favorite band as "a religious experience." That's because in a very real way, live music and even the modern concert is a type of shamanic performance. The singer-songwriter or band is using the invisible power of music, storytelling, and visual arts, to heal the spirit of the audience—we've simply developed it into a technologically advanced version of what was already an ancient, universal practice. When I reflect back on all the years I've sat behind the drums on a stage or in a studio, it's the drum set that I see as the religious altar for me.

These were my thoughts as I drove towards Hopkins Village, the famed center of Garifuna culture, about an hour south of Dangriga. I was immediately struck by the raw beauty of the landscape, and I saw several rows of thatched-roof bungalows neatly aligned along the narrow, sandy roads, all immaculately clean, with no litter or garbage to be seen anywhere. The sugar-sand beach was just a few meters from the last row of houses, and the crystalline-blue ocean beckoned me for a swim. Yes, this was definitely the epitome of the tropical paradise we've all seen on postcards, and Hopkins Village could have substituted for any of those places.

I went straight to the only business I could find in the small village, a modest restaurant right on the beach. I mistakenly ordered a soup with turtle meat, a slight regret, but apparently turtles are in large abundance here. I asked the proprietor if she knew of a drummer whose name I had heard in Dangriga, a young man named Joel Coleman. She immediately knew whom I was talking about, and in about 30 minutes, a young man appeared, no older than a teenager as far as I could tell. It was Joel, a cheerful and pleasant young man with an easy smile and a gentle way about him. He was all of 18 years old, and I was an ancient 30 years at the time.

I invited Joel to join me for lunch and we agreed on a payment for him to give me some drum lessons. I paid more than was asked, because I've always believed that music lessons, particularly from a person whose traditions should be respected, is one of the many ways that a musician can honor a fellow musician. After lunch, we walked a few hundred yards to Joel's practice space—a small, single-roomed hut where he kept his carved Garifuna drums and a very weathered old drum set, its heavily tarnished cymbals and hardware the result of the salty sea air that breezed through the open slat windows.

I told Joel about my first experience in Dangriga hearing the exciting Punta rhythm and watching its accompanying dance, and we started our first lesson by playing that rhythm together, he on one of his "Premiero" (primary) drums and I on a slightly larger "Segundo" (secondary) drum. The Punta, it turns out, is a fairly complex rhythm to master, because even though the rhythm sounds simple in its repetitiveness, the subtlety of the swing in the rhythm is quite difficult. We played with a double open-handed technique, which for someone used to drumsticks was a difficult transition for me to make. This is also something that I've found to be very true over the years - how a rhythm can be explained with words and technique, yet it's the soul of the drummer who truly makes the drum sing. The subtle movements of the hands against the animal skin head, the microsecond shifts in the rhythm itself, and of course the actual strikes of the palm against the head—all of this is a lightning-fast dance. Here I was in a small village in Central America, playing traditional rhythms for the first time in my life, and the drum master before me was an 18-year-old kid who was playing circles around me.

A traditional Garifuna drum is carved out of a hollowed-out mahogany log about 16 inches in diameter and length, which creates a drum about as wide as it is tall. It's then stretched with a single cow hide or goat skin head held taught by wooden pegs, with a single catgut strainer across the top to give it a vibrational buzz, a sound found in other traditional African instruments. The bottom of the drum is left open and tilted slightly backward so that is sits between the drummer's legs, with the hands resting comfortably in a forward position on the head. These handmade drums had a very organic and earthy quality to them, and the sound that came forth was powerful and hypnotic. I began to notice in myself a trance-like feeling from the pulse of the rhythms.

Over the course of the following week, I made daily trips from my motel in Dangriga down to Hopkins village, where I would find Joel either at his mother's house or near his practice hut, and we would begin a few hours of drumming together. During this relatively short period of study, Joel showed me several of the main Garifuna rhythms, including the Punta, the Shumba, the Paranda, the Huga Huga, the John Canoe, and the powerful trance-inducing rhythm, the Dugu.

Joel didn't tell me this immediately, but he eventually revealed that he was a drum priest in the village, as was his father and grandfather before him. Joel was an honored member of his community, having been recognized as a master of the rhythms that propel his people's religious ceremonies, and as such, he had been initiated in the ways of their most sacred ceremony, the Dugu. But that didn't stop Joel from also playing dance music on his weather-worn drum set, and we had a great time taking turns on it, I showing him some of my American grooves while he played the Garifuna drums, and then we'd switch roles and try our best to remember what the other guy had just played. Occasionally, another one of Joel's drummer friends would join us, playing along as we jammed out our unique grooves. I smile remembering how much fun we had inventing our Garifuna-American grooves; it was definitely a special moment in my life as a drummer.

As Joel explained it to me, the Garifuna's Dugu ceremony is the most important ceremony in Garifuna culture, and it is only called for when an individual, family, or the greater community is experiencing serious problems, which could be physical, emotional, marital, financial, agricultural, business, or just general bad luck. When these problems persist, a spirit medium called a *Buyai* is consulted for advice, and if a Dugu ceremony is called for, then Joel and his drummers would be needed.

Buyais are selected by the ancestral spirits themselves, usually in the form of a dream that has deep symbolic meaning. A common theme I encountered through my research is that of a driver coming with a horse-drawn cart, the driver being recognized as an ancestor, such as a beloved grandfather or grandmother. In the dream, the Buyai-to-be will climb aboard the cart and pay attention to where the ancestor takes him or her. This dream journey is equivalent to the shamanic journey and the information and wisdom imparted in the dream will help explain the destiny of the Buyai, and perhaps even some of the spiritual powers they will develop in the future.

If a Dugu ceremony is called for, the announcement goes out several weeks, or even months ahead of time, so that all of the family members can attend, to show of community support for the sick individual. Traditionally, there would be about three days of fishing before the onset of the ceremony itself, and this is a way for the relatives and community members to re-bond with each other. It also reminds them of their historic connection to the ancestors who survived incredible hardships across the Caribbean Sea.

At the onset of the Dugu, a ceremonial space is created inside the *terreiro*, or cult house, and the pouring of libations is done to honor the ancestral spirits, another practice found in almost all the Afro-Caribbean religions. This is usually done by drinking rum or sprinkling it on the ground, often combined with smoking cigars because the spirits like to smoke and drink! All of this combined with the drumming, singing, and dancing creates an atmosphere of social harmony between the people, and a pathway for the ancestral spirits to descend.

Joel explained to me that as a religious drummer, it was his job to play the various rhythms necessary over the course of the Dugu, and these rhythms are played by three drummers, with Joel on the Premiero playing the lead rhythms, and two Segundos playing the supporting rhythms. When played in their proper sequence, the rhythms cause the spirit mediums to be induced into a trance-possession state.

The ceremonial dance itself is called the *Mali*, and it usually lasts for about two days, with the dance being repeated about eight times for every 24-hour period. During these all-day and night sessions, multiple trance possessions will take place, which are caused by the rhythms and the sacred songs that call the ancestor's spirits into the medium. The ancestral spirits will then speak through the mediums, imparting information, knowledge, and wisdom to the extended members of the family and community. This trance-like state, known as *ASC* or *altered state of consciousness,* goes something like this:

1. The medium becomes disassociated from themselves and the people around them. A trance begins and they enter a liminal condition, neither here nor there, where they exist between the material world and the spirit world.

2. The medium exhibits a lack of motor control and there are exaggerated body movements known as hyperkinesia, which are sometimes exhibited as violent jerking movements and spasms.

3. The medium begins to act out in the character or personality of their ancestor, and this is a character that is markedly different from their everyday behavior. This is the ancestral spirit taking control of the medium, possessing them, and beginning to speak through them.

4. After the ancestor has finished speaking and advising the community, the medium experiences a loss of memory as to what happened or what was said during the trance. This is a highly effective veil of protection too, since the medium is seen to be a sacred voice of the ancestors and they are released from anything that was said, nor are they personally bound to any of the words, decrees, or judgments cast down by the ancestor they channeled.

This phenomenon of people communicating with spirits is far from unusual, and it is found throughout the histories of Judaism, Christianity, Islam, Hinduism, and Buddhism. God spoke to Moses through the element of fire in a burning bush; angels appeared before the saints; churchgoers occasionally speak in tongues; and the bible is built upon the premise of a holy ghost. The Islamic myths talk of the Jinn, who were genie-spirits that ranged from very bad to very good. Hinduism has countless stories about the various gods appearing in different manifestations, and the Buddha was visited by multiple spirits and deities on his path to Enlightenment. Even now in the New Age movement we have gurus channeling entities who tell their congregation exactly what they want to hear—for a price.

Whatever our social conditioning might make us think about these kinds of mysterious ceremonies, there is one thing that we should all know from experience: when people get together to do a ceremony of any kind, it inherently strengthens their bonds of love, compassion, and a sense of community between the people. Ceremonies, especially musical-shamanic ones, inherently cause people to feel closer to the spirit world, and when they emerge from the ceremony, they are always stronger, healthier, and most importantly, happier. People such as the Garifuna have developed their own unique system to deal with the same basic problems that affect all of us—they just found a very musical and joyous way to do it.

Joel Coleman, his wonderfully kind mother, and the warm-hearted people of Hopkins Village were a truly incredible experience for me, and I learned more in two weeks from those people than I learned in the previous decade of professional music. Joel taught me far more than just the basic rhythms of the Garifuna people—he taught me how rhythm and dance is a very real way to heal people.

Joel definitely possessed the wisdom of a much older man, of that I am sure, and this just reinforced the Garifuna belief that the ancestors can reincarnate back into their villages to teach the members of their communities. Hopkins Village seemed to have a natural balance between the buoyancy and optimism of youth, compared to the slow and deliberate wisdom of the elders. It is between these two polarities that real truth and wisdom are exchanged, the youth looking forward into the future with the elderly offering a gentle and guiding hand of how to get there safely.

On my way back to Belize City, I stopped in Belmopan to say goodbye to my cousin at her Banana Ranch. During my last evening there, I picked up an old Mariachi bass guitar that had mysteriously appeared on the porch of my bungalow and I wrote the composition, "Escuro", which in Spanish means "mysterious darkness." It's the only word that I could find to describe the beautiful, enchanted place called Belize.

After a visit to Guatemala and the Mexican Yucatan to look at ancient Mayan temples, I finally returned to Seattle. As a gift for Joel, I mailed him a beautiful leather drumstick bag full of several new pairs of drumsticks, mallets, brushes, and some hardware for his drum set—things that he really needed. In his modesty he had only requested a single new pair of drumsticks, so I hoped to surprise him with a large bag of them. It was a small gift from his American friend, a gesture of kindness for his musical and spiritual generosity. Unfortunately, the bag was returned about six months later with a stamp from Dangriga that said, *Postage Undeliverable.* It had made it all the way to Dangriga, but not the short, final distance to Hopkins Village.

I'm hoping that Joel called for a Dugu ceremony to sort out the mail delivery problems in Belize. I hope to ask him that the next time I see him.

6. Garifuna Punta Rhythm
7. Belizean Rainforest
8. Barrett Martin Group "Escuro"

VERSE 6

DARK BLUES: A VERY MAD SEASON

Mad Season, Live At The Moore Theater in Seattle, 1995. Left to right: John Baker Saunders, Layne Staley, Barrett Martin, Skerik, Mike McCready.

"Pain is self-chosen. At least, so the prophet says."

—Layne Staley

When I returned from Belize in the winter of 1997 it became apparent that the Screaming Trees vaunted *Dust* album wasn't going to take off as we had hoped. Despite our extensive touring over the previous year, the album sales were flat and new opportunities seemed slim. Facing an uncertain future for the band, I was extremely sad and actually quite depressed. I think the other band members felt the same way and it was generally a very a dark time for everyone. Kurt Cobain's suicide three years earlier still seemed to linger over the city like a dark, heavy cloud, and several other non-famous Seattle musicians had also died from overdoses, and many others were struggling with various drug and alcohol addictions. Perhaps the saddest part of it all was the inability of those suffering to appreciate their remarkable musical achievements, their immense skills and talents, which was the very thing that made Seattle the world center of music in the 1990s.

I don't know what it is about American society that makes it such an addictive, self-destructive place, but over the course of my almost half a century of life, I have seen far too much of it. I think it has something to do with a capitalist society that can provide any product you can dream of, but cares little for the welfare of the people themselves.

Of the five major rock bands that I played in—Thin Men, Skin Yard, Screaming Trees, Mad Season, and Walking Papers—the singers for Thin Men, Skin Yard, and Mad Season eventually died of drug-related deaths. Mad Season actually lost two members—our singer and our bass player, both to heroin overdoses—and several members of these five bands had their own battles with drugs and alcohol, including myself.

The great irony of this is that the stereotype of the drug-addled rock star is the biggest cliché in music. It's been done so many times, that it's become a ridiculous cartoon. I always thought that rock & roll was supposed to be a form of rebellion against an overbearing, restrictive power structure. But what is rebellious about being signed to a corporate major label who decides your financial fate, while you're strung out on your drug of choice, losing all your royalty and show money to disgusting drug dealers? Where's the rebellion or independence in that? This character sounds more like the fool who is manipulated by others, bled dry of their money, power, and self-respect and that, by definition, ain't rock & roll.

It took me a while to figure all this out myself, and as clear as my mind can be, the hard path of alcoholism taught me some very difficult lessons. But when I did finally figure it out, I got sober and I stayed sober, and everything in my life greatly improved from that moment onward, so many years ago. This next story took place between 1994-1999, so it spans about five years. It's about four young men who were figuring out the very hard lessons of addiction, as we made one of the most definitive albums on that subject.

Alcohol was my drug of choice, so I decided to stop drinking in 1994. It was my first attempt at sobriety, and to be honest, it would take me a few more years until I finally accomplished total sobriety. I did it, not because anything bad had happened to me, but rather because I didn't like having an unclear mind when I was surrounded by so many people in the music business who had varying degrees of insanity and addiction. I wanted to be the opposite of that; I wanted to be a true musician who was independent, creative, and not controlled by anything. I wanted sobriety and clarity of mind as I figured out the next stage of my life and I was, for the first time, seriously thinking about applying to music conservatories to finish my education. And then one day I got a call from Mike McCready, the lead guitarist of Pearl Jam, who used to come and watch Screaming Trees shows from behind my drum riser. He had an idea he wanted to present to me in person and he asked if I would be interested in meeting him for dinner.

We picked a night and met at a seafood restaurant in the Fremont neighborhood of North Seattle. After we caught up on life, Mike told me that he wanted to do a side project with me, because he had recently completed rehab and was now clean and sober and inspired to write music again. Great, I said, I was sober now too.

Mike had been writing songs in rehab and he wanted to try them out with me on drums, and he also wanted to ask Layne Staley of Alice In Chains to sing vocals. I had, of course, been on a world tour with Layne the year before on the Alice/Trees tour and we had become pretty good friends. Mike also wanted to bring in a bassist from the Chicago blues scene whom he had also met in rehab, a man named John Baker Saunders. I liked this idea a lot, because I always loved the blues and that influence was deep in the Screaming Trees.

We decided to initially just have me, Mike, and Baker jam together to work out some musical ideas, and by the second jam, Layne was with us as well. That is how the band Mad Season came to be, and this is the story of the five years we were officially a band.

Mad Season was born into Generation X and we were fortunate in that our lives were shaped and reinforced by a continual soundtrack of rather exceptional music. We grew up during the golden age of music in the late 1960s and '70s, experienced the power of punk and new wave in the '80s, and then the roar of alternative rock in the '90s. We were truly a blessed generation of musicians. We're all getting older now, a little grayer around the temples, and as we approach our middle age we see our own children growing up into their youth, with their own music. It makes me reflect back on a time when we too were young and full of hope and optimism, when everything seemed possible, and age and wisdom had not yet tempered our fiery spirits.

Music defined the sound and character of our generation, and it empowered us in that very special way that only music can. Now, in the noonday sun of life, I especially remember these gifted friends who left us much too soon. Those talented bright stars who shone with so much power, beauty, and grace. That's how I like to remember them anyway, because unlike the rest of us, they never age in the time capsule of memory, they never make mistakes, and as time passes, we only remember their greatest qualities. The historical revisionism in our own memory seems to work favorably for them in that regard, although it's rather unreasonable for the rest of us, who are still forging ahead in the hurricane of life. Perhaps that's how it should be—we remember only the best in our departed friends, and what we remember most poignantly is the music we all shared together.

During the late 1980s and early 1990s a powerful musical landscape began to unfold in the Pacific Northwest, and many great bands and visionary artists emerged under the umbrella of what we called "alternative music." Seattle in particular seemed to have a corner on the market, inventing its own unique style of music, and you probably knew many of the bands from that era. Some of those bands are still working today, others knew intuitively when their time had expired, and a few ended under more tragic circumstances. One thing is certain, however: all of those bands left behind great bodies of work, some of them classic albums that still reverberate today, 30 years later.

There were also a few side projects that came out along the way, one of the more notable being Temple of the Dog, a tribute to the late singer Andrew Wood of the band Mother Love Bone. Another album came from our band, Mad Season, and that album was built around a desire to understand the spiritual nature of pain, expressed through music. Our only studio album *Above* is now considered to be a classic of that time, and that's because it was all about playing the blues.

It was 1994, and Mike and Baker had just gotten out of a rehab facility in Minneapolis, where they had become fast friends with their love of the blues and the bright clarity that comes from a newly sober mind. Layne and I had toured with our regular bands the previous year, playing shows around the world together. But we were exhausted from the grind of the road and I think all four of us were looking for a different kind of musical expression. We convened in the fall of 1994 to write a few songs and see where it all might lead. During those first kinetic rehearsals, we talked as friends about our previous job skills before rock & roll had changed our lives so dramatically.

Layne and I had both been carpenters in Seattle, pouring concrete foundations, framing houses, and generally working as laborers until the touring life had taken over. Mike had worked at a Seattle pizzeria before he found his overnight success with Pearl Jam, and as they say, overnight success takes about 10 years of hard work before it magically happens "overnight." Baker, although a working bassist in the Chicago and Minneapolis blues scenes, had frequently worked odd jobs to earn a living, because economic times were tough for any musician in the 1980s and '90s. It meant that you had do a little of this and a little of that to get by. It's really not much different today.

Whatever our past jobs and bands might have been, Mad Season was now focused on making our own album, and after several highly productive rehearsals we played a series of secret shows at Seattle's now legendary Crocodile Cafe. The intent was to tighten up the songs and try out the new material on a live audience, and during these shows we realized a singular, musical vision that would manifest in the studio a few weeks later.

The recording sessions were booked at Seattle's Bad Animals Studio, at the time owned by Ann and Nancy Wilson of the band Heart, a truly heroic band for those of us who grew up in the Northwest. The recordings were overseen by engineer Brett Eliason, who had previously worked with Heart, as well as running the front of house sound for Pearl Jam and Screaming Trees during our bands' early tours. The first 10 songs were recorded quickly, two of them featuring additional vocals from Screaming Trees vocalist Mark Lanegan, as well as some exceptional saxophone work from a Seattle jazz musician known as Skerik. In just over two weeks of recording, with an additional week for mixing, the album was finished and ready to be presented to the world.

Above was released internationally on March 14th, 1995 on Columbia Records and it immediately struck a resonant chord with the public that sent the album to Gold status (500,000 units) within a few weeks. It peaked at #24 on the Billboard Top 200, and the album's first single, "River of Deceit," was a bona fide radio hit in the United States, reaching the #2 spot on the modern rock chart. All of this happened without the band having played an advertised show, much less touring to support the album. Thus, we decided to play a proper, advertised concert.

On the evening of April 29th, 1995, Mad Season stepped out onto the stage of the Moore Theatre in downtown Seattle to perform what is considered to be one of the greatest live shows of that decade. The Moore is an old but elegant theater on 2nd Avenue in downtown Seattle. It was built in 1907, holds about 1,400 people, and is a Seattle landmark where every notable Seattle band—and almost every national touring band—has played at some point during their career. It's a beautiful place to both play and hear music, and I still go there from time to time to see shows.

Our show was sold out, in fact, tickets were gone within an hour of being released to the public. In the audience were our closest friends, girlfriends, parents, and at least one grandparent, so three generations of people were there with us. My grandfather, who had served in WWII in the South Pacific campaign, absolutely loved the concert. He always wondered what rock & roll was all about and this show really proved it to him. I also met one of the great loves of my life at that show, and I think maybe a few other people found love there as well.

When Mad Season walked out onto that stage we honestly didn't know what to expect. Prior to this we had only played those handful of unannounced club dates at the Crocodile. But when we did finally walk out on stage, the loudest, most thunderous audience I had ever heard greeted us. It sounded more like a Viking horde, roaring with excitement—it's something I will never forget.

I've always said that Mad Season was the heaviest blues band that ever came out of Seattle, because our songs were dark, haunting, and totally built around blues-based riffs. Anchored by the deep, swinging rhythm section of Baker's bass lines and my drums, overlaid with Mike's alternately blistering and ambient guitar work, and Layne's haunting words and melodies, Mad Season essentially played a grungier, heavier version of the blues. Our unusual chemistry made us sound totally unique for the time, in an era of post-grunge formula rock that was beginning to dominate popular music back then.

Above is the only complete album of Layne Staley's introspective, mystical lyrics, but they were paradoxically very uplifting songs. That's because, just like the blues, when you hear a song about suffering or sadness, it kind of makes you feel better because you realize you are not alone in this world. That's the power of a great song - it uplifts the spirit of the people and shows them a new way of seeing, even if the theme is a dark one.

At the Moore Theater show, in addition to the four principle band members, we also had the talents of saxophonist/percussionist Skerik, who had played on *Above*, and the vocals of Mark Lanegan, my former Screaming Trees band mate. Both musicians added spectacular color and voice to our explosive, visceral quartet.

It was also very fortunate that we made a last minute decision to film and record the entire show. It was an expensive decision to make back in 1995, when the technology was still analog and we had to buy costly reels of celluloid film and magnetic recording tape to document the evening. It was a real gamble for a band that was playing its first announced show on a large stage, but looking back, it was a great decision because we definitely "bottled the lightning" on that special night.

When we made the set list, we only had the 10 songs we had recorded for *Above*, plus our version of John Lennon's "I Don't Want To Be A Soldier," thus we really had to take our time and extend some of the songs and guitar solos to make a normal length concert. One of the highlights of the evening came in the encore with the two-song medley "All Alone" and "November Hotel." "All Alone" is perhaps Layne's most beautiful vocal performance from the show, and it segued perfectly into the explosive closing song, "November Hotel." The title of that song was named after the distress call a pilot makes when he's been shot down in combat, just as Mike McCready's father had been shot down in Vietnam. Fortunately for us, Mike's father was also in attendance, so we dedicated the song to him.

When you watch the film, *Mad Season: Live At The Moore*, you can really see what it was like in 1995, at the peak of the '90s Seattle music scene, right in the heart of Seattle. Everyone who was there knew that this was a zenith that would eventually fade. But for a little over an hour, Mad Season captured on film and tape that essential moment in history.

Before we came out for the final encore, we all agreed backstage that the audience that night was a very special one indeed. And when Layne spoke to them, he said, "This is the most awesome crowd!" and you could hear the emotion in his voice. He said it because those who were there touched us deeply that night, just as we touched them back. Those kinds of moments change you forever, because there we were, all of us, alive in that moment in one place, feeling the magic together.

What few people know is that in the spring of 1996 a second Mad Season album was started. Again, Brett Eliason was engineering and Mike, Baker, and I started recording the basic tracks for about 20 new songs, this time at Seattle's Ironwood Studios, since renamed Avast Studios. My friend Peter Buck, guitarist of R.E.M., came down and helped us write a beautiful song, and Skerik returned to bang on some percussion and add his colorful approach to our expanding sound.

Unfortunately, because of his ongoing addiction and declining health, Layne was not able to sing on any of the second album recording sessions. After a very creative but ultimately frustrating month in the studio, we each took divergent paths. Mike went back to Pearl Jam, I went back to the Screaming Trees, Layne went back to Alice In Chains, and Baker joined the superb Seattle folk rock outfit The Walkabouts.

A couple years passed with the lingering hope that maybe, eventually, that second Mad Season album would get finished. We all hoped it would happen, and I would occasionally get a call from Columbia Records asking if any progress had been made. But communication between the band members had become fractured and disjointed. We missed what we once had together but we couldn't find a way to get back to that place. It was very much like the end of a great love affair—lost connections, misinterpreted messages, sadness, and eventually isolation. And then a very dark day came, when the one true god, Death, made his fateful appearance.

We lost Baker to a heroin overdose in the early winter of 1999, and then just three years later in April of 2002, we lost Layne in the same way. Many of us were spiritually and musically crushed for a considerable amount of time. Sometimes, when I remember too many of the details, I still am. But maybe that's also why we write about the people who died before us. Maybe they were just too good to not write about, their memories demanding to be told through words and stories.

My memories of Baker are rich and full of great humor. He was about 12 years older than the rest of us, which made Baker closer to 40 when we recorded *Above*, as opposed to me, Mike, and Layne who were all 27 years old at the time. We thought we had lived hard lives in our own self-suffering, myopic way, but Baker had truly lived it.

Born into a working class family in Montgomery, Alabama, Baker found his musical calling in the electric blues of the Chicago and Minneapolis music scenes, where he played with several respected bands, making the chicken scratch that bluesmen earn. When I played with Baker for the first time, I could immediately hear his deep and ancient soul singing through his resounding bass lines, and when the Mad Season rhythm section played, we swung like a battleship, physically moving everyone in the room. The first notes you hear when the *Above* album begins to play is Baker's lonely bass line starting the song "Wake Up," which was the first song he wrote and introduced to our band. Baker set the mood for the album, and everything else followed in step with that.

The other thing about Baker, something that anyone who knew him would attest to, was that he was a very gentle and kind person with a deep and caring soul. He really loved people, especially older folks, and I think it was because he knew how tough they must have been to have survived the Great Depression, WWII, and to make our country as strong as it was.

Baker and I bought houses pretty close to each other with the advance from our album, and he would often come over to my house in the morning for coffee, driving his 'deliberately 1970s' burgundy Plymouth sedan. It was classic Baker style. We'd start with black coffee, he'd flirt with my girlfriend, and then I would make us some scrambled eggs and toast. He'd tell me some hilarious story about the old guys he used to play with in Chicago and we'd start the day off with a good laugh. Always Baker made people laugh, with a story or anecdote to go with everything, but he tempered that humor with a deep respect for human beings and a linguistic wit that was a cross between his polite upbringing in the American South and the mean streets of Chicago. I have never met anyone before or since that even comes close to Baker's character—he was truly one of a kind.

Baker and I were supposed to meet for breakfast the morning he passed away. I had insisted we go to a nearby restaurant rather than me doing the cooking, because I had just gotten back from a tour. Sadly, he never showed up at my doorstep. He had died the night before, flat on his back on his kitchen floor. The drug dealer who sold him the heroin left his body without calling the police or an ambulance, stealing Baker's cherished Fender jazz bass as he fled like the vermin he was.

I really wish Baker was still around today because he would have been the greatest friend to get older with. In many ways, Baker was the wisest of us all, but I only understand that now, almost 20 years after his death.

When Layne passed away, so many people around the world were devastated. He and I had wandered through the great cities of the Western world when we toured together, but that is just a cold memory now. As I said, we only remember the greatest qualities in our departed friends, so here are some of Layne's best.

He was an extremely intelligent, humorous, and gracious human being, and he cared about things like politeness and kindness to strangers, qualities that seem to be fast evaporating in today's narcissist, social media driven culture. He laughed easily and talked openly with his fans, and his guest list at shows was always reserved for the young, marginalized people who couldn't afford to buy a ticket. Those were Layne's people, the ones without a voice, and through the power of poetic music, he gave them voice.

Layne once told me a story about his first tour in South America, after a show in Rio de Janeiro. Some fans took him to the beautiful botanical gardens on the outskirts of the city, and as they sat on the Earth talking under a canopy of trees, a tiny marmoset only a few inches tall leapt onto Layne's shoulder and resided there for quite some time, much to the delight of everyone present. Layne said it was one of the greatest experiences he ever had on tour, and years later I saw many of these tiny creatures when I toured Brazil, but they always seemed rather terrified of humans. They apparently loved Layne, however.

My best personal memory of him was when we were making *Above* and he was in the studio lounge reading Kahlil Gibran's iconic book, *The Prophet,* a book I highly recommend everyone read at some point in their lives. I told him I had read it as a college student, and I liked the part about the arrows you fire into the world to keep the darkness at bay. Layne said that as musicians we were like burning arrows, arcing across a dark sky. We talked about what it meant to be an artist with a spiritual message, and I can tell you that he had a deeply felt spiritual message to convey in his music, even if his lyrics were dark.

This theme is evident in all of Layne's songs, both with Mad Season and Alice In Chains, and its because he existed in a realm between darkness and light, a liminal state where he could see both sides. Darkness must always exist first, in order for the light to emerge in contrast to it - the two are inseparable parts of the same continuum. It's also important to remember that Layne was very young when we wrote and sang those words, yet he said a huge amount with that incredible voice. Listen to his words, because he was singing a particular kind of truth that anyone who has lived under difficult circumstances can understand. And somehow, like the blues, Layne's voice makes you feel better.

A few years after Layne's passing I got a call from my old friend, Bill Zildjian in Massachusetts. Bill had a couple of young children at the time, and while on a family drive through the countryside, he was playing *Above* on the car stereo. When the last song on the album "All Alone" came on, one of his little ones in the back seat asked if there were angels singing on the song. Bill relayed this to me over the phone: "Yeah, he was a certain kind of angel," I said, "A dark one to be sure, but an angel all the same."

Even though we lost Baker, Layne and several other Northwest musicians in those bitter Seattle years, one of the truths I've come to learn is that a person's talents are not reduced by their personal obstacles; those are merely the outer challenges that serve to temper and forge the spirit within. A person in darkness is often very close to the light, and that is why I choose to remember Baker and Layne as exceptional human beings first and foremost, and musicians second to that. They were tremendous artists who loved the Earth and its people, even if the world was a bit hard on them.

I spoke at Baker's funeral and I wrote the eulogy for Layne's, and both times I quoted another great Seattleite, the historical Chief Sealth of the Duwamish people, after whom the city of Seattle is named. The Great Chief famously said, "There is no death, only a change of worlds." I would only add to that truth that I believe we live in many different worlds, some of them dark, and some of them light. The sharpest minds can see both.

In 2012, Mike McCready and I reconvened to sift through the original magnetic tapes from that unfinished second Mad Season album. We decided to finish three of the best songs from those sessions, including the one that Peter Buck wrote, "Black Book Of Fear," as well as two others, "Locomotive" and "Slip Away." We felt that these songs best exemplified the direction the band was going before Baker's and Layne's untimely deaths. This time around, a clean and sober Mark Lanegan returned to honor his friend's memories with his own words and voice on those three songs. We then created a deluxe version of the album, which contained those new songs, as well as a forgotten guitar interlude that Mike had recorded during the first album sessions.

Additionally, we found some lost film footage from the *Live at The Moore* concert, and a never-before-seen show from a New Year's Eve gig on December 31st, 1994. We didn't even know the film footage existed, but I distinctly remember that Layne rode his Harley Davidson motorcycle up to the back of the stage moments before we were to go on. It was one of the most rock & roll moments that I can remember.

We also had one more instrumental song from the second album sessions, a song that Mike and I finished in Baker and Layne's memory. It is titled "Ascension" and it is exclusively a part of this book soundtrack.

We've all lost friends and family members; loss and grief are universal experiences we all go through eventually. We still love our departed, we always miss them, and we remember them through the stories we tell about them. When I remember the legacy of my departed friends, I still think of them as burning arrows who arc across the darkened skies.

9. Mad Season "Ascension"

VERSE 7

SENEGAL, GHANA: THE DRUMMERS TELL THE STORIES

Wolof Griot teaching basic Kora technique to Barrett in Dakar, Senegal 1998

"The original holy trinity is the forest, animal, and human kingdoms. The wooden body of a drum represents the forest kingdom; the antelope skin represents the animal kingdom; and when a man plays the drum, he unites all three kingdoms."

—Drum Master, West Africa

I had dreams of going to Africa long before I finally had the chance to go. Part of it stemmed from watching Stewart Copeland's 1985 film, *The Rhythmatist*, in which he, as the drummer for The Police, goes to Africa to hang out with native tribesman, play traditional rhythms, and even play his drum set for a pride of lions, while safely secured inside a cage (Mr. Copeland was in the cage, not the lions). I also knew about drummer Ginger Baker's African odyssey to Lagos, Nigeria in the 1970s to play with Afro Beat pioneer Fela Kuti and his groundbreaking band the Afrika '70. I suppose I could have gone to Africa sooner, on one of those well-planned safari trips, but that is not how I wanted to go the first time. I wanted to go there with a musical purpose, and I knew that it would somehow be connected to my work as a drummer. Africa is, after all, the mother source of all rhythms, and of all human beings, for that matter. We all walked out of Africa about 100,000 years ago, and we became the modern human who learned how to write language, harness electricity, and eventually walk on the moon. Fortunately, we remembered to take the drum with us, and all the incredible rhythms that go with it.

It was about 1997 when I started thinking seriously about going to Africa. I had started taking African drum lessons and buying a lot of drums and percussion for use in my studio sessions—a djembe here, a rattle there, and eventually a basement full of drums and percussion. I also started reading books on African culture and mythology to see if Africa would beckon me. And so she did.

The creation myths of Africa are the oldest on Earth, even older than the Australian Dreamtime, although many are quite similar, and we can see some cultural connections. In Africa the myths often start with a huge Cosmic Serpent or Python, often described as a Rainbow Serpent, very much like the Aboriginal creation deity, or the anaconda deity of the Amazon-dwelling Shipibo tribe. The Tutsi people of Rwanda believe that their first ancestors fell from the sky, and the Kongo people of Zaire saw their universe as being divided into two regions, with an upper world and a lower world separated by a great ocean.

The Dinka people of Southern Sudan believed in a High God who became angered by the irreverence, stupidity, and general clumsiness of human beings after he was struck on his big toe by a gardener's hoe. In disgust, the High God climbed a rope ladder back up to heaven, pulled up the ladder, and severed his connection with humanity forever. In southern Africa and Zimbabwe, stories abound of people who built immense towers to try to climb back up to their High God, and for the Luba people of Zaire, this tower was built by musician-architects. However, the High God became annoyed with all the racket the musicians were making, and as they drew closer he destroyed the tower, sending everyone hurtling back to Earth.

Other myths come from the Zulus of South Africa, who believed that their kings had the power over rain, and the Yoruba people of Nigeria who believed that the Orisha *Changó* ruled thunder and lightning, his queen *Osun* ruling fresh water and fertility.

The Dogon people of Mali saw the universe as formed out of a giant cosmic egg that they called Amma, and the Bambara people of Mali revered the Great Antelope deity who brought the secrets of agriculture to their people. Alternately, there was Pale Fox, a trickster who stole the sacred seeds from the cosmic egg and incorrectly planted them on

Earth. By planting the seeds wrongly and without proper intention, Pale Fox created chaos and disorder, which put humans on an evolutionary path whereby they had to transform the chaos of nature into sustainable, balanced agriculture. This is how humans learned how to become caretakers of the Earth rather than exploiters, and in doing so evolved in accordance with the Creator.

Through this process of evolution and transformation, Africans were the first to harness fire and forge iron with the art of blacksmithing. After that discovery, an entire mythology emerged out of the mystical power of the blacksmith, his ability to make tools as well as weapons, and perhaps most importantly, his ability to make the gongs and bells used for the musical incantations and religious ceremonies. *Ogun*, one of the Yoruban Orishas who represents civilization, also rules the element of iron because we need iron to make everything from the blade of a knife to a jet airliner. For the followers of Ogun, one doesn't swear on a bible when testifying, but instead kisses a piece of iron, which is the most solemn oath in telling the truth.

When you're studying African music and dance, you're talking about an aural (listening) tradition that goes back many thousands of years. With African music and drumming, you have to listen to what people say, how they play their instrument, and then memorize it. It's not written down, it is written in the mind, and when you learn music in this way, there is no disruption in the continuity of the tradition. These traditions contain both musical and cultural information, and they encourage the greatest of mental faculties—things like observance, patience, and wisdom. That's why Africa and her immense musical traditions are so vitally important in the history of human expression— this is where it all started.

Back in Seattle, I had seen a flyer in the window of a local drum shop that I frequented named John's Music, where I had been buying all those African drums. The flyer advertised lessons from a Senegalese drum master who also happened to live in Seattle. His name was Mapathe Diop and he was offering classes in Sabar drumming, the traditional drumming of the Wolof people of Senegal. Mapathe was also a Griot, which is a kind of musical storyteller, entrusted with preserving the stories and musical traditions of his community. Mapathe had immigrated to the United States with his family, but he continued to make annual trips back to Senegal where he would take his students for more advanced training with traditional Wolof drummers.

For most of 1997-98, I studied with Mapathe, his son Thione, and a small group of local Seattle drummers, most of them Anglo-Americans like myself. We sweated it out in the basement of Mapathe's modest home as we studied the traditional Sabar rhythms of the Wolof people. These rhythms also propelled a beautiful and energetic dancing style, which would often happen during our simultaneous practice sessions.

In African culture, like many other indigenous cultures, drumming and dancing are synonymous, expressed in different ways as rhythm moving through the hands of the drummer, or through the body of the dancer. The tall, hourglass-shaped Sabar drums were elegantly carved out of long, slender logs, and then stretched with a thin goatskin, which was held in place with horizontal wooden pegs. Played with an open left hand and a thin, short stick in the right hand, these drums could be made to "speak" in a variety of ways that were both quiet and hypnotic, as well as loud and thunderous. I immediately loved this style of drumming and took to it quickly. I was especially energized by the African dancers who were taught by Mapathe's wife, as they jumped, gyrated, and lunged across the floor, propelled by our rhythms. When the opportunity came for me to go study with Mapathe's extended Griot community in Senegal, I didn't even think twice. We left Seattle in October of 1998, making one stop in New York before boarding our plane for Dakar, the capitol of Senegal.

There were only about a dozen of us in the traveling group—half drum students and half dance students. I was the only professional drummer in the group, although the younger men who had studied with Mapathe for a few years were quite a bit better in the Sabar style than I was. They were quiet and serious young men, and I respected them for their commitment to a tradition and the years of practice it takes to really learn something deeply, just as I had done with the American drum set. But African drumming is a very different style altogether, and it is much older than the world's other rhythmic systems. Those who study it over the course of a lifetime say that mystical truths are revealed as they go deeper into the practice. I never went that far with African drumming, but I can say that with over 40 years playing the American drum set, certain mystical truths have been revealed to me about music, life, love, and the pursuit of wisdom. I think the same is probably true with any artistic path—the deeper you go into it, the more truth will reveal itself in a way that only an artist can understand.

The first thing that hit me when I got off the plane in Senegal was the heat and the smell. It's not a bad smell, however it's totally different from anything else I had ever experienced. It smelled both ancient and mysterious, and also strangely familiar. It smelled a bit like seduction. There was the usual chaos at the airport, as porters and taxi drivers clambered over each other to help us with our bags and drive us to our destination, and then we were off.

We drove in four taxis through the rough, potholed streets of Dakar, and I saw immediately that it was a very poor country indeed. On the outskirts of town, I saw entire communities that were built out of tarps and plastic remnants that we as Americans would have taken to the dump. However, here in Africa everything has a secondary usage, sometimes as your main source of shelter. These were not refugee camps, but the equivalent of the Dakar suburbs, where people lived in houses made of cinder block, wood, and discarded plastic. Clearly the infrastructure of the country was falling apart, and as I would later learn, this is generally true of most of West Africa, which only gained its independence from French and British colonialism in the early 1960s. Since that time, West Africa and its many nations have been left to govern themselves, and now in the 21st century, we're seeing the ill effects of centuries of colonialization, as well as systemic corruption at the highest levels of government.

Africa can appear very poor to the naked eye, but under its soil it is perhaps the wealthiest continent in the world because of its natural resources, minerals, and gigantic underground aquifers. This is a fact not lost on the international oil, mining, water, agricultural, and timber industries that are currently operating there, or rather I should say, exploiting these natural resources for themselves. In the meantime, Africa's citizens receive very little of the products or revenues taken out of their countries. But there is a saying and I do believe this is true: Africa cannot be saved by anyone other than Africans themselves.

After an hour's drive out of the city we finally arrived in the small coastal village of Diamagen, where Mapathe had rented a small residential house on the beach for us to live in. We were greeted by throngs of children from the village's families and we spent our first evening resting, eating our first truly African meal, and walking on the gray sandy beach as a smoky, red sunset enveloped the horizon. Very early the next morning at about 5 a.m. we were awakened by the Muslim call to prayer, blasting through the blown-out PA speakers in the town, which gave the prayer-singer's voice a distorted quality that was almost rock & roll in its delivery.

My knowledge of Islam up to that point came from a comparative religion class in college, some books on Sufi poetry, and I had read a good portion of *The Thousand And One Nights*, but that was about the extent of my knowledge. Senegal is an Islamic country, but more in the Sufi mystical tradition of Islam. In honor of my host, I started waking with the call to prayer and whenever I was with Mapathe, I would kneel with him and pray in the direction of Mecca, the holiest city in Islam. Mapathe seemed to appreciate this gesture, even though I'm pretty sure he knew that as a rock musician, I was never going to convert to any organized religion. But I also believe that showing respect for another culture and their religion is the highest spiritual practice of them all.

Our shared home was a modest one, with only two bedrooms and one bathroom for all 12 of us. The best feature was the huge, wide-open floor in the middle, and this is where we did most of our drum and dance classes. We had no electricity and only cold water, which wasn't really a problem considering that the daily temperature was well over 100 degrees, so a cold shower was all anyone ever wanted. Our drinking water was filtered through our individual water purifiers, and we usually boiled it as well, because tap water in Africa is extremely risky to drink no matter where you are from. It's another unfortunate problem with the collapsing infrastructure—sewage leaking into the drinking water systems. At night, we shared the floor space around the house, sleeping on cheap strips of foam rubber under mosquito nets, as we urban-camped inside our new home.

Senegal is just north of the Equator, and here the sun rises and sets at almost exactly the same time every day, about 6 a.m. for sunrise and 6 p.m. for sunset. Thus in the evenings, and because of our lack of electricity, we had a variety of candles placed around the house and in the outdoor courtyard, creating a very warm, Victorian atmosphere for our little habitude. At night, I read my African mythology books using the light of a small flashlight, the only sounds being the occasional peal of laughter in the distance or a lonely dog barking in the warm, African night.

Mapathe's niece, a lovely and quiet young woman, would cook for us daily in the small kitchen of the house, making us coffee and bread in the morning, and an evening meal which usually consisted of fish or chicken mixed with rice and an assortment of vegetables. It was all served together on an enormous clay platter and we had to eat with our hands, which is Senegalese custom. We initially followed this tradition of eating by hand, but the truth is, it's a very messy affair, especially with the dripping sauces. I later found out that most households use silverware just like the rest of us, so I was the first to break with tradition and buy everyone giant tablespoons that were available at the local farmer's market.

At one point I went to a tiny local grocery store to buy some cookies and candies for our little expatriate tribe, and I was shocked at how expensive everything was. Indeed, the price I paid for a small bag of groceries was more expensive than the backpack of folk art I had bought at the local art market the previous week. It wasn't because I was a tourist, because the prices were clearly marked on the packages. It's because imported food in Africa is very expensive, and most people just eat the food that they grow locally, catch, or buy at the numerous farmer's markets around the city. It's very opposite of how we're raised in the U.S., where a grocery store or deli in every neighborhood is where we "grow our food."

Within the first couple of days, I and a couple of the other drummers went with Mapathe to the house of a Wolof elder known as a *Mirabou*, which is a kind of medicine man in Wolof culture. This Mirabou had made small leather amulets for us to wear while we were in Senegal, as a kind of talisman called *gris-gris*. It's based on a folkloric belief that when a person is undergoing serious training in a spiritual tradition (drumming being considered a spiritual tradition in Africa), they are engaging with the ancient spirits associated with that tradition. Conversely, there are more malevolent spirits who would try to disrupt and interfere with that training, and thus the gris-gris must be worn at all times for personal protection against those evil spirits.

I wore the amulet around my neck the entire time I was in Africa except for a brief moment when I took it off to take a shower in our little house. As I was about to step into the shower, I slipped and fell on the tile floor, jamming my toes into the doorjamb and dislocating one of my toes. Fortunately it snapped back into position on its own, but for anyone who has ever broken a toe, you know what an inescapable pain that is. It takes months for it to heal, and especially when one is wearing hiking boots and walking everywhere, the pain is rather relentless. Needless to say I wore that amulet 24 hours a day for the rest of my time in Africa and I even wore it for a little while after I got back to the

United States, just in case any of those spirits followed me home.

About a week into my stay in Senegal, I started taking trips into Dakar, just to walk around and see the city and visit the amazing folk art markets. I had a bit of a limp, the result of a bad ankle that had been shattered six years earlier on a Screaming Trees tour on our last night in Paris. The damaged ankle, which plagues me to this day, combined with my dislocated toe, gave me a kind of loping, wounded stride, which was probably quite obvious to see. And although it made traveling a bit more difficult and long walks somewhat painful, it also gave me a certain kind of empathy. Because in Africa, you see countless people who are truly injured and wounded, much of it the result of polio that still ravages those who are not given the easily available free vaccine.

There are many reasons for this, the main one being a superstition that Western medicine is secretly laced with disease, and therefore many mothers never take their children in for the free vaccinations. The results, however, are just absolutely awful, and there's no way to describe it except to see it directly. When you see an innocent child, their spine looking as if it has been melted and bent in half, walking on their hands and feet in a filthy street—its one of the worst things you will ever see. It shocked me so deeply the first time I saw these kids that I had to avert my eyes and walk into an alley to compose myself and process what I was seeing.

Over the next few weeks I met many people who graciously smiled and sometimes shook my hand with their own withered hand: a gorgeous young woman with a deformed arm; a strong young man with his spine and hips twisted in the most cruel way; a woman barely able to walk, but still carrying a heavy load of vegetables on her back. All of them were generally cheerful and accepting in whatever fate had been delivered to them, but in my mind, it just wasn't right, especially when Dr. Jonas Salk had already invented the polio vaccine decades earlier. All of this, I thought, was a preventable and terrible injustice. And it still is.

One day as I walking down a particularly crowded and slightly crazy street, a tiny little girl, perhaps not more than five or six years old began to follow me, asking me for spare change. I smiled and shook my head no, because I had learned within a few days of being in Dakar that if you started giving out coins, every child follows you and asks for more. In this case, I had some coins jingling in my pocket, and that was my dead giveaway. I began to walk faster, the girl gave chase, and we both began to laugh at the absurdity of a giant man running from a little girl down the street. Then she ran in front of the taxi.

The taxi screeched to halt, inches from her tiny head. I was absolutely horrified, in fact I froze in the street. The little girl's face was confused and terrified—it burned itself into my memory. People stared at me, some shaking their heads, but within a few seconds everyone went back to their business as if this were commonplace. Just then, a well-dressed African man reached into his pocket and handed the girl some coins. He spun her back in the direction she had come from, and marched her back to her corner. He didn't even look at me and I can understand why, but the whole incident taught me a huge lesson in compassion. Give when you can, even if its just some coins, and try to imagine what it might be like to be a hungry child on the street.

After seeing so much poverty and physical suffering from these children I was really at a loss to understand it. Then I remembered what I had learned from a Zen master I had been studying with in Los Angeles—that the world is full of sickness and suffering, both physical and mental, and everyone will suffer these things sooner or later. Even if you are born with a healthy body, any number of things can happen to you, whether it be a disease, an accident (like my own damaged left leg), and eventually old age, sickness, and death claims us all. It also makes you realize how precious and fragile life really is, how we must cherish every day of life. Life is a dangerous business even in peacetime, but in Africa it seemed like it was always on the precipice. All I could do was just smile and wipe away tears as I limped along through the dusty streets and alleyways of Dakar.

One of the people who helped me to navigate around the city was a young man, a fixer if you will, named Ali Baba. Ali spoke English well and he helped me find some special musical instruments. He also gave me good advice on where to visit, and he helped set up some music lessons with a Kora master, the 21-stringed African harp. This master spoke no English but he was able to teach me some basic Kora skills, just from watching and listening. I ended up buying that very Kora from him, and according to my journal entry it cost me exactly US$50, a gray T-shirt, and two cans of sardines. Ali Baba, for his part, only asked for a small amount of money for his services, but he really took a liking to my cargo pants. Since I had a pair of hiking shorts on underneath, I gave Ali the cargo pants as well.

I also spent a few days exploring Gorée Island, the infamous slave fortress just off the coast of Dakar where slaves were held before they were shipped off to the New World. The island has been transformed into a beautiful artist colony and teaching center, but there is still an old slave fortress with a doorway in its bowels that is referred to as the "Door Of No Return." It was through this doorway that the slaves were forced to walk in chains onto a ship, never to see Africa again. It is a sad and terrible place to walk, and one can feel a dark misery in the place. But above ground, Gorée Island has been revisioned with colorfully painted buildings, parks, and artist markets, which is proof that a terrible place can be transformed into a beautiful one. I bought a large, hand-carved drum there, which was made by a man who lived in the turrets of two enormous naval cannons. The cannons had been placed there by French forces during WWII, and later made famous in the movie *The Guns of Navarone*. It was quite a unique place to build a home, inside a gigantic gun turret, but it had been artfully converted into a residence. It all reminded me of how beauty can be created in the unlikeliest of places.

Back at our little house on the beach of Diamagen, our drumming and dancing lessons continued, where the dancers would practice in tandem with our drum ensemble. The classes were led by the drummers and dancers of Les Ballets Senegal, the famous dance company, most of them from Griot families. And one of the most fascinating things about Griot culture is how diverse it is. It's a gigantic system of music, dance, storytelling, and historical narratives, all of which is unique to each region in West Africa. It is considered to be one of the oldest and most intact musical traditions on the planet, and it is always being reinvented with each successive generation. The system is generally divided into three different categories, which includes speech, musical instruments, and repertoire, which I briefly describe here:

KUMA

Kuma basically means a form of speech, which the Griot combines with poetry, music, a clever wit, and the ability to sing long narratives. This *Griotness* means they are a genealogist, historian, advisor, spokesperson, diplomat, mediator, translator, musician, teacher, and sometimes even a warrior. Patricia Tang explains this beautifully in her book *Masters Of The Sabar*, where she refers to a Griot as a kind of a *time-binder*.

The word "time-binder" is a fascinating one, in that it places the Griot at the epicenter of people's lives, anchoring them to a place and time in their village, their region, their nation, and their cultural identity, all of which becomes a shared, collective story.

With Wolof Sabar drumming in particular, we hear the rhythms being used as a form of language through the enunciation of specific drum patterns. These rhythms, called *Bakks*, are sound mnemonics that represent old wisdom proverbs. When a series of Bakks are played in sequence (as we did in our lessons), they become a set of proverbs known as *Rhymes*. It is common for vocal shouts and praises to be interjected throughout the Bakk and Rhyme sequences, and it's extremely powerful to hear these shouts over the thunder of the drumming.

The Tama, or talking drum, is another drum I studied a little bit as well. This drum hangs under the arm, with small heads on either side of the hourglass drum shell that are laced together. When squeezed under the arm, the laces tighten and the tone of the drum can be instantly raised or lowered. The Tama technique is built around the idea that tone and rhythm can be a substitute for actual language; it works like a kind of "surrogate speech", and this is because many African languages are tonal languages. Talking drums were traditionally used to announce people of importance, and whenever kings and queens traveled, they frequently had a talking drummer communicating for them. Now it has evolved into an instrument that can even be used in jazz ensembles.

This is a common theme you will find across the African continent, where the idea of drumming as a form of communication is found in several African cultures. For example, when the British colonial troops were occupying Ghana, the indigenous Ashanti Army outsmarted the British by using drum stations in the jungle that warned the Ashanti of British troop movements. The rhythms traveled at the speed of sound, and each station passed on the "message" to the next station, so the message traveled much faster than the British troops. This confounded the British to the degree that they began to refer to the drum stations as the "bush telegraph" and they outlawed them, but of course to no avail.

FOLI AND DONKILI

Foli and *Donkili* basically refer to the various instruments (Foli) and the songs/repertoire (Donkili) that can be played on those instruments.

Here we enter into the realm of an abstract musical language and it can be a tricky transition, especially as Westerners who are used to being hit over the head with the obvious. The instruments used by Griot musicians are extremely subtle and unique to West Africa, and they all have their own tuning systems, which are directly linked to their various geographic locations. These tunings and regional melodies are often spoken like different languages or dialects and they become musical interpretations of the local culture.

The main instruments here are the Kora (harp), the Balafon (marimba), and the various drums, such as the Wolof's Sabar, the Fulani's Djembe, and the Hausa's Tama. Each instrument has regional importance, with a specific repertoire, tuning system, and particular rhythms, all of which define the cultural aesthetics of that region. The same is true with the various drumming styles, as there are as many rhythms as there are different geographical locations, and these rhythms are learned by the traveling, migrating drummers as they move through the savanna, sahel, jungle, and coastlines of West Africa.

These instruments may also be connected to other cultural traditions, such as hunting, where the Kora is used to appease the Nyama (the essential spirit) of the slain animal. Or in agriculture areas, drumming is sometimes used to appease the Nyama released during the tilling of the soil. It's an ancient and beautiful way of connecting music to the spirit of the flora and fauna of the landscape that sustains the people.

One of the best places to hear this kind of music in Senegal is at the traditional Sabar party, which is very much like a block party. It includes a wide variety of foods, ferocious Sabar drumming and singing, and highly energetic dancing by the local women who demonstrate their individual styles with great laughter and amusement. There is also the Tannibeer, which is a party exclusively for women, which starts in the evening and may go late into the night. It is a more formalized dance than a Sabar party and it contains a sequence of traditional dances.

Then there is the fascinating and totally unique national sport known as Lambe, which can only described as a form of Greco-Roman wrestling (a system of wrestling throws within a ring) that uses ferocious Sabar drum ensembles as the soundtrack. In Lambe, every wrestler has his own Sabar drummers, and it is said that the best wrestlers are the ones with the best drummers. The whole thing is a spectator sport as the wrestlers dance, prance, and flex their muscles, and the drummers raise the energy of the crowd with call and response rhythms and shouts. Meanwhile the Mirabou cast their spells and incantations in favor of their preferred wrestler. It's an amazing spectacle to behold.

With the explosion of global pop music and even electronic dance music, a new platform has been created for the modern Griot musician. Well-known Griots and their family of musicians have become internationally famous, such as the Kora master Toumani Diabaté, guitarist Vieux Farka Touré, and the Kouyaté family, all of whom hail from Mali. There is the Kora master Foday Musa Suso of Gambia, whom I have played with, and of course the Wolof Sabar masters in the Diop family who still live and teach in Seattle and Dakar. These musicians have taken the music out of their villages and put it on the global stage, and it's amazing to see and hear them. The word Griot is even being used in African American communities, where rappers and street poets are deified as spokesmen for the marginalized, and a new breed of historians, storytellers, poets, and jazz masters continues the tradition of the Griot in America.

GHANA

After a few weeks of Sabar lessons in Senegal, there was a lull in the teaching when a group of drummers from Les Ballet Senegal had to travel for some performances. I took this opportunity to book a flight to Accra, Ghana, just a little farther east in the Gulf of Guinea. I had already gotten my Ghanaian visa, anticipating a trip there because it's another country that is known for its amazing drumming systems. Now was my opportunity.

It was a very long and rickety plane ride on the now defunct Ghana Airways as we made bus-like stops in Bamako, Mali; Abidjan, Ivory Coast; finally landing in Accra. When I got off the plane, I was greeted by a small military escort in red berets carrying a sign that read *Martin Bartlett*, an all too familiar misspelling of my name. I was a bit worried at first; I had never been met by a military detachment, but when I introduced myself it turned out to be an escort that a friend of mine at the World Bank had set up through the vice-president of Ghana. The kindly vice-president had sent a full diplomatic escort to whisk me through customs and get me situated for my musical studies in Ghana.

My first stop the next day was at the National Theatre, where I was given a tour by its director Dr. Amoaku. This fine gentleman arranged for me to take drum lessons at the University Of Legon, one of the academic cornerstones of Africa. There I met Dr. Willie Anku, who was the head of the music department at the university, and he set me up with a crash course in Ghanaian drumming.

For the next two weeks, I would meet with the drummers on a large grass lawn at the university under an immense flowering tree where we'd practice the traditional rhythms of the Ewe and Ashanti people. We focused on traditional rhythms like the Gahu, Kplongo, and Agbadza, and usually there were just three or four of us, but other drummers would occasionally join in. We spent a lot of time talking about the nature of rhythm, the sacredness of drumming, including the quote at the beginning of this Verse, which came from one of those conversations.

One of the deepest realizations I had came from a discussion about *clave*, the distinct rhythmic subdivisions that are played on a cowbell during the practice of these, and many other rhythms. Clave is a mystical thing, and in fact, entire books have been written about it. It's the rhythmic emphasis that is most recognizable in African, Cuban, and Brazilian music, and you would recognize it immediately from its feel—you just have to know what it is. The thing that fascinates me about clave is this: clave has just two, and only two, possible variations, which are felt as either 2/3 or 3/2 accents within the rhythm. These clave accents vary depending on the rhythm, but they define the feel of the rhythm itself. It is essential to the way the human body feels and moves to the rhythm—clave is the thing that makes us dance.

Parallel to clave have been the discoveries in quantum physics where subatomic particles—quarks, leptons, and bosons—tend to cluster into groups of either two or three, depending on their magnetic polarity. In quantum mechanics this is described as either a 2/3 or 3/2 electromagnetic charge. As a drummer, I began to connect the two: clave can only be felt in the body as a 2/3 or 3/2 subdivision, and the subatomic particles of the universe (which are, of course, in our bodies) were also clustered into twos and threes.

Almost 20 years after my Africa trip, I had a conversation with the conductor of the Seattle Symphony, Maestro Ludovic Morlot. I had worked with "Ludo" when we played Mad Season songs along with the Seattle Symphony. One night after hearing the Seattle

Symphony perform Beethoven, I told Ludo about my clave-quantum physics observation, and he told me a similar allegory that existed with symphony conducting. When conducting, there are only two movements in the conductor's wrists that are of critical importance. There is the two-way, up-and-down movement of the wrist, and the three-way rotational movement of the wrist. Again we see the two and three pattern in a conductor's movements, and Ludo also reminded me that every musical time signature that exists has some fractional variation of that 2/3–3/2 pattern: 3/4, 4/4, 5/4, 5/8, 6/4, 6/8, 7/4, 7/8, and on and on and on….

Is it possible that Africa's earliest drummers were in fact *feeling* the atomic structure of the universe? Can we still feel it when we play those old rhythms today? Maybe there is a reason that music and rhythm seem to organize themselves in these patterns, which seem to reflect the very fabric of the universe. These questions I have had for many years; they started in Africa, and they continue to this day. Maybe someday a physicist-musician will figure it out.

After a couple of very mystical weeks in Accra, I decided to take a short trip into the countryside, going north to the city of Kumasi, the capital of the old Ashanti empire. The bus ride was long and tedious and I was the only white person on a completely packed bus of Ghanaians, all of whom were very kind and polite to me. This was an amazing lesson for me, to be a total minority in an African country, and there were days in northern Ghana where I never saw another white person. I never had a mean word spoken to me, as the Ghanaians (and the Senegalese too) are some of the kindest and most respectful people I have ever met on this planet. They are absolutely wonderful people.

Although not nearly as large as Accra, Kumasi seemed to be quite a bit busier, with an enormous food and arts market that seemed to stretch for a couple miles as I walked it end to end. Packed with people buying food and household items, it was a wild and chaotic place with much yelling and bargaining.

Walking through that market I eventually found the workshop of the national drum maker of Ghana, a quiet and elegant man who had carved the magnificent, gigantic drums I had previously seen in the National Theatre. Made out of enormous single tree logs and carved with the most ornate Ashanti symbolism, the drumhead pegs were made of cast gold leopards, their open jaws grasping the wires that held the drumheads taught. After watching him work on some other superbly craved drums, I convinced him to sell me a small drum that he was going to burn because it wasn't perfect. I persuaded him to sell it to me and it's a piece of history that holds a very special place in my heart, mostly because it was made by a master, and because I saved it from the fire.

I visited the Ashanti Cultural Center where I learned about Adinkra symbolism, which are designs that represent colloquial wisdom in the Ashanti tradition. Their most famous application is in the wood carvings and exquisite fabrics that are famous in Ghana. Adinkra symbols are timeless, often funny proverbs that are full of wisdom and truths that transcend all cultures. I have a series of them framed on my wall to remind me that the earliest wisdom is indeed, African.

I also convinced the administrator of the cultural center to allow me to play and record the famous leopard drum, a drum that was used as an announcement of the approaching king. Stretched with a loose antelope head, it is not struck, but rather, an L-shaped stick is dragged across its head in an elliptical movement, which produces a sound incredibly similar to a leopard's growl. I've included the recording I made of this leopard drum on the book soundtrack.

During the couple of months I spent in Senegal and Ghana immersed in drumming and music, I kept thinking about my former Los Angeles landlord, Milt Holland. Milt had been a famous percussionist in the early Los Angeles recording scene starting in the 1950s and he played well into the 1990s. He had been one of those adventurous types who had gone looking for the rhythms of the world right after World War II, when that kind of travel was especially risky and not for the faint of heart. He had studied traditional rhythms in Africa, South America, and India and he was already a legend by the time I met him.

For the last half of the 20th century, Milt played on countless film and television soundtracks, and dozens of classic jazz and pop albums. He was a member of the famed Wrecking Crew group of studio musicians, and he worked with everyone from Leonard Bernstein (Milt played the signature bongos in *West Side Story*), to Henry Mancini, Frank Sinatra, Quincy Jones, and so many rock and pop stars that I can't even list them here - you just have to look him up. Basically, Milt was the first-call percussionist that everyone wanted on their album or film soundtrack to make the music sound exotic and cool. He had recently retired when my friend Mich Rogers and I rented a house from him in about 1997, because Milt had wisely put his wealth into real estate and he owned numerous houses throughout the Hollywood Hills.

I was starting to do the same kind of percussion work as Milt in the late 1990s, playing on a few film soundtracks here and there, and adding some exotic color to albums by R.E.M., the Stone Temple Pilots, Queens Of The Stone Age, Air, and a bunch of other bands you've never heard of. The golden era of recording was already a dead form by the time I got to Los Angeles but I still tasted a small glimmer before it faded into the world of digital recording and sampling. I wanted to be like Milt Holland but that time had passed, and Milt was a dying breed.

At the first of every month I'd go and pay the rent at Milt's home higher up in the hills. I could have mailed the check, but then I wouldn't get to see Milt. He and his wife Mildred had a gorgeous home that was more like a museum of indigenous art and musical instruments that Milt had been collecting and using in the studios for decades. It was an incredible place, like nothing I had ever seen. Being that I was a drummer and a percussionist too, we became friends, so he and I would always chat for a bit, Mildred bringing us some coffee as we sat in his sunny living room. I would ask Milt about some famous album he had played on, or about his travels in search of new sounds. He'd tell me various stories with a twinkle in his eye, but the one I remembered most was when I asked him why he got into the whole exotic percussion thing. "Barrett, this is a serious thing playing drums and percussion. It's a mystical thing. The spirit will find you when the time is right."

Milt left us in 2005, but he was a master who learned from the old masters and then brought it back to all of us, through the various recorded art forms. *So, wherever you are now Milt, I just want to let you know that yes, the spirit definitely did find me and its still got me. Thank you for the set up.*

10. Sketches Of Senegal
11. Wolof Sabar Bakk
12. Barrett Martin Group "The Conjuror"
13. Ashanti Leopard Drum
14. Ewe Agbadza Rhythm
15. Barrett Martin Group "Agbadza"

VERSE 8

CUBA: THE ART OF MUSICAL DIPLOMACY

Cuban reunion in Hollywood, left to right: Barrett Martin, Mich Rogers, Cuban keyboardist, the Cuban drummers Eugenio and Oney, 2000

"At the risk of seeming ridiculous, let me say that the true revolutionary is guided by a great feeling of love. It is impossible to think of a genuine revolutionary lacking this quality. We must strive every day so that this love of living humanity will be transformed into actual deeds, into acts that serve as examples, as a moving force."

— Dr. Ernesto "Che" Guevara

I returned from West Africa in November of 1998 and I fell ill almost immediately after arriving in Los Angeles, where I had been working as a studio musician and producer. My doctor thought it might be some virulent form of malaria or some other unknown illness, even though I had taken anti-malaria medication while I was in Africa. I was given a very strong dose of the strongest anti-malarial medication you can take, which made me feel a bit like I had drunk Drano. It made me quite sick for a few weeks, and my happy, golden memories of Africa became a strange blur. Slowly, however, I recovered and it was right around that time that I received news that I had been nominated to travel to Cuba as a musical ambassador for the Music Bridge program.

The Music Bridge was designed to put musicians and songwriters from different countries together to build exactly that—bridges between their cultures. And I firmly believe that we should always work to build bridges between people, and never walls. Our trip to Cuba happened in March of 1999, the last year of Bill Clinton's presidency, and it was sanctioned by the U.S. State Department as a way to foster good will between our two countries. The Baltimore Orioles baseball team even went along to play the Cuban national team in Havana, and in turn, the Cuban team came to the U.S. to play in Baltimore.

This kind of diplomacy works well, and that's because musicians, artists, writers, and athletes are usually at the forefront of social and political change. The American Civil Rights Movement is a perfect example of this. Cuba was an ideal setting for our project and it worked wonderfully, that is, until George W. Bush came to power the following year and reversed many of the positive steps we had made, sending U.S. foreign policy back to the 1960s. In 2016, President Barack Obama made some excellent progress in normalizing relations with Cuba, and we again have the chance to get back on the right side of history.

During our trip to Havana in 1999, there were about 100 musicians from the United States and Great Britain. People like Stewart Copeland and Andy Summers of The Police, Mick Fleetwood of Fleetwood Mac, Peter Buck of R.E.M., The Indigo Girls, Bonnie Raitt, Peter Frampton, Gladys Knight, Michael Franti, Joan Osborne, Paddy Maloney, and even the great songwriter Burt Bacharach were just a few of the luminaries who were selected to participate. It was an incredible group of musicians, truly a historical gathering of artistic souls who wanted to make a change for the better.

It's also equally important to understand why we were there in the first place, because our relationship with Cuba is very much like a fiery love affair gone wrong. Here's the abbreviated version:

At the time of our visit, Cuba had been under the dictatorship of Fidel Castro since the Revolution of 1959. I abhor dictatorial tendencies from anyone, whether foreign or American. It's how spiritually weak men try to control their people. But as musical diplomats our job was to represent our country in the best possible way, regardless of whether we agreed with our host or not. However, it is important to understand that Mr. Castro and Che Guevara did, almost 60 years ago, liberate Cuba from the grip of American imperialism and the mafia goons who enforced our oppressive policies.

The fact is, United States foreign policy created many of the terrible political and economic conditions that existed in Latin America and the Caribbean during the 20th century. Those conditions led to military coups and countless atrocities committed against innocent people throughout Central and South America. The Cuban Revolution was simply a push back against that oppression, and it was very successful in this regard.

It started with United Fruit, a neo-colonialist American corporation that began expanding throughout Latin America and the Caribbean in the early 20th century. United Fruit was infamous for exploiting the land and labor of the countries in which it set up shop, and they had been abusing the Cuban people for many years by the time the American mafia and their political stooges moved into Havana. They wanted to make Cuba a playground for American and European elites, and for a time they did. They looked at the women as prostitutes and the men as busboys, until a revolutionary army assembled by Che and Fidel finally obliterated them.

Their revolution began in Mexico, where they trained in guerilla tactics before sailing to Cuba on a small yacht called *The Granma*. It was November of 1956 when *The Granma* landed on the southern coast of Cuba with only 86 men ready to fight. Despite the incredible odds and setbacks, their ragtag army slowly grew in size as they moved stealthily through the mountains and jungles of Cuba, until they reached Havana in January of 1959. At that point, the busboys and prostitutes put their knives to the mafia throats, who promptly tucked tail and sailed back to the safety of the American shoreline.

In truth, the Cuban revolution was essentially about the very same things the American Revolution was about—throwing out a colonial occupier who was abusing the people and treating them unjustly. Cuba just did to the United States what we did to England back in 1776. Thomas Jefferson wrote about this when he mused on the importance of revolutions in his autobiography: "Even this evil is productive of good.

It prevents the degeneracy of government, and nourishes a general attention to the public affairs. I hold it that a little rebellion now and then is a good thing, and as necessary in the political world as storms are in the physical."

Only a couple of years after Cuba's revolution, the CIA tried to invade and retake Cuba using Cuban exiles and CIA agents during the botched Bay of Pigs invasion of April 1961. The U.S. (and this time the CIA) were soundly defeated by the now solidified Cuban Revolutionary Armed Forces. Anger, resentment, and distrust flared in both countries until 1962, when it reached a boiling point with the Cuban missile crisis.

Cuba had rather naively tried to import ballistic missiles from Russia, which would have put those missiles 90 miles off the U.S. coastline. The U.S. initiated a naval blockade to prevent the missiles from arriving on Russian ships, putting a trade embargo on Cuba as well. But even after the missiles went back to Russia and the naval blockade ended, the U.S. continued its unethical trade embargo, which has made innocent Cuban civilians suffer for almost 60 years.

Cuba is no military threat to the U.S., and we still have our own embarrassing blemish of Guantanamo prison, which we still maintain in eastern Cuba. And we continue to punish generations of innocent Cubans with a fossilized, conservative worldview that has been terrible for both of our nations. The lifting of the trade embargo is something that needs to happen as soon as possible, right on the heels of opening up travel and normal diplomatic relations. We need this economic reform between our nations, but its also a humanitarian issue. This is because the vast majority of Cubans alive today were not even born when the U.S. trade embargo was first implemented in 1962. Thus, its grinding toll has been exacted upon children and the youngest generation of Cubans in a kind of collective punishment. The U.S. has directly contributed to hunger in Cuba, something I saw firsthand when I was there. Food is expensive and not in abundance, and what kind of a country are we if we deliberately cause hunger in another country simply because we don't like their political beliefs? That's not very high-minded. Embargos should be reserved for rogue military states and dictators, not Caribbean islands with musicians, doctors, and PhDs.

Let me clarify what I mean by that. Revolutions are not static things that start and stop neatly on a certain date. They are fluid, moving, evolutionary philosophies that change with the spirit of the people.

Since the Revolution of 1959, Cuba has developed one of the finest medical corps on the planet, famous for deploying doctors around the world in times of global crisis and disaster. They started doing this before Doctors Without Borders even existed. Cuba also has a free education system up to the doctoral level, so Cubans have the highest literacy rate in the world (over 99 percent) and they are educated in all academic fields.

I also learned from my own direct experience that Cuba has one of the finest music and artistic cultures on the planet. I witnessed virtuosity at a level so high, that it's going to set a new watermark in excellence when they do finally make it to American soil. Cuban artists like Chucho Valdés, Los Van Van, and jazz titans like Paquito D'Rivera and Arturo Sandoval have already brought Cuban musical excellence to the American stage through special concert arrangements. But it's time for a constant exchange of musical and artistic ideas to happen, and when it does, it's going to be amazing for both countries.

I took long walks in the streets of Havana, and I've seen the buildings in the central plaza where bullet holes from the street battles of 1959 have been deliberately left unrepaired, to remind people that a real fight took place here, where blood was spilled and native Cubans were killed by American guns and bullets. In order to make peace with Cuba, we have to understand that her revolution was because of our own oppressive policies. If we can understand that and learn from it, then we can meet our former enemy and become friends again.

If the U.S. is truly a free democracy (and that is questionable as of the writing of this book), then we shouldn't be threatened by Cuba for having a different political philosophy. We can no longer say that it is because Cuba is a communist nation, when our biggest trading partner, China, is the biggest communist nation in the world. If we are friends with China, then we should easily be friends with Cuba. And that brings me back to why we were playing music in Cuba in the first place. It went something like this….

Every morning all the musicians, including those from Cuba, would meet in the great hall of the Hotel Nacional in downtown Havana. There, two large bowls held small cards with our names—the Cubans in one bowl and the American/Irish/Brits in the other. A drawing would take place every morning, in which two or three Cubans would be paired with two or three from the other bowl, whereupon we would recuse ourselves to a writing space in our hotel rooms, or in the beautiful gardens that surrounded the hotel. There we would spontaneously write a song together, complete with music and lyrics. In my first drawing I was placed with the singer and guitarist Peter Frampton and two incredible Cuban jazz musicians.

My job in that first writing group was to keep the beat on two congas provided for me in the absence of a drum set. I did my best to play a basic *tumbao* pattern, the most common of the conga patterns. The funny thing, however, was that our Cuban bassist played electric bass with his left hand in a kind of hammer technique, while he simultaneously played congas with his right hand. It was incredible to watch—he was so much better on the congas with his one right hand than I was with two! Thus, I decided to just sit and watch while this master played both instruments and I just enjoyed the music that was being created. Peter Frampton led the vocal approach, while the other Cuban—the wife of the bassist—played magnificent piano on her portable keyboard. I never got to record that song, because the next day I was pulled into another Cuban band called Synthesis, which was one of the top fusion bands in Cuba, with a famed rhythm section that included a Santería drummer and an amazing Latin jazz drummer.

I immediately hit it off with the band's drummer Eugenio, who was hands-down the best Latin jazz drummer I had ever heard in my life. I was told later that he was considered to be Cuba's very best. Oney was the band's percussionist and a Santería drum priest who was equally impressive and very soulful. We formed an instant brotherhood, and spent nearly every musical moment together after that.

I was humbled by the skill and craft of these musicians, for their ability to play American jazz, rock, and of course their own Cuban folkloric music. I spent most of my time just watching and listening, only playing when prodded to do so. I was surrounded by genuine love and acceptance by these brilliant musicians and in ten days time, I learned more about Latin drumming and percussion than I had in all the years I spent in music school.

In the following days we would record these songs using a portable studio set up in the ballroom of the hotel and the results were quite exceptional. It was a predictable mixture of Western rock and pop with a Cuban rhythmic undercurrent, but it was also highly original. One of the highlights for me was when I got to play drums with the great singer and bassist, Meshell Ndegeocello, as we served as the rhythm section on a song by Synthesis.

This daily ritual went on for about a week until we had accumulated, between all of the songwriting groups, enough music for a full concert. And that is exactly what we did on our last night in Cuba, as we performed in front of a live audience of global ambassadors and political luminaries at the Karl Marx Theatre in Havana (formerly known as the Charlie Chaplin Theater prior to the Cuban Revolution of 1959).

It was a marvelous show, and the always-gregarious Michael Franti was elected to be the MC of the concert, a job he did stupendously. Many great songs were performed that night including the song with me, Meshell Ndegeocello, and Synthesis. I also got to play drums for the amazing Indigo Girls, accompanied by Mick Fleetwood, who played the second drum set next to me. I believe a CD and DVD of the songs and live concert is now floating around on the Internet if you want to see it for yourself.

After the show we were invited to meet El Presidente Fidel Castro in a traditional diplomatic receiving line at the presidential palace. There was Fidel, down at the end of the receiving line, wearing a three-piece suit and not the military fatigues he was famous for wearing. When my moment came I told him in English (which was then translated by his interpreter) what a beautiful country Cuba was and how honored I was to play with the Cuban musicians, who are undoubtedly the finest in the world. And then I said, "And now I have shaken the hand that fought beside Che Guevara!" At this last remark, Fidel chuckled and winked in acknowledgement and I smiled back. I had met history, once again.

Dr. Ernesto "Che" Guevara had been assassinated in Bolivia in 1967 by CIA paramilitary forces working with the Bolivian Army. Che was a truly great man, a Renaissance man whose intelligence, compassion, and fierceness are perfectly summarized in the quote at the beginning of this Verse—revolutionaries are guided by great feelings of love for the people. As Fidel grew older and grayer and eventually died, it is the young, eternal face of a beret-clad Che Guevara that has become the most reproduced image in the history of the world. It is the image of revolution incarnate. *Che Viva*, indeed.

All I can say about Cuba is that it is one of the most beautiful and musically incredible places I have ever visited. Go there immediately if you can. It's true that there are vintage American cars that look as if time stopped in 1959, but that's really because the American trade embargo has prevented new cars from arriving. As a result, the Cuban mechanics, like the musicians, are some of the best in the world. This is because the mechanics know how to *make* parts for their cars, in the absence of being able to buy pre-manufactured parts.

Along the gorgeous Malecón waterfront and throughout Havana's many plazas are extraordinary artists, wood carvers, and painters who ply their wares at tables and booths to the international tourists who wander the streets. It was there on the street where I bought my first Santería drums and an entirely new journey began.

During my time with Oney and Eugenio, the drummers of Synthesis, I was taught some truly magical rhythms. Oney was an exceptional fusion percussionist, but he had also been initiated as a traditional Santería drum priest. Santería is a New World religion that combines West African beliefs with Catholicism, syncretizing the two religions together to create an entirely new one. In this case, the gods of West Africa, known as the *Orishas*, have similar personalities as the Saints in Catholicism and the two overlap each other perfectly and beautifully. Unfortunately, it all began with the slave trade.

During the four centuries of the Spanish colonial period, Cuba received approximately 700,000 slaves. Of those people, the major ethnic group were the Yoruba people in what is now Nigeria in West Africa. They came to Cuba with nothing but the sacred songs and rhythms of their religion, known as *Ifá*. When they arrived in Cuba, they were forced to adopt Catholicism as the colonial religion, but like all people with a strong and ancient history, they simply bended Catholicism to fit with their own Ifá religion. The new name given to this syncretized religion is *Lucumí*, or the more popular term, *Santería*.

Just as it was in the old days, the Orishas can be summoned using their sacred rhythms and songs, which call them down into the bodies of the trance mediums. The sacred drums used in the Santería ceremonies are called *Batá*, and these drums are based on the same design as the drums in Yorubaland, Nigeria. This configuration uses three drums, each in the shape of an hourglass with drumheads on either end, and one end being slightly larger than the other. This allows for the drums to be played by three people, each with two hands, creating up to six different tones, and a complexity of rhythm that is unrivalled by any other drumming system in the world. The drums are always played in a trio, the largest drum being called the *Iya*, representing the archetype of the father. The middle drum is called the *Itotole*, representing the archetype of the mother, and the smallest drum, the *Onkonkolo,* represents the archetype of the child. The Santería rhythms are fast and rapid, and they soon induce a trancelike state, even with the uninitiated.

When we weren't rehearsing songs with Synthesis, Oney would show me and another visiting drummer the primary rhythms of the Orishas. He did this first by playing the rhythms himself on my recently purchased batá drums, and then invite us to take one of the drums and learn our respective rhythms. It was utterly and completely enchanting. What I found to be even more captivating was the research I did on the Orishas in the ensuing years, which I have summarized here.

In the Ifá religion, there are 401 different entities known as the *Irunmoles* who helped to bring about the creation of the Earth. 256 of them eventually became the sacred texts of Ifá, as well as the Orishas themselves. However, there is a group of about a dozen principal Orishas, who are universally recognized in West Africa and in the New World as the principle gods of the Ifá pantheon. These Orishas have certain personality characteristics that make them very human and completely beloved, and that is why they still exist today—because they represent the full spectrum of human personalities. When you read about them, I think you will find that one of them matches your personality pretty closely.

The word Orisha (or *Orixa* as they spell it in Brazil) can be broken into two words: *Ori*, which means "head", and *Xa*, which means "the power or potentiality." So the word Orisha literally means to have potential power in your head or mind. The Orishas themselves report to the supreme god, *Oludumare*, who lives in a celestial realm call *Orun*. We as human beings cannot touch that sacred realm, so the Orishas have been provided to us as emissaries through which we can communicate.

Below is a very short summary of the main Orishas in Cuba, as well as some stories and myths I found in my continuing research on the music and religions of the Caribbean and South America. I also listed several books in the bibliography which have excellent, in-depth stories about the Orishas, and I especially recommend *The Handbook Of Yoruba Religious Concepts* by Baba Ifá Karade, and *The Way of The Orisha* by Philip John Neimark, both of which have excellent descriptions of the Orishas. I think you will find the Orishas to be incredibly beautiful, powerful, and very wise beings.

OLUDUMARE aka OLORUN

Oludumare is the supreme deity or godhead in the Ifá pantheon. He/She is so infinite and complete, representing the entire universe and beyond, that he/she is not even approachable by human beings. That is why the Orishas were created, to act as emissaries between humans and Oludumare, and also as a buffer against the profanities of human existence. In fact, Oludumare is so vast of an entity that surprisingly little can be found to describe him/her, except in gigantic, sweeping interpretations. He/she is the spirit that is in everything, in every rock, every plant, every animal, every human, every planet, every star, every galaxy, the entire universe, and all the space that contains the universe. Oludumare is the totality of all existence, in the physical as well as the spiritual.

ELLEGUA aka EXU

Ellegua is the first Orisha who must always be honored before any of the other Orishas can be called upon. When Oney taught me the rhythms of the Orishas, it was Ellegua's rhythm that he always played first. Like the devil at the crossroads in the American blues myth, Ellegua is the guardian of the crossroads, or the "intersections" between this world and the world of the spirit. Ellegua is not like the Christian devil and he is not evil. Rather, he is more like a trickster, a Mephistophelean character with as much wisdom as mischief—he keeps everyone alert and awake. He is also the Master of Death, and he carries out those orders upon the request of *Obatalá*, the Orisha Of Justice, who is both his friend and opposite.

It is said that all of the Orishas have a little of Ellegua in them, like the little black drop of *yin* in the white *yang* that gives people their kinetic power. Ellegua is that kinetic power, and therefore he must be honored first, or rather "dispatched," so that the other Orishas can come into this world without Ellegua disrupting the festivities. In other words, Ellegua must be honored, pacified, and appeased with libations—alcohol, tobacco, and many other special offerings that he particularly likes. His colors are red and black, and because of his fierce nature, he is often syncretized with St. Anthony.

Ellegua also has a wife, or feminine aspect, and she is known as *Pomba Gira*. She is also a trickster, with a particular liking for men, liquor, and dark alleyways. It is said that she haunts the doorways of nightclubs and drinking establishments, and is usually depicted as a curvaceous woman with long, raven hair and full breasts, a sign of her provocative sexuality. In other words, she is the proverbial man-killer.

OBATALÁ aka OXALA

All of the Orishas have a profound influence on the followers of Ifá, but one Orisha rises above the others and is venerated as the King of the Orishas. He is *Obatalá*, the god of the sky, representing justice, purity, wisdom, and clear thinking. He is one of the few "cool-headed" Orishas, a rare exception in the usually hotheaded male pantheon. His domain is in the mountains and forests where he can find peace and solitude, and his color is white. In his blending with Catholicism he is syncretized with Jesus Christ and his symbol is comprised of the stars in the Southern Cross, which made him hugely influential with Christian missionaries in the Southern Hemisphere. In Brazil, he has an especially powerful influence.

Obatalá is the leader of the category of warrior Orishas, which also includes *Ogun*, *Ochosi*, *Changó*, and *Oya*. Obatalá is known for his older age and advanced wisdom, and a sense of humor that has mostly to do with his eons of observation on the human condition. He is not a jokester or a trickster, but more like a kind uncle or grandfather whose wise witticisms say everything. He also represents the pure and calm way to enlightened transcendence, which is in opposition to some of the hotter Orisha temperaments. He is also the final judge of humanity, a job entrusted to him by the Creator, Oludumare.

Obatalá had many sacred duties during the creation of the Earth, and Oludumare entrusted him with perhaps the most important of all, which was the creation of human beings. Oludumare told Obatalá to make the humans out of clay, and then when they were finished, to call upon him to breathe life into them. Obatalá, known for his meticulous and almost obsessive work ethic, started to make humans out of clay. After some amount of time had passed, Obatalá became a bit weary and decided to drink a little palm wine. He returned to his work, drinking more wine as he continued. But in his slowly deteriorating, inebriated state, Obatalá forgot to add arms and legs to some of the figures, and sometimes those that had all the exterior parts were neglected on the inside.

In the morning, a rather hungover Obatalá called Oludumare to breathe life into the figures, which Oludumare did, never even thinking to inspect the work of his most trusted Orisha. His mistake resulted in people being born with physical and internal handicaps, and because of the remorse and shame that Obatalá felt, these special people are considered the sacred children of Obatalá and he watches over them with particular love and care.

To honor Obatalá in ceremony, he is never offered alcohol or tobacco as a libation—he usually gets coconut milk instead. He is now the sober Orisha eternally on the wagon, but he is also the wisest for the deep lessons he has learned. It is a traditional thing for pregnant Yoruba women to pray out loud to the great Orisha of the Sky: "Korisa yana ire lo nio!", which means "May Obatalá create for us a good work of art!"

YEMOJA and OLOKUN

Yemoja is the Great Mother, and with her partner Obatalá, they become the divine parents of the other Orishas. Yemoja's personal domain are the oceans, the seas, and all the salt-water bodies. She represents the nurturing, motherly aspect of humanity, but she is also the most wrathful. She is the keeper of the oldest secrets and greatest powers, which she keeps hidden in the dark, silent, unfathomable depths of the oceans. There her powers remain unless she chooses to unleash them through her wrathful aspect, *Olokun*. From Olokun arises the greatest destructive powers of the ocean, including hurricanes, tidal waves, typhoons, waterspouts, and underwater volcanic activity. Yemoja is represented by two colors - blue for the oceans and crystal clear for the water itself. And because she is the Great Mother, she is syncretized with the Mother Mary.

In the Yoruba creation myth, the sky god Obatala was watching over the ocean-covered Earth when he became attracted to Yemoja's voluptuous form and their sacred union created the other Orishas. From her breasts sprang the "sweet waters"—the fresh water rivers, streams and lakes, which became the domain of her beautiful daughter, *Osun*. Yemoja also represents the amniotic fluid in the womb of a pregnant woman, and the process of pregnancy and motherhood. She also has control over the secrets of magic and sorcery, which she passed on to her daughters Osun and Oya. She is the natural maternal instinct in all animals and human beings, which is to be nurturing and caring, but if threatened, she is ferociously powerful and even deadly.

In Brazil, Yemoja has become the national deity, and every New Year on January 1st a nationwide ceremony takes place. There, people make tiny paper boats with cakes, fruits, and candies, which they push out upon the ocean waves, along with their prayers for the New Year. If the boat is "accepted" and continues out to sea, it is believed that their prayer will be answered by Yemoja. If, however, the boat is sent crashing back onto the shore with the incoming waves, then the prayer has been rejected and the person will have to try again next year.

CHANGÓ aka XANGO

Changó is another of the warrior Orishas, and he is perhaps the most volatile and flamboyant of them all. Known for his quick temper and ferocious spirit, he is a master of strategy on the battlefield and he leads his troops in battle. His symbol is the double-headed battle-axe but he also has power over thunder and lightning, so he is syncretized with St. Barbara, the patron saint of storms.

Changó also controls the power of the sacred Batá drums, the rhythms of which call down the Orishas. Because he is so fond of drumming and dancing, he is frequently the Orisha of musicians, and drummers in particular. His main colors are red and white.

Changó and his wife Oya were thought to have been an actual king and queen at one point in history. The story goes that Changó was the fourth ruler of the kingdom of Oyo in Yorubaland, Nigeria. He was married to Oya, a beautiful and powerful queen in her own right. But through a series of deceptive plots, misdeeds, and military mistakes, Changó was defeated by two of his own generals. Humiliated, he and Oya were sent into exile and as a gesture of his contrition, he committed suicide by hanging himself from a tree. His wife Oya followed suit by drowning herself in the Niger River. Upon their deaths, they both ascended to Oludumare where he made them eternal Orishas.

In another version of the story, Oya was previously married to the warrior Ogun, the Orisha who controls metal. Changó stole Oya away from Ogun, and this created a rivalry much like the jealousies in a classic Greek myth. Because of Changó's power over the Batá drums, and Ogun's power over metal, it was decided that all traditional Batá drums used in ceremonies would never have metal on them, lest a cosmic battle rage between Changó and Ogun. Changó was a bit of a ladies man and he eventually dumped Oya for her sister, Osun, but that's another story entirely....

OGUN aka OGUM

Ogun is another of the warrior Orishas and like Obatalá, he is considered a warrior of justice and a liberator of the oppressed. He's the most physically powerful of the warriors and he has dominion over all metals, and iron in particular. Because of this power over metal, he is also the Orisha of civilization, because without metal we would not have swords or plowshares, computer chips or jet airliners. In fact, it is a common practice for followers of Ogun who, when called to testify in a court of law, will often kiss a piece of metal rather than place their hand on a Bible. This is common in Nigeria, where swearing over iron is considered a sacred act. His domain, like Obatalá, are the mountains and the forests, and his colors are green and black. His symbol is two crossed swords, and he is syncretized with St. Peter, or sometimes with St. George, the dragon-slayer.

Ogun is the one who slashes and carves out civilization through the jungles of the wilderness. He is also a "hot" god who occasionally loses his temper. One evening as Ogun was walking through the forest, he came upon a group of men sitting in a circle, drinking bottles of palm wine. Ogun, tired and thirsty from his journey, asked for a bottle to drink from. The men looked nervously back and forth and giggled without saying a word. Enraged at this act of defiance, Ogun drew his sword and beheaded each and every one of them. He then reached for a bottle only to finding it empty. Each bottle he tried proved the same result—empty, until he came to the horrific conclusion that his people had not been rude but simply didn't have any more wine to offer him. In his contrition, he threw himself on his sword, killing himself, only to be reborn even more powerful because of the wisdom gained. This story is also the reason why followers of Ogun always set an empty bottle on its side when finished, so as to not confuse or anger Ogun should he pass by them looking for a drink.

OCHOSI aka OXOSI

Ochosi's realm is the wilderness, and as such, his domain is the forest and he is the protector of all of the plants and animals that dwell within. He is another of the warrior Orishas, particularly blessed with the ability to see great distances and with incredible hearing. Oshosi is a loner, but it is said that he sometimes hunts with his blood brother, Ogun. His color is green, his symbol is the bow and arrow, and he is syncretized with Saint Sebastian, the martyr who was tied to a tree and slain with arrows.

Ochosi is the hunter, the stealthful tracker, and he also has a close friendship with Obatalá. It is said that, like Ellegua, Ochosi is often tasked with carrying out the judgments of Obatalá, catching or dispatching the guilty with swiftness and skill.

In addition to the African Orishas, Ochosi is also allied with the *Caboclos*, the indigenous Native Americans of South America. These natives were extremely helpful to the newly arrived Africans because they recognized a kinship in each other, each being enslaved and colonized by the Europeans. The Caboclos taught the Africans which plants and herbs to use for healings, and their shamans, the *Ajes*, shared the secrets and visions of the psychotropic plants. Because the use of plants and herbs in the African religions is so important, the newly arrived slaves had to find substitute plants in the New World that could serve the same purpose as the plants in Africa. And because Ochosi is the guardian of the forest and all its plants, he also has an alliance with Osonyin, the Orisha of plants, herbs, and medicinal healing.

OSONYIN aka OSSAE

Osonyin is the Orisha of all plants, herbs and medicine, and as such he controls the "axe", or magic contained within them. In *Candomblé*, the Brazilian version of Ifá, the use of plants and herbs for making ritual baths is one of the most sacred traditions. Without the sacred leaves of Candomblé for bathing and making offerings, the Orishas could not manifest in their followers. Because of this, Osonyin is one the most important Orishas in the entire pantheon and he is syncretized with St. Joseph. Like Ochosi, his color is green.

Osonyin is depicted with only one arm, one leg, and one eye, a result of his many battles for control over the plant kingdom. His obsession over the secrets of the plants and herbs has made the followers of Osonyin a highly secretive order. Osonyin is also aligned with the Ajes, who must petition for his approval when creating their magic potions. One of the female Orishas, Oya, is the only Orisha to have successfully bested Osonyin's powers, as this story illustrates.

Osonyin had kept all of his herbal secrets in a large calabash gourd high in the top of an Araba tree. The Araba is the tallest tree in Africa and can reach heights of up to 120 feet tall. This particular tree was known as *Iroko*, the sacred tree, symbolizing the *Axis Mundi* or the Tree of Life, and because of this, it was imbued with great spiritual powers. Oya, hearing of Osonyin's secret calabash at the top of Iroko, called upon the winds (which she has dominion over) and the winds blew the calabash out of Iroko, smashing it on the ground and releasing all of the herbal secrets. The other Orishas scrambled to gather whatever they could before the angry Osonyin was able to re-gather the remaining secrets and scuttle them away once again. This is why all of the Orishas have power over certain herbs and plants, but the greatest keeper of those secrets is still the single, watchful eye of Osonyin.

OMULU aka BABALUAYE

Omulu, also known as *Babaluaye*, is a rather dark and somewhat frightening Orisha. He is the Orisha of diseases, specifically smallpox, leprosy, and tuberculosis, which were three of the most devastating diseases in the New World. Because of his association with deadly diseases, he is also connected to *Ellegua*, the Master of Death. More recently Omulu has become associated with diseases of the blood, specifically AIDS and Ebola. He is depicted on crutches with skin lesions, creating a most disturbing countenance. However, he is highly revered and respected because of his ability to cheat Death, and therefore he holds the secrets of immortality. Because of this immortal feat, he is syncretized with another Saint who cheated death, St. Lazarus. He is also the leader of the *Egums*, known as the "Battalion of the Dead," and his colors are black and white.

Despite his outward appearance of death and disease, Omulu has a small but very powerful group of disciples. They are believed to have immense knowledge into the secrets of time and the true nature of Death, and Omulu's initiates guard these secrets zealously.

OYA aka IANSA

Oya is the refinement of feminine strength and power, and her name sounds like the wind itself. She is another warrior Orisha, outside the quartet of men, yet she alone is allowed to take the battlefield with the other warrior Orishas. Her color is purple or reddish brown, and she is syncretized with Joan of Arc, another female warrior who led men into battle.

Oya was previously married to Ogun, but as I explained in a previous story, she left him for Changó, thus creating an eternal rift between the two male Orishas. Changó later left Oya for the beautiful river goddess, Osun, and Oya was so brokenhearted that she stole weapons from both Ogun and Changó. From Ogun she took a sword, and from Changó she took lightning from his secret cache of weaponry. As a result we have the image of a furious Oya on horseback, a sword in hand, lightning striking wherever she directs it, and a tempest brewing all around her. Would you like to meet that on a battlefield?

As a gift from her mother, Yemoja, Oya was given dominion over the wind, tornados, hurricanes, and even certain forms of witchcraft. In a parallel way, this also gives her dominion over the marketplace, where fortunes are made and lost, much like the unpredictability of a storm. In old Africa, as it still is today, there are gigantic markets that are run entirely by women, with one "head woman" as the overseer of the entire system. These markets were the foundation of the first financial institutions in Africa, and Yemoja and Oya are both closely aligned with these markets.

Lastly, Oya has a special affinity for the dead, the Egums, of which she is entirely unafraid. She is not Death per se, since that is the responsibility of Ellegua. However, once a person dies, it is Oya who waits for them and takes them to the land of the dead, where they wait until a reincarnation can take place. As such, she is also the guardian of cemeteries and graveyards, places she finds quite peaceful.

OSUN aka OXUM

Osun is the goddess of the sweet waters—the fresh water rivers, lakes, and streams. She is the daughter of Yemoja and the sister of Oya, and she is known for her enchanting beauty. Her symbol is the heart for love, her color is yellow, and she is syncretized with St. Catherine, who was also known for her beauty.

Because of her sexual allure, Osun is the Orisha of fertility, and specifically, conception. But Osun is too coquettish for the duties of motherhood itself, so that realm remains for her mother, Yemoja.

Instead, Osun assists through beauty, charm, cleanliness of body, and sexual energy to bless humans with the renewal of human life.

There is a story that tells how Osun used her charms to save humanity, when all the other Orishas had failed. It was all because Ogun had been working very hard for thousands of years, hacking away at the jungles of chaos to create the modern civilization that man would inhabit. Disgusted by the greed and wastefulness of humans, Ogun decided to quit work entirely and retreat to his forest solitude, causing civilization to come to a grinding halt. None of the other Orishas could convince Ogun to come back and restart civilization, and most of them were far too afraid to even approach the fiercest of the warrior Orishas. Finally, Osun decided that enough was enough, and so she crept into Ogun's forest abode, setting up camp not far from where he slept.

Each night Osun would do an erotic dance, her body undulating to the rhythms of the Earth, as she showed Ogun the perfected form of a woman. Each night, Ogun would creep a little closer to watch the dancing Osun, until finally, when he was within arms reach, she smeared her lips with honey and kissed Ogun with a deep kiss no god could resist. Pacified and hypnotized, Ogun agreed to return to the building of civilization once more. That is the power of Osun - using love to tame the fiercest beast.

What I find most fascinating about these Orishas is how closely they resemble the people I personally know, some of whom follow Santeria and have even been ordained. I could probably tell my friends which Orisha watches over each of them, but in order to truly know your Orisha, you should always go and see an Ifá priest, known as a *Babalawo*. They can do the proper readings and divinations and tell you for sure which Orisha watches over you.

If you find this beautiful and ancient tradition to be interesting, I assure you, the more you read and learn about it, the more the Orishas will captivate your heart. I think Santeria, Lucumi, and Candomble are some of the wisest and most compassionate systems of faith I have ever experienced, and it has affected me profoundly over the years.

*

It was now nearing the end of my time in Cuba, so I said sad goodbyes to my Cuban drum-brothers and the rest of us flew back to Miami to catch our respective flights to our home cities. The members from Synthesis would come and play a show in Los Angeles the following year, and Eugenio and Oney and I would have a joyful reunion. But that was the last time I saw the magical drummers of Cuba. Eugenio made an escape to Miami on the same trip, where he received political asylum. I would help him out by sending him a brand new box of Sabian cymbals to help get his drumming career off the ground in the U.S. Oney, however, returned to Cuba where I like to imagine he is still playing the sacred rhythms of the Orishas in the Santeria ceremonies.

For myself, I continued my work as a studio musician in Los Angeles, playing on albums for several rock bands, various singers and songwriters, and even a few movie soundtracks. One of the more interesting albums I worked on came from Nando Reis, an up and coming Brazilian singer-songwriter who asked me to play drums and percussion on his new solo album. Although we recorded the album in Seattle with my old friend Jack Endino producing, I would soon be heading to Brazil for the first time to promote Nando's new album. It was an exciting time, especially since I had already been baptized in the rhythms of Africa, Cuba, and soon would be going to Brazil. It was also the end of the millennia, the end of the 20th century, and very soon we would all be entering the glittering digital age of the 21st century.

16. Cuban Obatala Rhythm
17. Barrett Martin Group "Che Viva"

VERSE 9

BRAZIL: A MAGICAL BUREAUCRACY

Barrett and a tree sloth in the Brazilian Amazon, 2016.

"I was a beach boy, and I believe I learned my songs from the birds of the Brazilian forest."

—Antônio Carlos Jobim

To write a compelling story about the incredible people and music of Brazil is an enormous undertaking, which can hardly be done in one Verse. All I can really do is tell that story from my personal experience, with a few historical markers thrown in for reference. Here's how I got there in the first place.

After my return from Cuba, I found myself working on several albums back to back in the Los Angeles studio scene. I had earned a good reputation as an adventurous percussionist, especially after making the first Tuatara album *Breaking The Ethers* in 1997 with Peter Buck of R.E.M., and then immediately playing on R.E.M.'s experimental album *Up* in 1998. Soon after that I got a call from producer Brendan O'Brien to play a marimba solo on a Stone Temple Pilots song called "Atlanta", which was recorded at the old A&M Studios in Hollywood, formerly the Charley Chaplin soundstage. That's the one thing I love about Hollywood—the history of the town and all the incredible albums and films that have been made there.

I was also making increasingly frequent trips out to Joshua Tree in the Mojave Desert east of Los Angeles. I had become friends with Fred Drake and Dave Catching, the owners of the now-legendary Rancho de la Luna recording studio, which was in Fred's house (and still is) on the edge of the Joshua Tree National Park. The Rancho had become the headquarters of a burgeoning new sound called "desert rock" and one of the architects of that sound was producer and Masters Of Reality front man Chris Goss. Chris had sung back up vocals on the Screaming Trees *Dust* album and he was now producing Josh Homme, formerly of the desert rock band Kyuss who was now leading Queens Of The Stone Age. Josh had also been the second guitarist in the Screaming Trees during our 1996-97 tour to support the *Dust* album. So you can begin to see how a bunch of very creative and influential musicians were hanging out together in the Mojave Desert—something was bound to happen. At some point in 1997, Josh took me out to the Rancho to play drums on some songs he was producing, and these songs became part of the Desert Sessions series. During those sessions, I hit it off with Fred and Dave, and thus began my long association with the Rancho studio, those extraordinary musicians and producers, and the desert rock sound in general.

It was in December of 1999 when Josh asked me to come down and play percussion on a new Queens Of The Stone Age album they were recording. The sessions were at Sound City Studios in Van Nuys, California and the Queens were in the middle of recording their now-classic *Rated R* album. Chris Goss was producing, Dave Catching was playing guitar, and I played a bunch of percussion not normally used on rock albums, which included vibraphone, steel drum, and even an Arabic dunbek, along with various shakers and tambourines. The sessions were exciting and very original sounding. *Rated R* turned out to be the breakthrough album for the Queens, and the album stands as one of the seminal desert rock albums of the time.

In addition to the desert sessions, there were the usual Los Angeles recording sessions with various singer-songwriters, and a brief stint with the French band Air, as we performed a few shows in Los Angeles and at the Sundance Film Festival. I was doing all kinds of work using mallet instruments and all manner of exotic percussion, much like my late friend Milt Holland had done long before me. But I wasn't doing very much drum set playing since there were a thousand drummers in LA, but not many percussionists with my training. It was a welcome change I suppose, because it forced me to think about rhythm and "sound coloring" in a totally different way.

Then I got one of those life-changing phone calls from my friend in Seattle, Jack Endino. Jack wanted to know if I'd be interested in playing drums and percussion on an album he was producing for a Brazilian singer-songwriter named Nando Reis. I hadn't worked with Jack for many years and I had never heard of Nando, but I immediately agreed to do it because I had the strong intuition that working with a Brazilian singer would require all the skills I had developed up to that point, and it would also deepen my knowledge of Brazilian music. The thing was, Nando's band needed a place to practice in Seattle while I was finishing up my sessions in Los Angeles, so Jack and I arranged for Nando's band to rehearse in my basement studio until I arrived back in Seattle.

I was a couple days late returning but I could hear the music emanating from my basement as I walked down the curved driveway. As I descended the stairs into the studio the first thing I saw was a tall, slim, orange-haired man with spectacles and a beard, dancing happily and laughing as he clapped his hands in great amusement. I started laughing immediately because I saw the deep joy in Nando's mannerisms, and in that nuclear moment my love for Brazilian music and Brazilian people was sealed.

We rehearsed the songs for Nando's album over the course of a week, and then we began recording those songs at Hanzsek Studios in the nearby neighborhood of Ballard. We worked quickly and efficiently, and I even got my friend Peter Buck to come down and play some 12-string guitar and mandolin on a few songs. The resulting album, *Para Quando o Arco*, was an amazing mixture of Brazilian and American rock that still maintained the beautiful, melodic essence that Brazilian music is famous for. It even spawned a couple of radio hits in Brazil and it is considered a Brazilian rock classic.

Since that singularly important year of 2000, I've played on over 100 albums as a drummer and percussionist, and I've made several albums with Nando as both his drummer and producer, touring all over Brazil and seeing much of that vast country in the process.

My adventures in Brazil began in September of 2000 when I flew down there on a three-month work visa to do the first tour in support of *Para Quando o Arco*. I and American keyboardist Alex Veley, who also played on the album, flew to Rio de Janeiro and we knew it was going to be an auspicious trip when we got into our taxi at the Rio airport and the first single from Nando's album was playing on the taxi's radio. It was already a hit.

In Rio, Alex and I shared an apartment in Ipanema, the famous beach community just south of the city. We would often fly to the various cities on the tour, but we always returned to our apartment in Ipanema, exploring the city's musical landscape every night we had off.

The Nando band, now named "Os Infernais" (The Infernals), played every major city in Brazil and we even recorded another studio album in between our shows titled, *There's Still A Full Moon Shining Over Jalalabad* (the album was completed during the American invasion of Afghanistan). On that first tour, I heard more Brazilian music than my mind could process, I saw just about every tourist sight that could be seen, and I completely absorbed the rhythms of Brazil into the core of my being.

In the Infernais band, I had the duty of playing drums and singing back-up vocals, which were of course in Portuguese and occasionally called for the making of birdcalls, something I hadn't heard since the Martin Denny records my father played during my childhood. As it turned out, I was quite good at this unique task, and like most people who learn a foreign language through music, I began to learn the Portuguese language by singing Nando's lyrics. However, being an English speaker by nature, my brain wanted to Anglicize every word I heard in Portuguese, hence, some of Nando's lyrics sounded like "Pancho Villa was my sister," and "They say that my Fuji can't boogie," which of course is not remotely close to the real meaning of the words.

Every day in Brazil was magical, largely because Brazil is a magical culture at its very core. Every night there was music to be found in all manner of venues, from small antique shops that switched over to samba-pagode clubs at night, to formal musical halls and theatres, to gigantic samba schools with marching bands and beautiful, be-feathered dancers. There were berimbau dance troupes that would perform at restaurant tables by the seaside, and funk bands that played the dirtiest rhythms you've ever heard high up in the favelas that hang on the cliffs above the cities. And on weekend nights when the music was the fiercest, the parties would go well into the early morning hours of the next day.

We spent many nights in the enormous Rocinha *favela*, which was the equivalent of a large city of about 100,000 people, complete with its own police force and community services. Built along the hillside above Rio, these favelas have the best views in the city but are sadly lacking in basic services like clean water, sewage systems, and electricity. They are also quite dangerous if you don't know where you are going. Considering that Brazil is the eighth biggest economy in the world, and was at one point predicted to become the world's biggest economy, it's a crime that so many people have to live under these squalid conditions. But this is the inherent problem with Brazil—it's a truly magical country with enormous natural resources and human potential, but its government is so corrupt it simply can't get out of the way of itself.

At the same time, the Brazilian people are some of the friendliest and most community-oriented people you will ever meet. I remember once taking a trolley car up a steep hill in the old Lapa/Santa Teresa neighborhood, which is where the famous movie *Black Orpheus* was filmed. On these trolleys, the tourists (like me) paid a small fee to ride, but the locals just jump on and off for free, getting from one neighborhood to the next. On this particular occasion, a young woman with her small baby was trying to jump onto the slow-moving trolley but could not quite reach escape-velocity to make the leap. Realizing that her moment to jump was quickly expiring, she caught my eyes and literally tossed her baby up to me, landing him perfectly in my lap. She then successfully leapt onboard herself, smiling as she collected her little boy from my arms. No words were ever spoken between us, it was just understood that I would catch her baby and then we would continue with our mutual trolley ride.

This analogy is the closest I can give to the Brazilian experience. It's slightly desperate, but there is a common understanding that everyone generally keeps an eye out for each other, catching a flying baby when necessary. The spirit of Brazilian music seems to reside in these kinds of people and places, high above the city where life is tough, but the music and beauty of the natural landscape takes over. If one can disregard the blemishes of urban poverty, municipal corruption, and simply listen to the incredible music coming through her people, then Brazil is the most exquisite country in the world.

These all-night forays we took exploring music around the city would eventually take us to a *feijoada* house the next morning. This is a special kind of restaurant that serves the cure for the Friday or Saturday night before. Feijoada is a Brazilian specialty that is essentially black beans and rice with heavily salted beef or pork with manioc flour, and slices of orange on the side. It is the ultimate fare after a long night of music, dance, and libations—it is the soul food of Brazil.

When we were not pursuing our musical adventures around Rio, the Infernais band would play shows all over the country, from cattle stations in the hinterland, to the famed music halls of Rio, São Paulo, Salvador, and other coastal cities. Sometimes we flew on commercial airlines, but much of the time we rode in a tour bus across some of the roughest highways I've ever ridden. Some of these trips lasted as long as 30 hours, on roads that could barely accommodate cars, much less a tour bus. I'm pretty sure we re-graded several high spots in the road with the bottom of our bus, and many times I awoke in my bunk in terror, convinced that we had left the roadway and were off in a ravine, only to find out that were just driving down a particularly rough patch of road.

Frequently we would get off the bus in the middle of nowhere, perhaps at the crossroads of a trucking or cattle ranching town and there, miraculously, we'd find a beautiful old amphitheater built decades earlier, with a crowd of local folks eager to hear us play. The electricity systems were outdated and the lighting was yellow and dim, but the experience of young couples swaying to the music on a warm evening under the Amazonian stars will stay with me forever. These people loved Nando's songs so much, and they were so appreciative that we made the effort to get there, that it made those hard hours on the road totally worth it. And I think that's what moved me so deeply about the Brazilian people—that even in the middle of a rural, agricultural environment, the people cared about music more than anything. It was life to them.

Once while on my way to a recording session in Rio, I got lost not knowing the exact address of the studio we were recording at. I knocked on the door of a large villa that was on the same street as the studio, but it turned out to be the official residence of the world-famous Brazilian composer Heitor Villa-Lobos. Although the great composer had died many years earlier, his house had been preserved like a kind of museum. The housekeeper politely invited me inside and sat me down in the composer's study, right next to the master's grand piano and a giant palm tree. She then brought me coffee and cake after which she called to confirm the actual address of the studio, and then called a taxi to take me there. This is a classic example of the kindness and elegance that most Brazilians have. I also took it as a sign to investigate the work of Villa-Lobos and I'm glad I did because I began to understand the complexity of Brazilian music that goes so much deeper than the samba rhythms the world is so familiar with.

When I had time off between the legs of the tour, I was also able to study some of the incredible percussion traditions of Brazil and my first and greatest teacher was the percussionist Ramiro Musotto. Ramiro was Argentinean by birth but he knew, even as a young teenager, that he wanted to be a Brazilian master percussionist. So he moved to Bahia when he was a very young man and began his apprenticeship as a Brazilian percussionist.

Ramiro went on to play with some of Brazil's biggest bands and he was particularly known for his virtuosic ability on the berimbau, the single-stringed bow-like instrument that has its origins in Angola but is the definitive sound of Brazilian percussion. When one listens to either of Ramiro's two superb solo albums, *Sudaka* and *Civilizacao & Barbarye*, you can immediately hear his amazing berimbau melodies blended with electronic beats, Brazilian percussion, and sound samples that he recorded during his travels in South America.

Ramiro toured all over South America, Europe, and he even did a few shows in the U.S., but he sadly passed away from cancer in 2009. He and I were almost exactly the same age, and he was one of my greatest teachers, if only for a short time. Therefore I must credit him for exposing me to the immensity of the world of percussion, and specifically with teaching me the magic of *clave*, that mystical subdivision of rhythm that makes us move and dance.

There was one day in particular, which I will never forget, when Ramiro's powerful energy manifested. It was on a day when we were playing *Candomblé* rhythms on traditional *atabaque* religious drums. Candomblé is the Brazilian equivalent of Cuban Santería, and Ramiro was teaching me the rhythm for Changó, the Orisha of thunder and lightning, and the protector of drummers everywhere. Changó was Ramiro's guardian Orisha and Changó loves it when you play drums in his honor, for indeed, he is the master of the rhythms. Ramiro and I were playing Changó's sacred rhythm when a mighty thunderclap exploded in the sky right above us. It was not your ordinary thunderclap—it was an ear-splitting explosion that roiled across the sky for several seconds. Ramiro's eyes became huge with excitement and he laughed wildly, yelling at me, "This is fantastic—Changó is happy! Lay down the thunder Barrett!"

Lay down the thunder indeed, Brother Ramiro.

Great songwriters and composers like Nando, Ramiro, and several other people who I worked with in Brazil are part of a long tradition of artists who have created some of the most original forms in the history of music. In Brazil they call it *cannibalismo*, and it's a term musicians use when they cannibalize all the music they come into contact with, whether it be classical, jazz, folkloric, rock, or electronic. When they are done chewing through the form, they spit out a new music, a music that is fresher, more exciting, and more original than the one they first devoured. It's why Brazilian music is always reinventing itself.

For example, samba is the original sound of Brazil—it's that marching-dancing rhythm that we associate with huge lines of marching drummers and beautiful, dancing, be-feathered girls. But samba is constantly being reinvented and repurposed in new forms of music - it's the rhythm that everyone from pop singers, to favela bands, to electronic DJs use to keep the crowds dancing and moving.

One of the biggest evolutions in samba happened back in 1958 when a guitarist named João Gilberto began to experiment with the rhythm by slowing it down and creating a new rhythm he called *bossa nova*, which literally means "new beat." The accent on the *clave* stayed the same, but it was slowed down to allow for more sophisticated chord progressions and melodies to be composed over the rhythm. The new sound was so cool and cosmopolitan that it affected Brazilian cultural as deeply as rock & roll affected American culture at the same time. A few years later, in 1962, Antônio Carlos "Tom" Jobim took the bossa nova sound and, along with the famed poet Vinicius de Moraes, wrote the international hit "Girl From Ipanema," the national song of Brazil.

By the mid-1960s, Brazil and its bossa nova songs were being heard around the world and its influence was so great that it became the universal sound of sophistication—nothing else sounded that cool. Even now the bossa nova beat is still the defacto rhythm for modern "chill out," ambient, and down tempo electronic music. Its feel is so timeless and hypnotic that no rhythm has even come close to replacing it.

But back in 1964, just as the Brazilian sun was shining the brightest on its musicians, a military dictatorship overthrew the democratically elected government of President Goulart and the military installed a right-wing dictatorship that lasted until 1985. The American president Lyndon Johnson supported the coup and the CIA contributed advisors to the military junta, which ultimately resulted in the imprisonment, torture, exile, and in some cases "disappearances" of many left-wing activists. It was one of the darkest periods in Brazilian history, and unfortunately the United States contributed to that darkness, and this is partly why the relationship between our two countries has always been a little strained. However, the musicians continue to bridge that divide with their collaborations and that has made a huge difference over time.

Twenty years was a very long time for Brazil to be under military rule, and the remnants are still visible today in the vast military police that patrol the streets of Brazil's largest cities. Many of those streets are named after generals, because, well, those generals liked to name streets after themselves. But like the forces of physics, there is always an equal and opposite force in politics that pushes back against dictators, and so it came to be with the musicians and artists of the legendary Tropicalia movement who waged a war of peace.

Tropicalia was a mixture of avant-garde poetry, theatre, Brazilian folkloric music, a healthy dose of rock & roll, and a psychedelic twist that gave the whole presentation a magical realism. The movement was lead by the very young but extremely talented singer-songwriters of Caetano Veloso, Gilberto Gil, Gal Costa, the producer Tom Ze, and the legendary band Os Mutantes (The Mutants). There were also playwrights, filmmakers, artists, and writers involved so that the movement encompassed the totality of Brazilian culture at the time. Their message was not overtly political or aligned with any political parties. Rather, it was about the individual person having the freedom to express themselves how they wished. That act of individual freedom was of course enraging to the military dictatorship, because dictatorships can only thrive when the people are ignorant, suppressed, and have no voice. These Tropicalia musicians gave the people their voice.

The Tropicalia movement owed much to the Nueva Canción movement, which had started in the early 1960s in the Spanish-speaking countries of Central and South America. Nueva Canción was a songwriting style that was used to speak out against the nationalistic, right-wing agenda that had begun to emerge in countries like Argentina, Chile, and Peru. The freedom-driven music of Nueva Canción and Tropicalia infuriated the conservative, fascist, military governments and in the case of Brazil, this led to the arrest and exile of Tropicalia's leaders, Caetano Veloso and Gilberto Gil.

The two friends fled to London but continued their careers in the UK and Europe, until they were finally allowed to return to Brazil in 1972. Somewhat ironically, thirty years later Gilberto Gil became the Minister of Culture under President Lula De Silva, and Caetano Veloso is now considered the greatest singer from Brazil, touring worldwide, with a voice renowned for its sublime beauty and extraordinary timbre.

In my explorations of Brazilian music, I was particularly taken by the fusion records that were made in the 1960s and 1970s, the two decades that are referred to as the Golden Age of Brazilian music. This is when a mystical blend of jazz, rock, folkloric music, and Afro-Brazilian rhythms emerged with such innovation that the entire world took notice. Albums by João Gilberto, Jorge Ben, Caetano Veloso, Gilberto Gil, Gal Costa, Milton Nascimento (and his amazing collaborations with the American jazz musician Wayne Shorter), Rita Lee, Os Mutantes, João Bosco, and many other Brazilian artists did incredibly adventurous work at that time. And when you look deeply into the rhythms, you'll hear that it is all rooted in African rhythms manifested as the samba, the baio, the bossa nova, the maracatu, the forró, and of course the drumming religion of Candomblé.

When I returned to Brazil for the second time in January of 2003, it was to record another album and play more shows with the Infernais band. We started by recording the basic tracks for Nando's next album, *A Letra A,* and this time we recorded in Rio and we made a plan to do the final overdubs at my new home in Taos, New Mexico, where I had built a studio to keep my vast percussion collection.

In March, just about a month after we completed the basic tracking in Rio, Nando flew to Albuquerque, New Mexico where I picked him up in my Ford F-150 as we drove the two and half hours north to Taos. Nando was clearly enjoying himself as he watched the American "Wild West" landscape rolling by as we drove through the mountains and canyons of Northern New Mexico.

We set up shop at my studio in Taos and we immediately started recording overdubs with myself doing percussion and backing vocals,

Alex Veley doing keyboards and backing vocals, and Kip Beelman engineering the whole thing. We finished everything in about two weeks, during which we took day hikes and short trips into the desert to see old Spanish churches and Native American pueblos, where Nando could take photos for the artwork of his album.

Shortly thereafter, Nando flew back to Brazil where he completed the mixing of *A Letra A* and went on to have a rather huge solo career. I would work with Nando on other albums, but I wouldn't return to Brazil again until 2016 when I flew down to produced his critically acclaimed album, *Jardim-Pomar.*

What I have come to know personally, and Brazil has taught me this directly: all things change and music does so especially quickly. The downward trends in popular culture eventually reverse course, and exciting new forms of music emerge where mediocrity once held sway. I also remember that Brazil not only gave us the incredible singers, songwriters, and musicians whom I've just described, but Brazil also gave us academic giants like Paulo Friere, who redefined true education with his famous treatise, *Pedagogy Of The Oppressed.* Brazil also gave us the spiritual writer Paulo Coelho who wrote *The Alchemist,* and Brazil also gave us the master architect, Oscar Niemeyer, who redefined an entire school of thought on what modern architecture should be. And let us not forget the soccer legend Pelé, who I once saw dance across a soccer field in Seattle when I was just ten years old. All of these musicians, thinkers, architects, athletes, and ways of expressing the human soul are treasures that Brazil has given to the entire world.

Perhaps the most important thing that Brazil has taught me is how the power of music can change a political situation. Because even powerful politicians eventually buckle to the will of the people when the power of music moves those people to march, protest, and resist the collective ignorance of their so-called leaders. Music enlightens us, and therefore, it evolves us.

And so it was that I returned to the United States in the spring of 2003, at the beginning of two disastrous wars in the Middle East— Afghanistan and Iraq. There was enormous loss of human life on all sides, and astronomical expense to the global economy, to which no one benefitted except the makers of the war machines.

Considering the grim outlook of the time, and also because I no longer had a rock band to play with, I decided to go back to school and learn about the world rather than participate in the destroying of it. And that is how I ended up in the Peruvian Amazon.

18. Brazilian Candomblé Rhythm
19. Barrett Martin Group "Favela Song"

VERSE 10

PERU: WOVEN SONGS OF THE AMAZON

Shipibo women painting a songline, Peruvian Amazon, 2004.
Photo by Bear Guerra.

"Once you have taken ayahuasca and heard the songs of the rainforest, the Mother is in your heart forever."

—Enrique Augustine, Shipibo shaman

My time in Los Angeles during the late 1990s was a fruitful time for me as a studio musician and producer, and those experiences would help me tremendously in the next phase of my musical life. But by 2003, I was living full-time in Taos, New Mexico, where I had bought a house, built a studio, and generally planted my flag in the high desert of New Mexico. I was only occasionally venturing out west to do studio work in Los Angeles, and in 2003 I had just come back from my second trip to Brazil. The dissolution of the Screaming Trees in 2000, and the back-to-back deaths of Baker Saunders, Layne Staley, and my good friend Fred Drake really made me feel like my time in rock & roll was finished.

I wasn't going to quit music altogether, but moving to the desert and starting my first indie record label made me want to hunker down and really build something that was both original and sustainable. It turned out that New Mexico was not the best place to start a business venture, much less a studio and record label in a music industry that was beginning a rapid decline. But I loved New Mexico for its unique mix of people and the incredible beauty of its landscape. It ended up being my full-time home for almost a decade and the greatest thing New Mexico gave me was my formal education.

I started attending classes at the Taos campus of the University Of New Mexico and within a couple of years I was close to finishing up the bachelor's degree that I had abandoned in Washington State in 1987, back when I first started playing music in Seattle. At UNM, I was accepted into their esteemed anthropology and linguistics program, with a focus in ethnomusicology. I suppose the switch from music to anthropology was largely because of all the traveling I had done around the world and my sincere interest in the people of other cultures. It just felt like a natural extension of what I was already learning out in the real world.

The only live music I was playing at the time was with a small jazz combo led by a wonderful New York pianist named Mary Bruscini. Mary had left New York many years earlier, and like me, she had set up shop in Taos. She was a kind of a resident celebrity where she did everything from giving the locals piano lessons, to a weekly Saturday night jazz residency at an old hacienda that had been converted into a restaurant and bar. My jazz chops were pretty rusty but Mary gave me a shot at playing in her combo, so I practiced and practiced until I could hang with the jazz cats.

That weekly jazz gig became the main party in Taos on a Saturday night and it was a beautiful place to learn and play jazz in the New Mexico desert. Our audience consisted of locals and Hollywood celebrities, and the room was always packed. Mary would occasionally expand the band and add a conga player and horn section so we could play some Latin jazz arrangements, but most of what I learned from that marvelous, elegant New York lady was in our small trio where we played the music of Thelonius Monk, John Coltrane, Miles Davis, Charles Mingus, and all the classic jazz standards that could be played with just piano, drums, and upright bass.

By 2004, I had produced and released the first few bands for my label, one of which was the first Barrett Martin Group album, which I had started at Fred Drake's Rancho de la Luna. I appropriately titled it *The Painted Desert* and I put together the first live version of that band with a great upright bassist named Luis Guerra, a saxophonist named Kanoa Kaluhiwa, and a pianist named John Rangel. I would book us gigs from Taos all the way down the Rio Grande corridor to Santa Fe and Albuquerque and even a few weddings out in the desert. Admittedly these were very small gigs, and some of them were in restaurants where the money was low and the playing was mostly for fun. However, there's something magical about the landscape and architecture of New Mexico and the people who live there and it can often make you feel as if you're playing in some exotic, faraway country. Generally speaking, I had a gig every weekend with one of these jazz bands, and as my mind settled into the land of enchantment, so too did my understanding that beautiful music can happen anywhere, and not just on a big rock stage.

At the beginning of the 2004 academic year, I was nearing completion of my bachelor's degree in anthropology. I would have to move down to Albuquerque to be at the main campus for my final year, especially if I wanted a chance at attending their anthropology graduate school. I was simultaneously presented with an opportunity that really only comes once in a lifetime, and that was an invitation to go to the Peruvian Amazon to work on a documentary film about the indigenous Shipibo tribe. So I met with my anthropology advisors to ask for permission and they all agreed that fieldwork in the Peruvian Amazon would certainly be a great step toward graduate school.

The Shipibo are renowned for their beautiful textiles, as well as for their acapella singing, both of which are used as a way to heal in their shamanic ceremonies. They are also famous for their mastery of the extremely powerful entheogen *ayahuasca*, which in the last few years has created a huge new trend in ecotourism in the Amazon. But back in 2004, ayahuasca and the Shipibo shamans were pretty far off the radar and not much anthropology fieldwork had been done on these extraordinary people. My field assignment was to be the sound engineer and ethnomusicologist who would record and document the Shipibo songs for the film, and this would also serve as my fieldwork study for an honors degree in anthropology. I would be required to write an extensive thesis of my research, some of which I used for this story, and then I would submit my field recordings and the documentation for peer review.

The Shipibo project and the Amazon Rainforest in general became an ongoing passion for me that would become the center of my work throughout graduate school and beyond. And although I have always been an environmentally conscious person who grew up responsibly in the Pacific Northwest, spending time in the Amazon Rainforest utterly changed me at the core of my being. Here's how it happened.

There were five of us who were selected to fly to Peru on May 21st, 2004, and this group included the film's director, Anna Stevens, the cameraman Tad Fettig, myself, a photographer named Bear Guerra, and his brother Luis Guerra, who was also the bassist in my solo group. More importantly, Luis was our Spanish language translator and an additional producer for our sound recordings. We flew from Albuquerque to Dallas and then on to Lima, Peru where we spent one night before catching our connecting flight to Pucallpa the next morning. Pucallpa is the last little town on the eastern frontier of Peru right before the Amazon rainforest swallows up all of civilization. To give you a little story about it, a few years back there was a commercial airline that made a crash landing near the Pucallpa airport, and the plane went right into the rainforest. When help arrived, there was virtually no one on the plane and confusion ensued until rescuers finally realized that the passengers had simply gotten themselves out of the wreckage and walked home to their villages. It's the Amazon after all, and if you want to get anywhere, you just have to start walking.

Fortunately, our film crew arrived in a less dramatic fashion, and after arriving in Pucallpa, we boarded a long motorized canoe for the two-hour voyage up river to the village of San Francisco de Yarina Cocha, which literally means, "San Francisco of Serpent Lake." Yes, there were snakes here, lots of them, and mostly poisonous, with several of the large anaconda variety. The anaconda is the Shipibo's main totem animal, although to be perfectly honest, the largest snake I saw on this particular trip was the stuffed anaconda at the Pucallpa airport.

Our Shipibo village was part of an extended tribal community consisting of about 20,000 people who were divided into approximately 100 villages throughout the Upper Ucayali River Basin. The Ucayali is an upper tributary of the Amazon, and in our village the population was around 3,000, which was the largest of the Shipibo communities.

As well as being renowned for their singing, the Shipibo are equally respected for their elegant weavings and ceramics, all of which are embroidered or painted with intricate geometric patterns that are a kind of musical songline. When I first saw these weavings and paintings I immediately made a connection back to the opposite side of the planet, in Australia, where I had first seen and heard the songlines back in the early 1990s. Here in the Amazon Rainforest I found songlines again, but these were expressed differently through the Shipibo concept of a living landscape and their own cultural representation.

The Shipibo songlines look somewhat like mathematical fractals in their design, and they contain numerous symbolic meanings, which I would learn about during my time with these beautiful people. These designs were painted on the sides of their small, thatched roof houses, on their clothing, and sometimes even on their faces and bodies. They were literally wearing their songs, and as we entered the village from the long narrow dock where our boat landed, they came to us, singing their welcoming songs. Whether it was from lack of sleep, the joy of finally arriving in the Amazon, or the beauty of their singing, I was weeping tears as we walked into their village. Small children took my hands to walk and sing to me, which made me immediately forget the heavy backpacks of equipment I had slung over my shoulders. I was floating in a timeless landscape.

In the Shipibo tradition, to weave is to sing and to sing is to heal, and so goes the timeless process that their shamans have used to heal their people for centuries. They do this by using a variety of curing songs called *icaros*, along with the numerous plant and herbal remedies they cultivate in their rainforest gardens. Every herb, plant, animal, and elemental spirit has its own song, as does every human being, including you, the reader. These songs emanate out from all life forms and are heard by the shamans throughout the rainforest. The shamans then harness the curing power of the song by visualizing their corresponding song pattern and then memorializing it with a painting or weaving. This musical-visualization process is called *synesthesia*, and it's a phenomenon that has only recently become a subject for research.

Synesthesia is something we've all experienced before, even if we don't remember it. When we were babies, our sense of sight, sound, smell, taste, and touch were all blurred together into one gigantic sensory experience. As our brains developed, we started to separate these senses into compartments so we can differentiate what seeing is, versus hearing, smelling, tasting, touching, and so on. For some people, however, those senses are blurred together a little bit. For example, when you hear a certain chord on a piano such as D minor, you might associate that chord with a certain color in your mind. Maybe that color is dark purple (which is the color that D minor causes in me). That's an example of synesthesia, and I have it, to a small degree. Some extreme examples of "synesthetes" report having taste sensations, like salty, sweet, or tangy, when they hear certain chords or sequences of notes. You can begin to see how powerful synesthesia can be.

As it turns out, the Amazon Basin tends to have a very high percentage of people, and women in particular, who have a strong synesthetic experience. When they hear songs, the emergence of geometric patterns arise in their mind. Perhaps it's because of the rainforest itself, where there are so many different examples of life, color, sound, and smell, and maybe growing up in that kind of environment allows a person's mind to experience all the senses without having to compartmentalize them as we do in the industrialized, Western world. It's a truly amazing phenomenon, and my research was just a small contribution to the study of it.

When I first saw the Shipibo song patterns, it reminded me of something a music professor had taught me years ago in one of my theory classes. He had explained that in some forms of world music, the structure of a composition is depicted with either arcing, curving, or stepped lines that show the rise and fall of the melody within the structure of the composition. It was a simple mnemonic (memory) device to show the musicians how the music was supposed to flow. Since most non-Western musicians usually play by ear, these designs were a kind of musical shorthand or tablature for them to follow. When I saw the Shipibo songlines, I began to see that I was looking at an Amazonian version of this musical shorthand.

Like most indigenous cultures, the Shipibo teach their songs through an aural, memory-based tradition, passed down from shaman to student through direct transmission. In many ways, the Shipibo were just like the Griots I had studied with in Senegal, or the old delta bluesmen I would play with in later years. That musical transmission through performance and memory creates perfection through repetition, and it not only strengthens the skill of the singer's own abilities, it also puts the culture directly into the minds of the people, passed down from generation to generation, without interruption. It's the same way I learned rhythms in Africa, Cuba, and Brazil—from listening, repeating the rhythm, and allowing my own muscle memory to remember. Western scholars can now write out almost any style of music using the old Vienna school notation system, but I still believe the best way to learn music is from memory, so that the mind is remembering the music, and not a piece of paper.

Or as the great Miles Davis used to say to his musicians: *There ain't any music stands on my stage.*

The Shipibo are an animistic culture in that they believe all things— the sun, the moon, the earth, humans, animals, plants, the elements, and everything else is alive with a spiritual energy that animates them. More simply put, if something has a form, then there must be some kind of intelligence behind that form. These people live in an aquatic world, with the heavenly realm above, and the watery underworld below. Dr. Lucille Eakin describes it perfectly in *People of the Ucayali*, "When there is an eclipse, the sun is closing its eyes; an unusual cloud formation is a spirit of some kind; and a whirlwind is a dancing demon who will try to snatch the soul of a child. Rain protects and cleanses the body and spirit; thunder is the conversation of the dead."

For the Shipibo, their musical inspiration comes from the biosphere of the Amazon rainforest and its flora and fauna. Their songs convey the spiritual principles of the Shipibo culture with a holistic worldview that sees a connection between all things. It's the purest, most natural spiritual tradition I've ever witnessed anywhere on Earth.

There are two very important Shipibo myths that really help you to understand how their musical and spiritual worlds intertwine, and the first one is about their creation deity, the anaconda:

In the beginning, there was only darkness, and in the middle of that darkness was a giant anaconda named Ronin, who encircled the Tree of Life. The anaconda reflected back on her beautiful skin and began to sing the beautiful geometric patterns that she saw, and her singing materializing into the heavens, the stars, the sun, the earth, the moon, and all the creatures who inhabit those realms. A world made of song was the result of Ronin's singing, and now every person and every living thing is imbued with their own distinct song.

A second important myth is the staircase to the sun myth, which goes something like this:

In ancient history, the sun was much closer to earth than it is now, so close in fact that food could be cooked directly upon it. At some point, however, the sun began to move farther away, so a pair of twin brothers decided to remedy the problem by building a staircase to the sun. They did this by shooting their arrows, point into nock, thereby creating a staircase made of arrows known as the *Kata Pekao*. The Shipibo were then able to climb this arrow staircase and resume cooking their food again, but then too many people were on the staircase and this caused it to collapse, killing most of the people in a tragedy similar to Icarus when he flew too close to the sun. Now only a remnant of the staircase remains, and only the knowledgeable shamans can ascend the staircase to the realm of the spirits.

The staircase myth is also very important in understanding the melodic structures of the Shipibo songs, because it is along these staircase songlines that the melody of the song unfolds, allowing the shaman to ascend the staircase to the spiritual realm. This staircase pattern can clearly be seen on the embroidery and paintings found on Shipibo song cloths and pottery.

It takes about one month for a Shipibo woman to embroider a song cloth, from inception of the pattern to completion of the cloth. The process is highly intricate, and during my stay in the village I saw many Shipibo women sitting for hours at a time as they embroidered a new song cloth while their children played on the packed-earth courtyards as chickens darted in and around the jungle's edge. The stitching, I was told, represents the interconnectedness of all things in the universe, and the cloth represents the fabric of the cosmos. When I observed a shaman "singing a cloth," they would often trace their index finger along the songline, the melody rising or descending in general accordance with the rise and fall of the songline.

The eight primary colors of the stitches have significance as well: black and white for the base colors; red representing blood, childbirth, and the historical conflict between the Amazonian tribes; yellow for sunlight; green for the rainforest; and blue for the rivers and lakes. Other new colors including purple, orange, and various neon colors seem to come from access to new, synthetic threads and yarns. Apparently the 1980s new-wave color scheme has finally made its way into Shipibo culture.

These song cloths can be wrapped around the waist as skirts or made into a *cushma*, the male poncho. These cloths have become the trademark item in the village markets, and indeed, it is not uncommon for a prospective buyer to be wooed into a purchase by the enchanting melody of a song, sung by its weaver-singer. It's a highly seductive audio-visual pitch, one that is certainly hard to resist. It worked quite effectively on me, to the degree that I bought about thirty of these cloths, as the beautiful singing-weavers relieved me of my American dollars.

The traditional Shipibo women wear a white skirt embroidered with colorful thread that depicts two sacred icaros—the wisdom icaro and the protection icaro. These are important songs to remember, because this is a matriarchal culture and the women carry the wisdom of their tradition. There are also black skirts with songlines stitched in white thread in an opposite color scheme, but in both cases the wisdom and protection icaros are the common theme. Indeed the use of a protection song is extremely important in the world of shamanism, where fighting the forces of darkness takes place on a daily basis. It is similar to the concept of a protection amulet, or a Native American medicine bag, or the West African *gris-gris* necklace that my Griot drum master made for me in Senegal.

There is a third, very important style of song cloth and this one is made like a traditional cloth but it is imbued with a mahogany brown dye made from tree bark. These cloths are referred to as "healing cloths," and they are used in the shamanic ceremonies when they are placed upon the patient's body to infuse it with the healing power of the icaro woven into it. Often a tincture of Amazonian herbs called *piri piri* will be used in conjunction with the song cloth and its corresponding icaro, as well a good bit of hands-on bodywork.

SHAMANISM AND THE AYAHUASCUA CEREMONY

In the modern, globalized, technology-obsessed world we live in, people play very fast and loose with the term "shaman." It seems like anyone who is slightly alternative to corporate culture might be called a shaman, and I've even heard people say that the millionaire housewife down the street is a shaman because "she channels stuff." None of this is true, of course, because a real shaman is extremely rare and requires years of training in a specific tradition. When you work with an authentic shaman, it changes your life forever and you will never forget the experience. Fortunately for us, there are still many true shamans in the indigenous cultures of the world, and in the Peruvian Amazon I was able to interview, work with, and record the songs of a few of them.

With Amazonian shamanism, the herbs, plants, and animals from the rainforest are the main source of healing power. But in addition to this, and some would say of even greater importance, is the use of a powerful curing song, or *icaro*. Usually the icaro will come to the shaman during either a walk in the rainforest, in a dream, or in the sacred ayahuasca ceremony. The icaro is heard in the voice of the plant or animal spirit from which it came, and at the same time it appears as a geometric pattern in the mind of the shaman—the synesthesia experience I talked about. This "capturing of the song" in the mind of the shaman is how the shaman increases their healing power and builds their library of curing songs.

The first thing you notice when you hear an icaro is the high, penetrating, falsetto voice of the shaman singing it. It literally pierces right into your mind and soul, and I've included one of these icaros on the soundtrack of this book. It was explained to me that this voice is closest to the spirit voice that the shaman hears when the plant or animal spirit begins singing its song to them. Sometimes the spirit voice will sound like a choir of voices, and at other times it may simply be a single voice, sounding neither male nor female. Dr. Jeremy Narby states in his book, *The Cosmic Serpent*, "They are like radio waves, once you turn on the radio, you can pick them up. It's like that with souls, with ayahuasca and tobacco, you can see them and hear them. You start singing along with it, and once you sing, you understand them. You can follow their music because you have heard their voice."

The two main shaman-singers that I interviewed and recorded were Herlinda Augustine, the matriarchal head of the village, and her husband, Enrique, who is a powerful shaman and *ayahuascero*, a master of the ayahuasca ceremony. Several of the extended Augustine family were also shamans-in-training, and they are certainly practicing shamans by now. Both Herlinda and Enrique were experts in the ayahuasca ceremony, the powerful entheogen and psychotrope that has become a global phenomenon. It was the Shipibo who perfected this ceremony and then passed it on to other shamans down the Amazon River Basin.

The first thing Herlinda and Enrique told us upon our arrival in the village was that we were going to do an ayahuasca ceremony that very night, to cleanse our bodies of the Western toxins and cultural programming we carried in our minds, and to integrate us into the Shipibo worldview. We deposited our backpacks and set up our mosquito nets and sleeping bags in a large, thatched-roof longhouse that had been recently built. We spent the rest of the afternoon meditating and preparing our minds for the powerful ceremony to come.

For the Shipibo, the ayahuasca ceremony is the highest spiritual practice in their culture. During the all-night ceremony the participants ingest ayahuasca tea, and dozens of icaros are sung throughout the night, often approaching eight to ten hours of almost non-stop singing. The corresponding song cloths for these icaros are laid upon any sick patients as a healing device imbued with the power of the icaros.

The icaros are almost always in a pentatonic (five note) musical scale, and often one shaman will start with one icaro, and then another shaman will join in singing the same icaro, or sometimes starting an entirely different icaro altogether. This creates an incredible polyphonic experience, where multiple icaros are being sung, creating a literal tapestry of voice, melody, harmony, and color. The singing gives you a kind of anchor to hold on to when the visions start to come, because when the visions come, it's one of the most powerful things a person can experience, except for perhaps death. Which is also why ayahuasca is often referred to as "the little death."

I had done ayahuasca once before in Taos, New Mexico with a group of martial artists who I had studied with for many years. Someone had smuggled a bottle of ayahuasca up from the Amazon and we drank all of it. Although our visions were extremely powerful, it wasn't nearly as powerful as doing the traditional Shipibo ceremony in the Amazon Rainforest. Doing this ceremony in the place of its origin, and more importantly with a trained Shipibo shaman, makes the visions much more powerful and meaningful. That is how it should be done.

The important operative word here is "vision." Let me explain. Harvard Medical School and the University Of New Mexico have both done extensive research on this very subject and they found that the active alkaloid in ayahuasca is Dimethyltryptamine, also known as DMT. DMT is often called the *spirit molecule*, because everywhere it is found in the Amazon, the indigenous people have figured out how to extract it for its visionary, healing properties. It is found in various plants, trees, seeds, and even in a certain frog's skin, which one must lick to receive the effects—now that's bravery! DMT is also created inside the pineal gland of the human brain, although science still does not know why. Perhaps it is a link to our ancient, shamanic past?

DMT also has a similar property to the neurotransmitter serotonin; in fact, the two work closely together. The DMT molecule makes a perfect lock over the serotonin molecule, enhancing and magnifying whatever information is being transmitted through the brain's neural network. It is believed by many people, from psychologists to shamans, that the DMT helps to reveal what is hidden in the brain's subconscious network, and that is where the visions come from.

I also use the word "healing" in the same context as when I speak about visions. And this is because when you have a vision, you usually see things about yourself, including your past and possibly your future, and when you see these things in a sacred way, it frequently manifests as a physical healing. Western medicine has finally begun to understand this principle, where they see proof that positive mental projection and visualization can also cause faster physical healing.

Back in our little village in the Amazon we prepared for our first ceremony, and I must admit, I was a little scared, but I also knew I had to do it. There was no backing out now. Our crew sat in a circle on our thin mats on the wooden floor of our longhouse, joking about how we got on an airplane in Albuquerque, New Mexico the day before, and via plane, taxi, and canoe we were now way up in the Peruvian Amazon about to ingest one of the most powerful natural psychotropes known to man, with a group of shamans we didn't really know. Thus, my Amazon adventure began.

It was very dark as the night settled into the rainforest, and there were fireflies buzzing around in our longhouse, flickering on and off like little welcome lights. The sounds of the night jungle engulfed us—and it was loud! That's something people don't realize when they first come to the Amazon—the incredible volume of the rainforest at night. It's relatively quite during the heat of the day, but at night, the rainforest comes alive. As the sun sets and the light starts to dim, the sound of the jungle collectively cranks up to the volume of a sawmill, and that's exactly what it sounds like—a loud, high-pitched buzzing sound that whines from deep within the leafy folds of the rainforest, punctuated by the sharp chirp of cicadas, night birds, and animals that you can't even imagine. It's incredible the first time you hear it, and you think there's no way you're going to be able to sleep at night. And then after a couple of hours, a primordial memory kicks in and it pulls you into sleep like a lullaby and you sleep better on those hard wooden floorboards than you ever slept in your life. I still dream about that place so many years later, and whenever I can't sleep, I imagine that I am lying on the floor of the rainforest and I am surrounded by the musical cacophony of life.

When we started the ayahuasca ceremony, we were instructed to sit in a large circle, with Herlinda and Enrique at the western side of the circle, facing the eastern doorway. We were told to pray to the spirit of the ayahuasca for a healing vision, while the shamans blew tobacco smoke on us to cleanse any dark energy that might disrupt our ceremony. Rose-scented holy water was also anointed on each person and a general feeling of calmness and serenity began to emerge in our collective consciousness. When it came time to drink the ayahuasca tea, it was dispersed in a small plastic cup that was literally taken from a cough medicine bottle, so you can see that the amount of ayahuasca you drink is quite small considering the amount of power that it contains. Herlinda and Enrique began singing the sacred icaros as we sat in upright, meditative positions waiting for the medicine to take us over.

At Enrique's request, I had been placed to his left, which made me feel quite a bit safer. Aside from my dabbling in psilocybin mushrooms and the one ayahuasca ceremony in Taos, I really didn't have much psychedelic experience. When the medicine came on about an hour later, it felt like a little tingling rain coming down upon my head—the *mariacion* or "little rain," as they call it. After the first initial tingles, it came on incredibly strong, like a spiritual tidal wave that terrified me, but I also knew I had to surf the wave and ride it. I stayed in my upright meditative position and breathed into the rush. I imagined that this might be what Death actually feels like, and that's when I had "the little death," and I immediately left my body.

I felt myself being shot vertically out of the top of my head and I was immediately out in the deep cosmos, with galaxies spiraling past me as I shot at a speed faster than light across the universe. I saw exploding stars being born in real time, new planets and moons spiraling into existence, and I saw the formation of entire solar systems. It was so clear and vivid that I was amazed at the clarity and definition. It looked as real as a film, except my mind was the projector.

I flew across alien planets and saw magnificent, gravity-defying landscapes. On one of these planets I saw the great Tree Of Life, the Axis Mundi, the center from which all life emanates—and she was a woman, a queen. Enrique was with me in the vision now, or rather, Enrique's spirit was guiding me as we descended into the tree and went deep into the lower realms. There were very old, ancient roots with glyphs carved into them, the beginnings of language I assumed. There were huge, empty cavernous spaces inside these roots, some of them the size of football stadiums, and although it was dark, I was not frightened at all. It did not seem to be an evil place, simply a place that held the origins of life—and it was all in black and white. Then we began our ascent up the tree and suddenly we were up in the branches and the colors became ultra-vivid. There were small children sitting on the branches and laughing, with birds and other creatures that were otherworldly and beyond description. But it was the color, the vividness and the vibrancy that was so striking and real.

Now we were leaving the ancient planet, and we were ascending up into its atmosphere. I flew like a rocket into the cosmos again and I saw more galaxies whirling past me. I also saw beings and entities that were from other times or other dimensions. Other things I saw were too personal to disclose here, but I will say that it was a life-changing experience and it profoundly affected the way I saw my own life and what it means to be a spiritual being on this Earth. I also realized that I was alone and Enrique was no longer with me.

As I continued to hurl out into space, I saw an immense structure in the center of the universe, a palace it seemed, although it was immense on an astronomical scale. It had a structure to it, lines and curves that were iridescent and brilliant in color. Its dimensions appeared to be light-years in length and height and there seemed to be an intelligence radiating from it, like a living being, but not humanoid—something much bigger. I felt like I was at the center of everything now, the center of all creation, or perhaps, the center of my own being, which is the same thing. I stayed there for a while, drifting peacefully in the void, staring at this crystalline palace in total amazement, observing it and trying to understand it. I was in total bliss.

The strange thing about it is, although I had traveled far beyond the boundaries of anything I could conceive of, I still knew that I had a body back on Earth, and that body was sitting next to a shaman named Enrique, in a longhouse on the banks of the Ucayali River in the Peruvian Amazon, on the continent of South America, on a planet called Earth. I completely and totally knew this in my consciousness, yet I was having this out-of-body experience where my consciousness felt like it was on the other side of the universe. I could hear Enrique singing faintly in my mind, in his high-pitched, gentle voice, even if it was trillions of light years away.

Suddenly Enrique's singing was loud and piercing, causing my right eardrum to become distorted and painful. He was also digging his fingernails into my right forearm, which I could suddenly feel and then, BOOM, I was right back in my body sitting next to him. I looked over at Enrique in the darkness of the room and he patted my arm in a knowing, reassuring way as he kept on singing. Yes, I was back in my body, instantly, and for the rest of that long night I quietly listened to the icaros as I re-entered the world of humanity through song.

The ceremony lasted into the early morning hours and then we slept, exhausted. I emerged from the longhouse around noon, as I lazily ventured into the courtyard of the compound where I found Enrique sitting happily, surrounded by his little grandchildren who chatted and played on the ground all around him. He smiled as I walked up and he motioned for me to sit in the plastic lawn chair next to him. Anna, our film director was up now too, and she handed me a cup of coffee.

My Spanish was, and still is, terrible. I can understand it but I can't speak it conversationally, and I always mix it with my Brazilian Portuguese and the two years of French I took in high school. This always made the Shipibo laugh at me, but fortunately Anna and Luis both spoke very good Spanish, so Anna translated for us. I told Enrique about the experience I had during the ceremony, and he just laughed and shook his head, letting out a high whistle. "Oh Marteen, you flew so far! I had to bring you back, you went too far your first time!"

Enrique's personal story is a beautiful one. He married Herlinda when they were very young and he learned shamanism and traditional healing in order to keep his children healthy. Medical care is expensive and extremely hard to find this far up the river, so traditional healing is more of a practicality than anything else. Enrique estimated that he had been given about 10 truly powerful icaros that were his main curing songs, with which he could heal. He also talked about how there were shamans in human bodies, alive right here and now, but there were also shamans that existed in another dimensions, without a body, and they can teach you too. He called these shamans the *Morayo*.

A week later, I would accompany Enrique out into the rainforest as he gathered the roots and leaves he used to make the ayahuasca tea. I watched as he cut down long stalks of the brown vine, *banisteriopsis caapi,* which literally looks like a serpent snaking its way around a tree trunk. Then we gathered leaves from a different bush, the *psychotria viridis,* which is the second plant needed for the binary recipe. We then hauled the raw materials back to the courtyard in cloth sacks that we carried over our shoulders and we began to make a new batch of ayahuasca tea.

First, Enrique chopped the vine into six-inch sections, and then he smashed them flat with a hammer before he handed them to me. Then we began to layer the smashed vines inside a giant aluminum cooking pot, topping each layer of vines with a layer of the leaves until the entire pot was filled with alternating layers of vines and leaves. The pot was then filled with fresh water and a lid placed on top. A fire was now burning in the central cooking area and the pot was placed right onto the fire, the flames licking up the sides. Soon the water was boiling and seeping out of the pot, which Enrique occasionally stirred as the vines and the leaves dissolved into a soupy, brownish-red liquid. After a full day of slow cooking, the pot was removed from the smoldering fire and left to cool overnight. The following day the thick, brownish-red liquid was strained through thin cloth and bottled in the most recycled item in the Amazon Basin—1.5 liter plastic soda bottles. This one pot would make a very large supply of ayahuasca, enough to fill several bottles, with one bottle being more than enough for a single ceremony.

A couple of days later we did the ayahuasca ceremony again, and most of us participated in more ceremonies over the following two weeks. Of all the ceremonies I did in the Amazon and back in New Mexico, none were as powerful as that first one when I left my body to explore the cosmos. But I would also say that with every ceremony I did, a deep intuitive understanding of myself as a musician began to settle into my being. Another shaman in the village named David explained it to me this way:

We have two hemispheres in our brain - the left side is more visual, spacial, and logical, and the right side is more intuitive, emotional, and even telepathic at times. David explained that, whatever you need in your spiritual evolution, the ayahuasca spirit will give it to you, and it does this by balancing and integrating the mind, the soul, and the body.

It is opening up your subconscious, layer by layer, like an onion. Thus, one ceremony might be highly visual, and the following ceremony might be more emotional and intuitive, with no visuals at all. Both are important and necessary for the development of a holistic, evolved mind if we want to live as enlightened human beings.

During my time in the village, I noticed a general happiness with almost everyone I met, and especially with the children. I've never heard so much laughter echoing throughout the forest, emanating from the jungle pathways, and in the village's tiny streets. There was a constant singing of songs, and walking together in small clusters of happy little people. Aside from the occasional soccer ball or a Frisbee, I never saw any plastic toys lying around, and I'm not sure they even wanted them. Here there was something much deeper going on, a deep happiness centered around singing and exploring the rainforest. To this day, I've never encountered such happiness anywhere in the world.

As the children became more accustomed to the Americans living in their village, they would jump out at us, poke us, and then run away laughing with delight at the coup they had just scored. During downtimes when I was sitting in the shaman's compound listening to people talk and doing nothing particularly important, some young mother would come up to me, hand me her baby to hold, and silently walk away for an hour or more. I'm sure that I held babies for at least as many hours as I recorded icaros, and I began to realize that famous truth I had read on a bumper sticker: *It takes a village to raise a child.*

Herlinda Augustine was the main shaman in our village and she was clearly the matriarch who made sure everyone was fed, well-behaved, and she dispersed money to the other women to make sure they had all their households needs. She was incredibly strong and wise, and she was also blessed with an amazing singing voice. It was Herlinda that provided us with most of the information on the Shipibo culture, and it is her voice that you hear in the icaros that come with the soundtrack of this book.

At one point during our stay, Herlinda took us for a long walk in her personal rainforest garden, which had been bequeathed to her from her father. It was a huge parcel of land that was quite a long walk from the central village. There she pointed out several different plants that she used for her healing practice, and she described them in depth. Some were used for such diverse remedies as treating high blood pressure, female health issues, hemophilia, and even one plant for men's erectile dysfunction (the leaf of this plant when folded in half would not break but would spring back totally erect, much to everyone's laughter when demonstrated).

She also told us about a time when she was walking in her garden only to discover an enormous anaconda swimming in the small waterway that joined the larger river. The anaconda reared up as Herlinda approached and the snake's body destroyed a small footbridge, the remnants of which we saw. That's how big the anaconda was according to Herlinda, big enough to crush a small bridge with its huge body. She estimated it to be about ten meters (thirty feet) long.

Herlinda's daughter, Magdalena, was the closest in age to me, about thirty-seven years old at the time, and she had three children of her own. She was a shaman-in-training when I met her, learning her mother's and grandmother's songs, as well as developing her own set of curing icaros. She had a lovely, kind nature about her and I liked her immediately, so we developed a good trust between us from the moment we met. After Herlinda passed away a few years later, Magdalena rose to take her mother's former position as the main matriarch and shaman in her family, and a leader in the village where she resides to this day.

Magdalena cooked all of our meals during our stay in the village, and this usually consisted of rice and either chicken or some kind of fish, with a side of vegetables grown in the garden. It was clean, healthy food, and we all lost weight, but it was the good kind of weight loss where one feels much more energetic. At one point, the infamous Shining Path guerrillas decided to build a roadblock near our village as a protest against the Peruvian government and its laws against coca-growing. Thus our village ran out of supplies very quickly, and for about a week all we had to eat was chicken broth and some quinoa sprouts, and we all lost about another ten pounds. Still, I can remember with amazing clarity how good I felt when I was in that village, how light, clean, and clear-minded I felt in that environment.

Magdalena told us a lot about childbirth and how traditionally-born Shipibo children are born into a song cloth that is woven by their mother during pregnancy. The mother starts to hear the child's unique song while it is still in the womb, and she begins to embroider it into a cloth. At the moment of birth, the baby is literally pulled from the womb and wrapped in the same song cloth the mother has made, so it is imprinted with its song right from the moment of birth.

As the days went by, my recording partner Luis and I would record dozens of icaros around the village. I would also interview the shaman-singers, Luis would translate, and I would write down with pen and paper the stories they told us about their songs. Simultaneously, our cameraman Tad Fettig would film spectacular footage of the rainforest, the people, and the general day-to-day life in the village. Luis' brother Roberto "Bear" Guerra took some extraordinary photos, including the one at the top of this Verse. It was pure magic, especially within the surreal beauty of the rainforest.

During the last few days of our trip, Luis and I set up our portable recording studio in an abandoned hut on the outskirts of the village. Up to that point we had been recording the shamans as we wandered around the village, but it became apparent that there were so many songs that we needed one place where everyone could come. We decided on the famous principle that if we built a studio, the singers would come, and come to us they did.

All of our equipment was battery-powered, so we hung a series of microphones from the rafters in the ceiling and put the word out that anyone from the village who had a song they wanted to sing—we would record it. People started lining up outside the hut and they included wise old men and women, a few random shamans we hadn't met, and several young children who had never even heard a recording before. Of all the famous recording studios that I have worked in around the world, our little rainforest studio ended up being one of the most enjoyable experiences of my life. It was just a magical place.

For three full days, Luis and I recorded more than a hundred Shipibo songs, ranging from shamanic curing songs to old traditional songs, and even some children's songs. After all the recording and filming in the village, we now had plenty of material for our film, the soundtrack, and my thesis. The resulting work became the documentary film and album, both titled *Woven Songs of the Amazon*. The film, which is still available as a DVD, is a great living document of a traditional culture that is still intact and flourishing in the Peruvian Amazon. And the album that Luis and I produced contains about thirty of the best songs and icaros, which give a very good example of the extraordinary music of the Shipibo culture. It still stands as one of the best recorded documents of traditional Shipibo music, and all the profits of the DVD, the CD, and the digital downloads go to the Augustine family and their children. Some of them are even going to college now, and at least one is going to law school.

It was now mid-June and it was time for us to go home. We walked out of the village and headed down to the boat ramp, our backpacks loaded down with song cloths and pottery where our Western clothing used to be. The children walked beside us, holding our hands and singing, just as they did when we arrived, sometimes crying because of our departure. I was crying, too; I didn't really want to leave, but I also had a thesis to write, a degree to claim, and a musical life to return to. But I had been changed forever.

We got in our little motorized canoe and made our way back to Pucallpa, where we caught a flight back to Lima over the top of the Andes Mountains. Tad and I continued on to Cusco, the Inca capital high in the mountains at over 11,000 feet. Our heads were dizzy and our footsteps heavy, since we had just come from the floor of the Amazon Rainforest and were now in one of the highest cities in the world. Tad needed to film some people in the indigenous Quechua villages for another documentary he was working on called *Ausangate,* so I tagged along to assist.

We visited Inca ruins and several mountain villages where we chewed coca leaves with the natives and did small ceremonies with them. The Quechua people were getting ready for a big pilgrimage to the sacred mountain of Ausangate, and I could see in their colorful, elegant clothing the vivid patterns and designs that were similar to the Shipibo songlines 11,000 feet below us in the Amazon Rainforest.

I could see, in that powerful moment, that all people are beautiful, all people are sacred, and all of us find ways to express ourselves through our language, our music, and our culture. Indeed, we must never forget that.

20. Peruvian Amazon Rainforest
21. Shipibo Shamans "Thunder & Lightning Icaro"
22. Shipibo Shamans "Remix"

VERSE 11

ALBUQUERQUE, JERUSALEM: THE ILLUMINATED HEART

Barrett in the holy city of Jerusalem, 2005

"There are invisible aspects to being sentient and embodied. Consciousness is invisible. Love is invisible. Both are immeasurable. Placed and passionate, cool and in motion, we move along, earthy and pure soul."

        —Coleman Barks

One of the greatest qualities a man can develop is his ability to listen to the beliefs of another person, especially when that person is from a completely different culture or religion. This is especially true now, but it has always been the case since time immemorial. Men and women who have developed this quality are the only reason why peace has ever existed on this Earth, even if it seems to be in short supply these days. I met a handful of these remarkable like-minded people who were American, Israeli, Palestinian, and Iraqi and it changed how I thought about the so-called Eastern-Western divide. It all started with a chance meeting with the remarkable poet and mystic, Coleman Barks.

It began as far back as 1998, when I had been recording with the band R.E.M. in their hometown of Athens, Georgia. They had asked me to play some drums, upright bass, and a slew of percussion instruments on their eleventh studio album, *Up*, which was a great honor for me. The band's singer, Michael Stipe, introduced me to Coleman Barks late one night in an Athens bar called The Manhattan, where Coleman was predicted to show up around midnight, which he did, almost exactly. At the time, Coleman was a professor of literature at the University Of Georgia, but he was also a renowned poet and the primary translator of the revered Islamic poet, Jalaluddin Rumi. *Rumi*, as he is more commonly known, was born in Afghanistan about 800 years earlier, but Coleman had somehow figured out how to channel the spirit of Rumi's poetry into English, and those 800 years of historical divide dissolved into the present moment.

I had already read and come to love Rumi's poetry long before I met Coleman, mostly because of the alternately spiritual and irreverent themes of the poems which, although written during the late Dark Ages, resonated with the spiritual awakenings of the 20th century. Coleman's most famous book, *The Essential Rumi*, was already one of the most successful poetry books in the history of US publishing, selling well over a million copies, which for a book of poetry is exceedingly rare. It's especially hard to imagine those kinds of sales now, but back in the roaring 1990s, a huge number of people were reading this poetry. Needless to say, Coleman and I hit it off immediately that night in Athens, Georgia and we became fast friends. I would call or email him over the ensuing years to ask for his opinions on essays I was writing and various other worldly observations, but mostly what Coleman taught me over the years is that the path of a true man is one of fearlessness, and a great love for humanity.

But let's go back in time a little bit, to about 800 years ago....

Rumi, in his time, was considered a giant of spiritual understanding, one of history's greatest Illuminators Of The Heart. His collection of poetry, known as *The Divan of Shems Tabriz,* is his greatest work, consisting of some 40,000 verses, and considered one of the greatest works in the pantheon of Islamic texts. His poems are often referred to as the "Persian Quran," since his native tongue of Farsi was the language in which he spoke his ecstatic verses.

His words transcend time, and some have even said that of all the great poets, writers, and playwrights, Oriental or Occidental, it is Rumi who is read by more human beings than any other. 800 years ago, it was poetry that carried the common man and woman through their days, because within the poems were interwoven the myths and stories that made up the tapestry of their reality. Rumi found that with poetry he had a way of reaching people, using words and stories to open their hearts and minds, transforming their lives in the process. His poems caused a spiritual awakening, and in a beautiful metaphor about prayer and language Rumi said it best: "Wool, through the presence of a man of knowledge, becomes a carpet. Earth becomes a palace. The presence of a spiritual man creates a similar transformation. Prayer has a form, a sound, and a physical reality. Everything which has a word has a physical equivalent, and every thought has an action."

All of Rumi's immense poetic verse can be traced directly to the meeting and ensuing friendship that developed with his greatest teacher and friend, *Shems of Tabriz*. Shems was an enlightened Sufi who roamed the countryside looking for prospective teachers and it was Shem's spiritual energy that ignited the poetic soul in Rumi. Hence the reason why Rumi titled his verses after the divine revelations of Shems of Tabriz. How they met and worked together is a matter of great historical speculation and some have called it the meeting of two Great Oceans.

Rumi was born in 1207 AD in the city Balkh, in the northern province of Khorasan, in what is now Afghanistan. It is interesting to note that the province of Khorasan is phonetically similar to the Latin *corazon*, which means, "heart." His father, Bahauddin, was a well-known Islamic scholar, who had a large following of students in his *madras*, or school, but a combination of events, including the menacing approach of Genghis Khan's Mongol Hoard, caused Bahauddin to move his family to a safer place. The family's caravan became a sort of traveling madras, with other families joining the pilgrimage at various stages of the journey in what would become a sixteen-year odyssey.

Their first stop was in the city of Naishapur in 1213, when Rumi was just five years old. There the family met with another famous Sufi, Fariduddin Attar, known as *the Chemist*. Attar took notice of the young Rumi, and he presented him with a "Book Of Mysteries" as a gift. It is said that upon the caravan's departure, Attar remarked, "What an astonishing sight! There goes a river dragging a mighty ocean behind it." Clearly the *Baraka*, or "divine grace," was already emanating from the young Rumi, affecting all who came into contact with him.

The family continued on to Baghdad, Mecca, Medina, Jerusalem, and Damascus, visiting all of the historic cities in the Muslim tradition.

During this time, Rumi married his childhood friend Gevher Hatun, the daughter of one of the families that had joined them on the journey. Soon after, they had their two sons, Veled and Chelebi. There is not much documentation about these years of travel, but it is generally understood that Rumi learned much from the various mystics and philosophers that visited his father, influencing the young Rumi as he grew into manhood.

Finally, in the year of 1229, the caravan reached Konya, Turkey where the growing family decided to settle amongst the Seljuk Turks and establish a permanent home. Just two years later, upon his father's death, Rumi assumed the mantle *King of Scholars* and took over as head of the madras.

At this point in his life, it would have been relatively easy for Rumi to continue along his predicted course, what with a growing family and a position in the community of religious scholars. But that was right around the time that Shems of Tabriz rolled into town.

Even less is known about Shems except that he was a kind of wild man or dervish who would search the farthest corners of the known world in search of spiritual wisdom. In principle, wild Shems was the opposite of Rumi's scholarly background. It's also said that he was born into the Assassins sect, the Assassins being known for their political murders, often rendering their services to the highest bidder. But it must also be said that within the sect was a school of great mystical knowledge, and more than one historian has suggested that the Assassins reputation was more of a cover to frighten anyone who might try to steal the secrets of their mystery school.

Now, there are many stories about the actual meeting of Shems and Rumi, which is a typical Sufi technique, where a story can be told with multiple allegories. But there is one that seems the most plausible, and I will paraphrase James Cowan, one of the more reliable historians on the subject:

The story goes that Shems went to Konya in 1244, specifically to find Rumi because he had had an auspicious dream that urged him to go. Upon arrival in the city, he checked into a room at a local inn and waited till daybreak the following day. The following morning, Shems was sitting in the courtyard in front of the inn watching people as they passed by. Around the time of afternoon prayer, a man approached riding on a mule, followed by a large number of students - it was

Rumi returning to his madras. Shems approached the entourage and without warning, grabbed the mule's reigns and demanded of Rumi one question: "Tell me who was the greater man, the lord Mohammed or Beyazidi Bestami?" Realizing that the question poised was a kind of riddle, Rumi replied that Mohammed was the greater because he progressed in stages of enlightenment, always thanking God and asking him to reveal more, whereas Bestami, intoxicated by his first level of attainment, simply thanked God and stopped his evolution from that point on.

At this point the witnesses say that Shems fell to his knees in admiration, that Rumi raised him up as an equal, and they walked arm in arm back to the madras. Whatever the true story may be, the most important thing is that these two great oceans of wisdom finally met, one wild and one learned, and they merged their collective wisdom. But it was not without obstacles.

Shems utterly dismissed acquired, academic knowledge and instead, followed a path of union with God through an intuitive, unbridled approach. He knew that knowledge could be transmitted directly from teacher to student, but to place all of one's understanding in a written book was an act of blind obedience, without worldly experience. It is said that at one point, Shems threw all of Rumi's books in the courtyard fountain as a challenge to Rumi's academic background. Rumi of course, could not retrieve the books because to do so would be to admit defeat in the eyes of the one who held real truth. However, this kind of irreverence for the traditional would become a serious problem for Shems and would eventually lead to his death.

It was about three years later, in December of 1247, when Shems was summoned to receive a dervish at the back door of Rumi's madras. Upon coming to the door, he was immediately set upon by several men with daggers and stabbed to death. Rumi heard his final cry, but when he reached the doorway, Shems' body was gone, and only a few drops of blood remained on the stones of the courtyard. Shems disappeared into death just as mysteriously as he had appeared in life and this threw Rumi into a great, inconsolable depression.

Although the murder of Shems was devastating for Rumi, it also brought him to his deepest realization—that there is a direct communication between a person and their God. One of the main precepts in Islam is that there need not be an intermediary between an individual and God—anyone can find this communion when they look deeply into their hearts. Rumi found this truth directly, and his method as described by Idries Shah was, "To bring the Seeker into the mystical current, in order to be transformed by it…. Understanding can come only through love, not by training by means of organizational methods."

And so it was that around the age of forty, Rumi began his first poetic verses. He would apparently cup his left hand around a column in his madras and then, turning in circles around the column, he would recite the free-form verses that his students would copy down in the Farsi language. This spiraling "dance" around the column was also the beginning of the Sufi Mevlevi Order, also known as the Whirling Dervishes. They call their spiraling dance the *Sema*, and it is always accompanied with music from the reed flute, or *Ney*. This flute metaphor appears often in Sufi poetry, because it is a metaphor for the human soul. A reed is cut from the riverbed to be made into a flute, which is analogous to man's separation from God. The flute is then drilled with nine holes, just as a human body has nine orifices, and the mournful, longing sound of the Ney is analogous for the human spirit calling back to God for reunion, as we toil along the muddy banks of the natural world.

Rumi's realization was that it is only in our hearts that we can truly find God, and that is Rumi's greatest gift to the world. In Sufi cosmology, the heart is the macrocosm of the Universe, or as God said to Mohammed in one of his revelations to him, "I created the whole Universe for you. The heavens and the earth cannot contain me, only the heart of my faithful servant is expansive enough to contain me."

Or as Rumi's said, "The Fruit is the cause of the Tree."

Rumi's poems range from the highest spiritual insights to profane and even obscene folk stories. The sacred and the profane existed side by side for him, and this is another reason why he is so beloved by everyone—because he made us laugh! When I read Rumi's poems I often laugh out loud, because great humor is the truest mark of a spiritual archer. This is why Rumi still illuminates us, Eastern and Western alike, like a single oil lamp burning in a wind blown, sand blasted, landscape. Indeed, I have often thought that the relationship between Shems and Rumi was much like the relationship between a great musical master and his or her students. One teaches the other, passing the torch of great insight on to the next, and every so often, one of those students explodes like a Roman candle of enlightenment.

After my foray into Sufi mysticism, I felt that I had found a deeper spiritual path, one that aligned with the Zen Buddhism I had already been practicing for several years. The Sufism and the Zen seemed like parallel rivers, separated by a thin sandbar. I wanted to learn more about Sufism and I had the idea of traveling on the ancient Silk Road, through Afghanistan and Iraq, and maybe even into Iran. And then the attack on the World Trade Towers happened in September of 2001 and almost overnight it seemed as if America was at war with the entire Middle East. Even though the attack was done by a handful of fanatics from Saudi Arabia, every other country in that corner of the world was lumped in as "terrorists."

In 2001, we invaded Afghanistan and in 2003, we invaded Iraq, where American troops are still fighting fifteen years later. How could it be that Iraq, the ancient center of western civilization could suddenly be our enemy? The answer, of course, lies in the economic and political policies of 20th century capitalism - but that is entirely different book. And what followed in those wars was a kind of madness that put Islam and anything vaguely Middle Eastern on a collision course with our so-called American values. Rumi's moment in the American spotlight began to fade very quickly, and with it, so did my dreams of going to those ancient countries.

When I was at the University Of New Mexico, I took classes in Arabic music taught by an Iraqi master musician named Rahim Alhaj, as well as classes in Muslim culture and Eastern philosophy taught by a former Special Forces sergeant who had spent time in the Middle East. Sgt. Voorhees and I hit it off immediately because we both agreed that Sir Richard Francis Burton of the Royal Geographic Society was our mutual hero. Burton spoke dozens of languages, helped to map inner Africa, discovered the source of the Nile River, and in his down time, translated the *Kama Sutra* and *The Thousand And One Nights*. Men like Burton just aren't made anymore, which is why Sgt. Voorhees and I agreed he was our man.

Within the few years it took for American forces to invade Afghanistan and Iraq, I had become good friends with a Sufi poet, an Iraqi master musician, and a former Special Forces soldier, all of whom knew exactly what the Muslim world was really like. I knew I had to go deeper myself.

It was now the end of the 2005 academic year and I was finally graduating with my bachelor's degree, eighteen years after dropping out of college in 1987. I had also been accepted into the university's anthropology graduate school to start work on my master's degree, which I would complete a couple years later. But it was June of 2005 and I had a brief pause before my graduate seminars would begin, and I was planning on enjoying the warm New Mexico summer. Then I got an email.

It came from a singer known only as "Adama" and she was a British woman of Nigerian descent who was making an album in Jerusalem where her Israeli boyfriend owned a studio. It turned out that Adama absolutely loved the Mad Season album, *Above*, and she wanted to sample a part of one song. I gave my permission, and somehow the conversation evolved into me coming to Jerusalem to play drums on her new album. Within the week I had a plane ticket from Albuquerque to Tel Aviv, literally a day after my graduation.

After a lengthy flight, I finally arrived at the Tel Aviv airport, and after many questions by a suspicious Israeli customs official, I was finally allowed to pass through passport control and retrieve by baggage. I was met by the beautiful Adama and her wonderfully hospitable boyfriend Gili, and we got into a car to head east into the desert. Tel Aviv was not the shining city by the sea that I had imagined, in fact, it was a rather grim, worn out looking city. Jerusalem, by contrast, was a shining temple of ancient white limestone surrounded by very modern architecture and verdant gardens. It felt both ancient and modern, and I fell in love with it immediately.

During the two weeks that I spent in Jerusalem, I got to see a lot of the Israeli and Palestinian countryside, including the West Bank and the Negev Desert. Our studio and accommodations were in East Jerusalem, which is part of the Palestinian West Bank and is still occupied by Israeli forces. It's a beautiful place for sure, and I felt a deep ancientness there. Still, it was disturbing to go through checkpoints with a .50-caliber machine gun pointed at our car every time we wanted to go into town for dinner. I could only imagine the indignities leveled upon the Palestinian people every time they want to move around inside their own country.

As we drove past Palestinian towns such as Ramallah and Jericho, you could see the inequality between the Israeli and Palestinian ways of life. The Palestinians were living amongst crumbling cement and cinder block buildings, many of which had either been destroyed in clashes with Israeli troops, or razed to the ground by Israeli bulldozers.

The Palestinians are usually not allowed to rebuild after these battles, or they are unable to because of the Israeli blockade that prevents building materials from being delivered to the Palestinian territories. These communities often lack reliable running water and electricity because the water and electricity is also controlled by Israel and can be cut off as a form of punishment. On top of all that, the Israelis continue to build illegal settlements on Palestinian land, chipping away at Palestinian sovereignty, piece by piece. The United Nations finally condemned this in 2016, but it remains to be seen if the Israeli state will abide by international law and give that land back to the Palestinian people.

When you see it with your own eyes, it changes your entire perception. The Palestinian areas look like a very rough and miserable way to exist, living between checkpoints and knowing their land and homes could be confiscated or razed at anytime to make way for the next Israeli settlement. I could immediately understand why there would be periodic uprisings against the occupying Israeli forces, because if you treat people this badly for decades, those people eventually rise up, and the end result is always terrible for both sides.

The Israeli/Palestine conflict has been an ongoing problem that I've heard about for most of my half century of life. It never seems to end. However, my personal experience in Israeli was wonderful. The people I met were intelligent and insightful, and they explained the difficulty in living between these two worlds, where a person might literally live between a beautiful orchard and a rubble-strewn war zone, a paradox I saw many times. All agreed that this was a terribly unjust way to treat people, and that it wasn't a tenable situation for the long-term safety of Israel or Palestine.

It is so unfortunate that these half brothers of Abraham cannot seem to live together in peace, yet here they are, karmically bound to each other in a relatively tiny corner of the world, each distrusting the other because they are taught, from childhood, to think that the other is the enemy. If only they could see how beautiful both cultures are.

Meanwhile, between dinner breaks and machine-gun checkpoints, we worked on Adama's album. The studio had been built at the end of a soda pop factory, with living accommodations built into an adjacent building. It was more like an industrial compound where one could live and work, and in our case, there just happened to be a recording studio there too. It made sense, considering the communal nature of a Jewish kibbutz, and I liked the feeling of working in a studio-factory environment.

Adama is a unique songwriter in that she dreams all of her songs. She can hear them come alive in the dream state, and then she awakens and immediately wants to record the music. Thus, we would usually record the drum tracks in the late evenings, when Adama worked best. During the day, we would take day trips to walk around and explore the deepest corners of this ancient city, and we also had our driver take us out into the Negev Desert, where we floated in the salty Dead Sea. On another day, we explored the ruins of Masada, where you can still see the traces of the Roman Army encampment around the base of the giant, natural fortress.

On one particular day, Gili said that he wanted to have lunch in the Arab quarter, which is said to have the best hummus in the world. This is because Jerusalem is divided into four quarters, those being the Jewish, Christian, Armenian, and Muslim quarters. The first three quarters are relatively subdued and not particularly festive—even a bit grim, if I must be honest.

As we were driving through the Jewish quarter, I saw a most peculiar sight. There, walking briskly down the street, I saw an elderly Jewish man in his heavy black coat and fur hat, waving his arms in the air and shouting wildly at the sky (all this in 100 degree heat). I asked Gili if this was a normal occurrence and he said, *yes, occasionally.* Apparently the man was having an argument with God and this is often how it is displayed—by yelling up at the sky and waving your arms in dramatic gestures. I loved the spirit of this elderly Jewish man and it taught me a little bit more about the nature of the Jewish people.

Soon we entered the Muslim quarter, where the market was full of life. There were brightly colored fabrics, carpets, and intricately embroidered Bedouin crafts, all of which were for sale and ready to be bargained for. It was, in opposition to the other three quarters, an extravagantly colorful, lively, and exciting place. We walked through the market, I bought a few Bedouin fabrics, and we went deep down into the bowels of the city, far below ground and beyond the daylight that was no longer visible. The market continued to sprawl downward at these depths, making us want to keep going to explore the mysteries that lay beyond sight. There, in the deepest part of Jerusalem, we found our hummus vender, operating from a simple cart with a few scattered tables around it. The warm hummus came with perfectly toasted pita bread and the freshest, crispiest vegetables you could imagine. There was no meat, and none was needed, because the pita, hummus, and vegetables were an absolutely perfect combination. It was divine, and it still stands as the best hummus I have ever had anywhere on Earth.

Many years later I researched the origin of the word hummus and found that it comes from the Latin word "humilitas" meaning, "grounded, and of the Earth." It is essentially just ground chickpeas and olive oil—a very humble food, yet it was often used as a sacrament in early Sumerian and Mesopotamian ceremonies. Perhaps, because of this humbleness, it is considered to be holy.

This very simple act of eating handmade hummus in the Arab quarter with smiling, happy Muslim and Jewish people instantly changed how I thought about these two cultures. Yes, there are machine guns up above us on the streets, and there is still that abominable wall that was built to separate the Israelis from the Palestinians. But at their core, these people are built around family, food, and their strong spiritual beliefs. The deep religious feelings here in Jerusalem will touch anyone with a soul, and when you look deeper into the people you will see that their spiritual beliefs are quite the same.

We finished recording Adama's beautiful album and I returned to the United States to begin graduate school, where I sadly found things to be worsening with American and Arab-Muslim relations. Blatant attacks on mosques and Muslim people seemed to be met with indifference, and I couldn't believe how far we had fallen since the more tolerant 1990s, when it was considered a good thing to respect different cultures and spiritual beliefs. Extremism was on the rise in both the United States and the Muslim world, and as we've seen over the ensuing years, it has not been good for either.

It was shortly after I returned from Jerusalem that I reconnected with my Arabic music teacher, Rahim Alhaj. Rahim asked me to release a couple of his albums on my indie label and I happily agreed because Rahim's story is a powerful one:

Rahim is exactly the same age as I am, and whereas I was educated in classical European music and jazz, Rahim was educated in classical Arabic music at the Institute Of Music in Baghdad, Iraq. There he studied with Munir Bashir, the "King Of The Oud," who was considered to be the greatest *oud* player of the 20th century. The oud is the Arabic lute, an eleven-stringed instrument often said to be the grandfather of the western guitar. Depictions of ouds are seen in ancient Egyptian hieroglyphs and at least one archeological dig has carbon dated an oud to be more than 5,000 years old.

After the first Gulf War in the early 1990s, Rahim was forced to flee Iraq because of his activism against Saddam Hussein. He had been imprisoned and tortured under the Hussein regime, and when he finally crossed the Iraqi border into Syria, he had to leave his beloved oud at the border and start his life from scratch.

Passing through Syria, Jordan, and other countries, Rahim eventually made it to the United States where he was granted political asylum in the year 2000 and resettled in Albuquerque, New Mexico, where an Arab community had begun to grow. Rahim is now an award-winning composer, a global ambassador for peace, and he plays with symphonies around the world. But it was there in Albuquerque at the University Of New Mexico where we first met and became good friends.

I had read about Baghdad many times of course, and I learned that it had once been the center of the civilized, intellectual world, that the world's first university was founded there, and that it had been a great center for Islamic scholars and scientists. Now it lay in ruins as a result of American cruise missiles and laser guided bombs, but back in the 7th century, Islamic scholars were preserving and codifying the great works of human civilization, while simultaneously, the Catholic Church was burning books—and sometimes people—who did not align with the Vatican's extremist doctrines.

Formerly known as Mesopotamia, modern day Iraq has a history as old as human civilization itself. The two main cultures that emerged from there were the Sumerian city-states that flourished between 2600-1850 BC, and the city of Babylon which was founded around 1894 BC, and later renamed Baghdad. Their myths are considered to be some of the oldest in the world, and they begin with a myth about the primeval sea, represented by the goddess *Nammu*, who gives birth to the male sky god *An*, and the female earth goddess *Ki*. Their union creates the other Sumerian gods, and this is much like the Yoruba creation story where Yemoja (the ocean goddess) and Obatala (the sky god), join together to create the sacred Orishas.

The main gods of these ancient Mesopotamians was a trio of astral deities, which included *Shamash*, the sun god; *Sin*, the moon god; and

Ishtar/Inanna, the goddess of war and fertility who is aligned with the planet Venus.

There was also *Enlil*, the god of wisdom, who is also the possessor of the sacred tablets and universal decrees, which determined the development of Sumerian culture. You can immediately see how the Moses archetype might have emerged from Enlil, and found his place in the early Jewish and Christian stories as well.

In the Babylonian creation myths, the union of *Apsu*, the sweet water ocean, and *Tiamat*, the salt-water ocean, creates a succession of gods, in which *Marduk* emerges as the king of the gods. Flood myths from this region are considered to be the catastrophic flooding of the Tigris and Euphrates Rivers, and the Sumerian/Babylonian myth of the flood in the Epic of Gilgamesh is very likely the source for the biblical flood of Noah and his ark. The Epic of Gilgamesh is considered to be the first great story in human history, and it details the exploits of two men, Gilgamesh and Enkidu, who started out as enemies but later became great friends. Their exploits together are metaphors for the evolution of human civilization as we emerged out of the wilderness of chaos and into what would become modern civilization.

Fortunately for us, the Islamic scholars did not not see the books and myths of the ancient world as good or bad, but simply as the highest works of humanity up to that point, thus worth preserving. They codified the earliest works of mathematics, chemistry, astronomy, the scientific method, and of course, music. Most notably, they preserved the ancient manuscripts of the Greek and Roman poets and philosophers, which had almost been burned into extinction. All of this knowledge, and much more was preserved, documented, and codified by that first university in Baghdad. It is especially important to remember this now, almost 1500 years later, that it was the Islamic scholars who preserved our ancient Western history, when we were trying our best to destroy it.

But that's just a brief history of that part of the world—the music is even more fascinating. Middle Eastern music, which is divided into Arabic and Persian music, is firmly rooted in the religious tradition of Islam and its many branches and sects. These would include the Sunni, the Shiite, and the various mystical orders of Sufism. These religious differences, combined with the three main language groups—Arabic, Turkic, and Farsi—can also be the source of great friction. The best quote I ever found to describe the differing philosophies of Eastern and

Western music comes from the noted scholar and musician, Dr. Jihad Racy at the UCLA school of ethnomusicology. Dr. Racy says, "European music focuses on representing images and concepts, whereas Middle Eastern music evokes intense emotions in both the performers and the listeners." Broken down into its most basic components, we can look at Middle Eastern music like this:

Tarab – is the emotional feeling of the music, and also, the pantheon of Arabic music itself.

Maqams – are the scales, much like the ragas of India, and these maqams correspond to different times of the day, the seasons, moods, emotions, and even celestial configurations. There are up to twenty-four different notes in any given maqam because they use quartertones instead of the western half tones. About seventy different Maqams are commonly used today.

Doulab – is the non-metric open period at the beginning of a song. It is in free time, flowing, and exploratory.

Taslim – is the initial melody of the song, performed in a slow manner.

Taqsim – is an improvised solo, very similar to the soloing in jazz or the improvisation in an Indian raga.

Hafla – is a musical party or concert, more for public and secular people, perhaps in someone's house or at a private party.

And so it was, fresh from my experience in Middle Eastern music that I embarked to make an album with Rahim Alhaj and Coleman Barks, combining the ecstatic poetry of Rumi with music that Rahim could conjure on his oud. All of this was backed up by my instrumental band, Tuatara, which also featured the extraordinary guitar work of Peter Buck.

We started in the winter of 2007 in Santa Fe, New Mexico, and Coleman's approach was to combine his Rumi poetry with some of his own poems about life in the bucolic American South. The idea was to create an album of poem-songs that would show just how similar the spiritual understanding of both the American and Muslim worlds could be.

I was the drummer, percussionist, and producer of the album, so Coleman sent me a list of the poems he wanted to record, since rhythm and spoken words are similar in their understanding of cadence and delivery. I already had some musical ideas started, and so did Peter Buck, so our recording process was basically to let Coleman get a poem started, we would listen to the pace of his words, and then, rather spontaneously, we created our music on the spot. Rahim had the remarkable ability to just start riffing on our musical themes, and the sound and tonality of his oud gave our songs their Arabic leaning.

The album was released in 2008 and although it was an artistic success, we were never able to play any live shows because of everyone's differing schedules. The album still stands as one of my favorite collaborations when I think of all the people whom I've ever worked with. And I suppose the message I want to convey with this story is that the world is a far better, much more interesting place when we exchange our differing ideas, allowing them to co-exist and even blend together. The Arab world and the greater Middle East are not our enemies, nor should we be to them. Each can learn and prosper from the knowledge of the other. Or as Rumi said himself: "Mankind has an unfulfillment, a desire, and he struggles to fulfill it through all kinds of enterprises and ambitions. But it is only in love that he can find fulfillment…when will you cease to worship and love the pitcher? When will you begin to look for the water?"

Or more succinctly:

"The book of the Sufis is not the darkness of the letters. It is the whiteness of a pure heart."

23. Coleman Barks & Rahim Alhaj "Death Of Saladin"

VERSE 12

THE DELTA: EVEN THE DEVIL GETS THE BLUES

CeDell Davis and Barrett Martin in Little Rock, Arkansas, 2012

"This business is all about the peaks and the valleys. You'll find out what you're made of when you're in in the valleys."

—Duke Ellington

During my decade in New Mexico, and throughout my studies at the University Of New Mexico, I made several trips down to the Deep South of the United States. I was there to either play shows or do some rather extraordinary recording sessions, but each and every one of those trips radically altered my views of music and the cultural fabric of the United States.

I first started going to the South to learn about the blues around the year 2001. Prior to this, I had driven through the South countless times on tour busses, stopping at roadside diners for breakfast, lunch, or dinner, and playing the occasional show in the major cities down there.

But this is not the same thing as purposefully driving into the South and spending an extended amount of time there. To do this properly, one must drive a car or motorcycle and visit several of the small towns and extraordinary landscapes that await you there.

Of course the main attraction to this mysterious place is the music, which is the origination point for all forms of American popular music, starting first with the delta blues, and then electric blues, jazz, rhythm & blues, soul, rock & roll, and everything else that came after that. All of these forms of music can place their birth in the American South, and particularly around the states of Mississippi, Arkansas, and Louisiana.

I always felt an affinity for Arkansas because my father's entire side of the family came from there. They were loggers from Fayetteville and they worked in the logging camps of the Ozark Mountains. My great-grandmother, born in 1890, lived to be almost 100 years old and she used to tell us grandkids stories about growing up in Arkansas without electricity or running water, then the invention of the radio, the telephone, airplanes, television, and finally, men walking on the moon. Her daughter, my grandmother, was actually born in a tent hospital in one of those logging camps, and later the entire family moved to the Olympic Peninsula in Washington State where a new logging boom had just begun. I've always felt a genetic pull to the South my entire life, and as a result, I ended up working with an original bluesman who would have had a lot more in common with my great-grandmother than with me. But as I have come to learn as a musician and a human being—when one is willing to open up and learn from another, amazing things almost always happen.

CEDELL DAVIS

The first part of this story is about CeDell Davis, a legendary delta bluesman and probably the toughest man I've ever met. Lots of people talk about being tough when they play the blues (or rock, hip-hop, and country music for that matter) but CeDell Davis, more than anyone I've ever met in my life, has literally lived and played the hardest blues I've ever heard. He's one of the toughest men in music, a fighter who will not quit, a man who never surrendered.

I started working with CeDell on my first trip to Arkansas in 2001, when he was about 75 years old and almost 60 years into his long music career. I was introduced to him by a percussionist named Joe Cripps, whom I had met on that trip to Cuba back in 1999. I drove all the way from Taos, New Mexico to Little Rock, Arkansas where I picked up Joe and then we headed out to CeDell's modest home in Pine Bluff. We presented CeDell with the idea that we would put a band together to back him up, and Joe would produce the sessions back in his college town of Denton, Texas. I suggested my instrumental band Tuatara, which I had formed with Peter Buck a few years earlier, so a plan was made to record in the coming months.

Again, I had to drive from New Mexico to Denton, Texas, this time with the bed of my Ford F-150 filled with drums, amps, guitars and keyboards. Peter Buck and R.E.M. sideman Scott McCaughey flew down from Seattle, as did keyboardist Alex Veley. Joe had already rented out a club space near the Denton town square and we filled it with my gear and a portable recording unit—this was to become our studio space.

For the sessions I played the majority of the drum tracks, Peter played electric bass rather than his usual guitar, Scott played pedal steel, Alex played various vintage keyboards, and Joe played congas, percussion, and produced the sessions. We also had the saxophone and harmonica player Jeffrey Barnes who added some amazing solos to the sessions. We recorded the entire album pretty much live over the course of three days and nights in that empty bar in Denton, Texas, and we concluded the sessions by having a live show for the locals.

I released the recordings in the summer of 2002 on my first label, and the result was the critically acclaimed album, *When Lightnin' Struck the Pine*. We followed up with an extensive tour of the United States using the same back-up band as on the album, with CeDell parked in a wheelchair at the center of the stage every night while he clawed his slide guitar and howled the earthiest blues you ever heard in your life. People absolutely loved it, but how CeDell ended up in that wheelchair is the more important part of this story.

When Lightnin' Struck the Pine was a great album title because it evoked the excitement of this delta music when it hits you just right. But lightning is also a metaphor for the day that polio struck CeDell when he was just a young pine growing into his youth, stunted with a physical handicap that would dog him like a hellhound for the rest of his life.

Every night on that American tour we would play for about four hours. Joe and I put together an opening band that was a Latin fusion project called the Wayward Shamans; Peter and Scott's band, The Minus 5, would play a second set; and then Tuatara would play an instrumental set before wheeling CeDell out to the stage. It was a lot of music to play, drawing from our various catalogs as well as from CeDell's own deep repertoire. At the end of every night, after CeDell had signed numerous CDs (and slugged back numerous shots of whiskey), we would all get back on the tour bus, which was designed to accommodate his wheelchair. We'd ride through the night, and CeDell would sip his beer (and more whiskey) and tell us tales of the Deep South back in the 1930s, '40s, '50s, '60s, '70s, '80s…. Well, you can imagine the history lesson.

On one of those late night runs, he told us about a time when he was 10 years old and he saw the legendary bluesman Robert Johnson playing at a house party in Helena, Arkansas. CeDell's father had owned a store in Helena that doubled as a juke joint at night, and Robert Johnson had played a lot of shows there during that period, so perhaps the story is true. Regardless, shortly after that is about the time CeDell decided to start playing guitar and singing the blues, and that's where the real story begins.

Born June 9th, 1926 in Helena, Arkansas, Ellis "CeDell" Davis was raised by a family of sharecroppers who worked at a local plantation. Sharecropping seemed to be the default occupation for many of the legendary bluesmen from that mystical part of the South, and they included Muddy Waters and John Lee Hooker, who both claimed the title of Sharecropper-Bluesman. CeDell's mother had been a traditional healer, a woman of the Faith, but she wasn't able to save young CeDell from the back-to-back ravages of yellow fever, when he was nine years old, and the excruciating pains of polio at the age of 10. The polio would hamper CeDell's ability to walk without the aid of crutches, and it destroyed much of the flexibility in his hands. He had just started playing guitar when the polio struck, so he learned, through his own ingenuity, how to use a butter knife over the top of the neck to fret the strings in place of making chords with his gnarled hand. In doing so, he pioneered the butter knife technique that many slide players imitate today.

By the age of 27, CeDell was apprenticing with the great Robert Nighthawk, playing exquisite slide guitar beside Nighthawk for a decade, between 1953 and 1963. They played throughout the South, following a circuit that took them to juke joints, house parties, speakeasies, and pretty much any place that would have them. CeDell told us about these gigs, where he'd make "Five bucks, a little whiskey, and a steak to take home" after a long night of playing the blues.

Then tragedy struck again, this time in 1957, when CeDell was playing a gig in East St. Louis. A gunshot in a gambling room in the back of a club resulted in a stampede of patrons, and CeDell fell under the panicked crowd and was trampled underfoot, breaking both of his legs with multiple fractures. After several months in hospital traction, and several months more convalescing at home, CeDell was now starting to use a wheelchair, where he ultimately sits to this day.

The most important thing to remember about all of CeDell's illnesses and injuries is that, while many other musicians committed slow suicide with excessive alcohol, drugs, and dangerous living, CeDell never fell victim to these vices. Instead, he was challenged by forces beyond his control, yet he refused to concede defeat, focusing on his deep blues instead. In the process, he became a stronger and more authentic artist, or as he said during the recording sessions for his most recent album, "I plan on living, man—dying will take care of itself!"

For many years, throughout the 1960s, '70s, and '80s, CeDell made blues albums for various European labels, yet still lived in relative obscurity, as most working musicians often do. Mostly he survived by plying his craft in the traditional way, playing countless live shows at clubs and house parties. Then in the early '90s, the famed *New York Times* music critic Robert Palmer rediscovered CeDell and his unique interpretation of the blues. In his book, *Deep Blues*, Palmer declared CeDell to be the finest hardcore blues vocalist of his generation and he set out to produce some songs for CeDell, which became the fantastic album, *Feel Like Doin' Something Wrong*, released by the blues revival label Fat Possum Records.

Fat Possum had been cultivating a strong roster of blues musicians who were creating a resurgence in delta and hill country blues, largely due to the efforts of Bruce Watson and Matthew Johnson, executive producers for the label. Under Palmer's production and Fat Possum's promotion, CeDell began to experience a second act in his storied career. Mick Jagger and Yoko Ono attended his shows in New York City, Iggy Pop pronounced CeDell's blues to be *unsettling*, and suddenly CeDell Davis was cool again. But as any veteran musician will tell you, popularity is a fickle thing, and anyone who goes the distance in music is going to be both cool and uncool many times over the course of their career. The only thing that truly matters is quality and commitment to the craft. Or, as CeDell once told me: "My mother told me not to play that devil music or I would surely be going to hell. I told her I'll certainly be going to hell if I don't!"

To me, that's the mark of an authentic man—the one who plays because he is driven to play and for no other reason than that. The music chose him and he answered the call. Fortunately for us he kept playing, giving us these great and gritty albums: *Feel Like Doin' Something Wrong, The Horror of It All, The Best of CeDell Davis, When Lightnin' Struck The Pine, Last Man Standing,* and *Even the Devil Gets the Blues.* Go get those records immediately; they're the real thing, and they'll change how you think about American music.

In 2005, CeDell had a stroke and it effectively ended his performing for a few years. During this time, CeDell was living in an Arkansas nursing home where he was found and befriended by Greg "Big Papa" Binns and his son Zakk, both Arkansas natives like CeDell, and both pursuing the same love of the delta blues. They got CeDell to start singing again, and as modern research into stroke patients has shown, singing can come back much sooner than speaking. As Greg Binns described it, hearing CeDell start singing made the nursing home turn into a kind of geriatric juke joint. The revitalized CeDell and his new band started performing at blues festivals around the South, and twice toured in Europe to sold-out crowds of ecstatic fans, many of whom were seeing the delta blues for the first time. The Binns have overseen almost every aspect of CeDell's new life, from his care at a modern assisted living home to a new motorized wheelchair he received from the Blues Foundation, as well as custom-fitted hearing aids he recently got from MusiCares. Sadly his guitar playing is gone, the result of the stroke affecting his hands, but this has also allowed CeDell to focus on his voice once again. It's a dusty and ancient voice as rich and fertile as the delta soil he grew up in.

It's now the summer of 2014 and I find myself recording with the great man again, but this time he is 88 years old and we are now in Water Valley, Mississippi, deep in the Mississippi Delta. In fact, we are very near the mystical place where the blues first began to form in the early 1900s, near the Dockery Plantation and the town of Clarksdale, where legend has it that Robert Johnson sold his soul to the devil at the famous crossroads of Highways 49 and 61. This is of course an old folkloric myth, more closely aligned with the African story of Ellegua, the trickster Orisha who hangs out around the crossroads. But old myths about the devil are hard to shake down here.

The studio where we are recording is Dial Back Sound, and it was designed and built by the same Bruce Watson who previously reinvigorated CeDell's career. He's helping us do that once again and the atmosphere is wonderful—the walls are hung with old guitars and vintage amps line the room recalling the golden age of recording. The studio is built inside the parsonage of an old Methodist church that still stands next door, listing slightly to its side, its whitewashed walls showing their age. But the church has its own haunting story that must be told, because the South is full of dark secrets.

Back at the turn of the century, when the reverberations of Reconstruction were still echoing through the post-Civil War South, the workers at the local steel mill in Water Valley began organizing to form a union. The preacher of the Methodist church, an enlightened man in his own right, allowed the workers to use his church for their union meetings. That is, until the day when a strikebreaker thug from the steel mill walked into the church mid-sermon and bludgeoned the preacher with a piece of lumber, killing him where he stood in his pulpit. Like so many other murders in Mississippi, this one went unpunished and the killer walked away free, probably to kill again as his kind are prone to do. But the spirit of the good preacher is still with us, and he guides us in these sessions, and we know he is pleased with our work from the subtle knocks and claps we hear late at night.

Here we are, about to play the very music that CeDell's mother scorned, right next to a church that she would have welcomed. The sacred and the profane exist side by side here in Mississippi, as they always have—as they always will. And that's because Mississippi is a paradox; it's one of the most beautiful and otherworldly places you will ever see, but it is also a place of unsolved murders, bodies buried in swamps, and disturbing tales told in hushed whispers. Anyone who has ever visited here will attest to its haunting beauty and the magical spell that bewitches you as soon as you cross the state line.

At night, I sleep on the floor of the studio's modest accommodations and I dream that I'm hearing music coming from the trees, beautiful music that seems ancient and in a strange tongue. I ponder this in the morning as I sip coffee on the front porch, because indeed, the blood of my ancestors is in this very land, it's in the roots of the trees that soak it up into their branches. The branches sing a haunting melody that is only audible in the liminal hours at dusk and dawn, when the fireflies dance and the cicadas chirp in harmonic unison. And sometimes, when the sunlight is just right and your spirit is in tune with that great, winding river, you can hear the music dancing on the small waves that rhythmically lap along the muddy banks.

As we wait for CeDell to arrive at the studio for our first day of recording, an absolutely torrential rain pours down upon us, making the metal roof of the studio groan under the weight. Lighting and a huge thunderclap follow, louder than any I've ever heard in my life—louder than that one with Ramiro Musotto in Brazil—and it rattles our very bones. I am in shock from the volume of it and then, two minutes later, CeDell arrives. He comes down the driveway like a rolling, black Buddha and he utters the sacred mantra: "Let's make a record." And so it begins.

The producer on this particular album is Jimbo Mathus, a born-and-raised Mississippian who declined an acceptance to the U.S. Naval Academy to pursue a career in music instead. I reckon he chose the harder path, and Robert Frost would have been proud of the road less traveled that he chose. Jimbo earned a solid reputation as the founder of the Squirrel Nut Zippers, who still play to this day, and as a knowledgeable bluesman and scholar of the form. He's made numerous solo albums and was the musical director for one of the all time greatest bluesmen, Buddy Guy, when they made the *Sweet Tea* album, in which Buddy does a cover of CeDell's greatest song, "She's Got the Devil in Her." Jimbo has also played with CeDell on and off over the years, so he knows CeDell's temperament well. Jimbo plays lead guitar on these sessions, and he laughs and jokes easily as he coaxes us through a series of delta classics. The rest of us—myself on drums, Stu Cole on bass, and Greg and Zakk Binns on guitars—follow along as we develop our musical chemistry.

We are intuitive and spacious, leaving plenty of room in the music for CeDell's words and Jimbo's guitar flourishes. I play simple, hypnotic grooves that complement Stu Cole's foundational bass lines and we all laugh frequently—we're having a great time. As Jimbo said to us at the outset, "You gotta have humor in your blues," and on these sessions, it is in abundance.

Everything is perfect and in balance, and it's all marvelously recorded by engineer Bronson Tew. He uses vintage microphones and compressors, many of which were shiny and new in the 1950s and '60s, when the blues was at its zenith. Now the equipment is showing its age, but inside the tubes and wires there's a humming, analogue electricity that is warm and embracing. The sacred and the profane, the ancient and the modern, acoustic and electric, all of it exists here in Water Valley, Mississippi.

The vast majority of the album is recorded live, with everyone playing together and CeDell singing along in real time. Only the keyboards and some hand percussion are overdubbed after we pick the final, keeper takes. We work like the steel workers who tried to unionize here a century earlier, playing for many hours straight, eating bologna sandwiches and salt peanuts from the local country store. We wash it all back with iced Cokes and beer, but on Sunday the beer runs out and we're in Yalobusha County, a dry county. For the first time in my life, I have to make a run across a county line to buy beer on a Sunday afternoon. It is a mission, indeed a holy mission, because CeDell can only sing with an ice-cold beer in his weathered hand. It's exciting to break this religious law, because some laws are just made to be broken, and this is certainly one of them.

Because these are live, human recordings, the songs do not always start cleanly and perfectly like a sterilized pop song. Indeed, they start and sometimes stumble into existence, but eventually they kick in with that distinct and heavy delta swing and the music, like the smell of a lover, ignites a feeling in CeDell. It is perhaps a long-forgotten memory, maybe about a girl he once loved, a man who crossed a moral line, or a funny anecdote that time has almost forgotten. CeDell starts singing when he is sufficiently inspired by the music, and that's because these songs are like life itself—it does not start or end cleanly. A great song, like a great life, happens in spontaneous moments of volume, strength, vulnerability, rage, and fiery passion. These songs are about CeDell's life, with all the beauty, grace, and messiness of it all.

The standard 12-bar blues that we've all come to recognize as "the blues" is really the codified Chicago version of electrified blues. But we're not in Chicago, and we are not following any rules. Down here in the delta there is only intuition and magic, so we "jump bars" and skip to new sections when CeDell decides to take us there. And that's because 12 rigid bars do not allow for the emotion to hold sway, and so we follow CeDell, intuitively, respectfully, and we change quickly, like a prizefighter in the ring. Delta blues is a tough musical form, tough as the men and women who invented it, who lived it. It is a hard-swinging form, like a scythe that cuts across the tall grass in big, arcing swaths, or a chain gang breaking stones with hammers in rhythmic unison. You can feel it in this place; it is in the soil, and it's in the music.

And the stories! In between takes, CeDell waxes about his life and we play quietly behind him as he tells a story. He talks about his days living in the haunted Aristocrat Hotel in Hot Springs, Arkansas: "If you don't believe in ghosts, stay at the Aristocrat - you'll see 'em!" Or moving to Tunica, Mississippi to live with his cousin and the friendships he developed with Washboard Pete and Doctor Ross "The Harmonica Boss." There he listensed to Charley Patton records on a wind-up gramophone, and he settled an old score with Sonny Boy Williamson: "He paid $500 for that name but he was a thief, a natural born thief!" At one point CeDell talks about being a young boy in Helena and hearing songs sung by former slaves, who were very old but still alive in the 1930s. The room becomes very quiet and we just listen, and we don't play any music for a time. The moment passes, CeDell makes a joke and we all laugh, the next song starts to unfold, and we're all swinging again.

We record for three days straight, and as the last day concludes, Bruce Watson comes to visit CeDell once more. They haven't seen each other in more than a decade and they both know these conversations are rare and more infrequent. The two men talk candidly for an hour in the main room of the studio, drinking beer and joking around with each other. All the other delta bluesmen Bruce has produced have passed on to the other world: Junior Kimbrough, T-Model Ford, R.L. Burnside, Pinetop Perkins—all of them gone from this Earth. CeDell is the last one still alive from that original crew of blues masters, and this despite the physical hardships he's endured. Bruce jokes earnestly, "You're the last man standing, CeDell," and they both laugh. "Yeah," CeDell replies with a chuckle, "I guess I am."

It's now the summer of 2015 and I've been playing shows on and off with CeDell, several of which we've filmed, because at 90 years of age, CeDell is singing the best blues of his career. Which just goes to show you that some forms of music only get better with the passage of time. It's the culmination of his life's work, a collection of his best original songs, delta classics, and spoken-word stories from a career that began in the 1930s and continues to this day. Although the process started several decades ago in the Mississippi delta, we're about to start a new album in Seattle, Washington, up in the great Pacific Northwest.

Like the delta, Seattle has its roots in a working-class culture that found its musical voice in the garage/indie rock explosion of the 1990s. But Seattle's musical legacy goes much further back, to the early 1920s, when a thriving blues and jazz scene flourished in downtown Seattle. That bluesy, working-class ethos is still apparent today, which is why we decided that Seattle would be the ideal place to make CeDell's newest album.

I asked some of my rock & roll friends to help us make the album, including Pearl Jam guitarist Mike McCready, R.E.M. sideman Scott McCaughey, Screaming Trees bassist Van Conner, Arkansas bluesmen Greg and Zakk Binns, harmonica master Johnny Stephens, Seattle guitarist and vocalist Ayron Jones, vocalist Annie Jantzer, saxophonist Skerik, trumpeter Dave Carter, upright bassist Evan Flory-Barnes, and bassist Deandre Enrico. The idea was to bring these rock, jazz, and blues luminaries together in Seattle to pay tribute to the roots of their respective musical forms. And also, perhaps, to give everyone a history lesson on life from CeDell Davis.

The album starts with the sexually charged double entendre, "Play with Your Poodle," followed by a spoken-word story about the first guitar CeDell ever bought: a Silvertone from the Sears Roebuck catalog that cost $2.50. Another spoken-word story tells the tale of Crap House Bea, the woman who allegedly poisoned Robert Johnson, and who also watched CeDell's debut performance in Helena, Arkansas. This is followed by CeDell's best-known song, "She's Got the Devil in Her," featuring a vocal duet with rising Seattle son, Ayron Jones. The album contains other CeDell originals, such as the rhumba-infused "Love Blues" and the haunting "Got To Be Moving On," both of which feature guest vocalist Annie Janzter and guitarist Mike McCready.

Switching between acoustic instrumentation and full-on electrified blues, the album also includes delta classics such as "Can't Be Satisfied," "Dust My Broom," "Cold Chills," and "Catfish Blues," as well as a down-and-dirty version of "Kansas City." The album begins to close with another original, the hilarious "Grandma Grandpa," featuring a vocal duet with Scott McCaughey, and then another spoken-word story with advice on how to live a full life. The album finishes with a rollicking version of the blues classic "Rollin' & Tumblin'," which features guitar solos from all three guitarists.

These songs and CeDell's remarkable life tell the story of the segregated South, to the invention of rock & roll, to the Civil Rights Movement, the sexual revolution, the invention of the Internet, and making music with some of the best rock, jazz, and blues musicians of this era. CeDell Davis has, in almost a century of music, truly lived his life to the fullest.

All of us are born into this world, and all of us will eventually die. That is the price of being given life. Most of us are born with youth and vigor, some are even born with beauty and charisma. Other blessed souls are born with physical and mental challenges right from the womb, or they are afflicted in their prime and have to adapt to a new way of life. These are the children of God, the children of Obatalá, the holy ones who teach us things that cannot be learned by other means. CeDell is one of these blessed ones, gifted with talent, wit, and an earthy humor, even as his body failed him. He's given us albums of music that teach us through humor, historical narratives, and sometimes, withering pain. It is very much the kind of music every American should own in their music collection. It is our first, original music after all.

IRONING BOARD SAM

Several months later I return to Mississippi to play some shows with CeDell and the Binns as we celebrate the release of these remarkable albums. We have shows around the South over the next two weeks, but before the tour begins, Bruce Watson has asked me to play drums on an album he is producing at the same studio where we recorded CeDell's new album. This time it's for another elderly but still vibrant singer named Ironing Board Sam. I arrive at the studio in late February of 2015, having just driven cross-country from Seattle with my drums in the back of my rented Chevy Impala. It took me about four days and nights to get here as I tried to outmaneuver a snowstorm that walloped the Midwest. I needed the cross-country drive because I had just ended a long relationship, and my latest rock band was also calling it quits—all within the same month. The road always helps to clear my head and I needed to get ready for another chapter of playing the blues. As I drove the final stretch from Memphis, I crossed the Mississippi state line and read her welcoming sign: *Welcome to Mississippi, the Birthplace of America's Music.* Indeed, I thought, I'm back home.

I finally arrive at Dial Back Sound in Water Valley and as I walk in I notice a sign stuck to the wall, which I had never noticed before but looks too weathered to be new:

Fun sticks to tape.

These immortal words were spoken by the late American record producer Jim Dickinson, who worked with everyone from Aretha Franklin to Big Star to the Rolling Stones. These words, and a disheveled photo of Mr. Dickinson, are thumbtacked rather unceremoniously to the wall of the control room and I am reminded immediately of this eternal truth. Fun kind of sticks to everything.

The first person I see as I walk through the front door is Ironing Board Sam. Sam was born in 1939 in Rock Hill, South Carolina, and he is already 75 years old by the time we meet. His father had been a sharecropper like CeDell's, and as Sam describes it, they only went into town for salt and pepper because they grew or raised everything else they needed. Sam has a beautifully aged voice, more like a smooth soul man than a gritty bluesman, and he immediately makes you smile when he sings. He was, at one point, famous for having a young Jimi Hendrix backing him up on the 1965 TV show, *Night Train*, right before Jimi moved to London and became a legend. But its now 2015 and Sam has signed to Bruce's Fat Possum Records. It's time to make his debut album for the label.

These sessions have the same superb house band that played on CeDell's *Last Man Standing* album: Jimbo Mathus is on guitar, Stu Cole is on bass, I'm on drums and percussion, and Bronson Tew is engineering and playing the "Pentecostal tambourine," as Bruce refers to it. Bruce is the lead producer on this album, but Jimbo and Bronson are offering their ideas too.

These sessions at Dial Back Sound are a great learning experience for me, because as much as I've learned in my 50 years on Earth, there is so much music that I simply haven't heard, and this is another case of me getting a crash course in soul music. Thus I must do what all good students of music do, which is to put aside my ego and just listen—truly, deeply listen. All of us in the band are learning how to play these old songs so that our new versions can sound original and exciting while still retaining the primal essence of the originals. More importantly, we have to adapt the songs to Sam's voice and his vocal range.

On our second day of recording, Jimbo is dressed up somewhat like an eccentric Confederate general with square-nosed boots, a red satin waistcoat, a pocket-watch chain, and a white Stetson hat replete with pheasant feathers—it looks like it came directly from Robert E. Lee's personal haberdashery. Jimbo sets the mood for the day just as Sam emerges from the guesthouse wearing his own distinctive outfit: a three-piece velvet suit, Santa Claus red, with a black leather porkpie hat that makes him look very much like a dapper Ellegua, hanging out at the crossroads. Sam's in a very good mood today, excited from the previous day's session. He tells me, "Music charges the battery of the heart, and the heart powers the brain. That's why I'm happy!" I hope I'm this cheerful if I make it to 75, and if I'm not, it'll clearly be because I didn't follow Sam's sage advice.

These well-dressed men remind me of those old photos we've all seen of the Stax and Motown musicians who would dress so smartly during their studio sessions, even though they were working in a windowless studio laboratory. They knew that looking sharp made the music even tighter. I make a decision right then and there to dress better for every recording session I do in the future, and for that matter, all the time.

The first thing you learn when you come to the delta is that the music here is an extremely visceral, physical thing. There is a codex of muscular movements and sinuous expressions, and it is retained and expressed in the body through dance and movement and the physicality of playing the music itself. Bronson, the engineer, is particularly good at teaching me these old beats and grooves by doing a series of comedic but true-to-form "dances" that are a combination of crouches, shuffle steps, and body spasms, all of which embody the hidden rhythms in this music. He dances a crusty shuffle, a stomachache funk, a hangdog shake, and a churchy baptismal stagger (to go with his Pentecostal tambourine). I learn about rhythms from watching his body movements and gestures, and we all laugh heartily, which explains the somatic meaning of this music.

And that's because delta music comes right out of the soil, and goes directly into the people themselves. It's retained in the bodies of these extraordinary men and women who take it upon themselves to preserve this first, great American music. Sam sums this up perfectly in one of the many conversations I have with him during our recording sessions. He says, "With a real hit, the beat and the rhythm come first, and then the band kicks in to lay down the music for the singer, who then seals the deal with their voice and words. But the beat always comes first, it's the prime mover—you gotta find that hot spot, Barrett, find that hot spot!"

We work diligently for hours each day, cutting the rhythm tracks live, and most of Sam's vocals too. This music has real life and spontaneity, which is exactly what the old hits had before the onset of digital recording. We're recording digitally too, but it has none of the sterility that many modern recordings have. And that's because this old-new music breathes. My drum tempos are solid, but they rise and fall slightly between the verses and choruses, just as the human body expands with breath and then contracts with exhalation. So, too, do these songs breathe like a living thing, because they are human-made and deeply, organically alive.

As we wind down the sessions on the third and final day of principal recording, Sam reads a poem that he wrote while in an altered, mystical state. It's beautiful and heartfelt, as true and exacting as any passage from the Bible. But instead of God, Sam refers to the "Super Spirit," which is the best term I've ever heard for describing That Which Is Unnamable. I won't tell you the poem's truths—you'll have to buy Sam's amazing album and hear his words for yourself. But he tells me afterward that it's important for young people to hear this poem because, as he said, "Peace will not come from guns, it will only come from what the young people decide to do." I am moved by his statement because, indeed, why do we not listen to the voices of the young people? It is they who will have to take over this mess of a world we are leaving them, and they should have quite a bit more say on the matter.

As I approach half a century on this planet, it often seems to me that the wisest words come from either the very oldest people or the very youngest, and those of us in the middle just seem to muck it all up. I was born in the North and I was educated as a musician, so I tend to think in terms of theories and the kind of academic analysis that gets drilled into graduate students. But this is the South, and here the contrasts are vivid. This is the land of William Faulkner and Muddy Waters, Mark Twain and John Lee Hooker, Cormac McCarthy and Stax Records, CeDell Davis and Ironing Board Sam. It is diametrically highly intellectual and full of wit, but it's also gritty, sweaty, and full of soul. It is real life, manifested through music.

When I come to the South, I feel a deep sense of release opening in my heart and mind and I realize that here, too, exist Americans who have a deep intellect and sense of humor that is perhaps more rooted in music, storytelling, and a deeply felt, bodily experience. It is a musical, danced experience, at least as important as any education system known in the world. The oral/aural traditions of storytelling and music reach far deeper into human memory than any textbook or classroom lecture can. No book can teach this stuff, because only the body can remember what the mind forgets. The body is compelled to dance, to play, and to teach, each of its muscles straining to express this deep American soul.

Here in the delta, the traditional codes of friendliness and community still exist in a social fabric that is as rich as the soil that grew the cotton clothes you're wearing, and the corn, beans, and peas you will eat for dinner tonight. Here in the delta, the seeds for each new season of music are dutifully planted and tended to, as the musician-farmer-philosophers wait patiently for the next crop to sing out.

24. CeDell Davis & Ayron Jones "She's Got The Devil In Her"

VERSE 13

NORTH AMERICA: THE INDIAN IS IN THE COWBOY

Raw Power on the roof of Pike Place Market, Seattle 2015. Left to right: Duff McKagan, Mike McCready, Mark Arm, photographer Charles Peterson, and Barrett Martin. Photo by David Coalter.

"When I hear music, I fear no danger. I am invulnerable. I see no foe. I am related to the earliest times, and to the latest."

—Henry David Thoreau

Back in the 1990s, when I was still in my twenties, I started to get involved with a Native American group in Washington State. I felt something deep in my soul that told me that in order to connect with myself and the Earth, and I would have to follow the indigenous ways. I was hearing that distant Cherokee great grandmother in the back of my mind, because she was there, all of her people were there, somewhere deep in my DNA.

I started to learn the sacred ceremonies of the Lakota people, as opposed to the Cherokee, because the Lakota are more present out here in the western United States. I learned through my teacher, Carolyn Hartness, who had been taught by the great Lakota medicine man, Wallace Black Elk. Now, when I say I learned the sacred ceremonies, I mean that I learned the basic concepts and how to participate as a novice. I am no expert and I have no intention of revealing anything secretive, but I will say that just by doing basic ceremonies, I went through a hugely transformational process, as I grew from a boy into a man.

It started, as it usually does, with the basic sweat lodge ceremony, known as the *Inipi* ceremony, which in Lakota means, "to live again." Over the decades (and countless sweat lodges later), I learned how to become a fire tender at the highest of all Lakota ceremonies, the Sundance. I attended three Sundances in the early 2000s, and I was given the responsibility of building the sacred fire, heating the sweat lodge stones, and carrying those stones into the sweat lodge, as I followed the exact instructions of the medicine man or woman leading the lodge.

One of the most profound spiritual experiences I ever had happened at a Sundance led by the Lakota medicine man, Buck Ghost Horse. Yes, the Lakota do have the coolest names in American history, that's for sure. Buck is now in the spirit world, but in addition to being a Lakota medicine man and Sundance leader, he had also been a Marine drill sergeant at Paris Island. He was a true warrior, all the way to his core.

At this particular Sundance, I had been working as a fire tender for the male Sundancer's private sweat lodge, which Buck oversaw. It had been an emotional dance, as many of the dancers were Vietnam vets and some were newly returned from the Gulf War. These warriors needed healing because of the trauma they endured in those wars, which had been devastating to their souls. They were at the Sundance to do their ancestor's most sacred ceremony. Buck decided that all of the fire tenders would sweat together as well, so that we were all purified and unified in this enormous task of healing.

As we sat in the darkened lodge, the glowing hot stones began to be brought in, one by one, by the lone fire tender who stayed outside to serve us. These stones are made from volcanic rock, so they glow like giant red-hot embers and they emit an incredible heat. That's why the Lakota call them the Grandfathers and the Grandmothers—because their immense wisdom will cleanse you through heat and sweat, and they will teach whatever your spirit needs to learn in the darkness of the lodge.

Once the first seven stones had been brought in, Buck sprinkled some tobacco on the stones and said a prayer in his Lakota language. And then an incredible thing happened, and I swear this to be true - the stones began to sing in human voices. It was not the natural squealing sound you might expect from super-heated stones. No, these stones were actually emitting a chorus of distinctly human voices, relatively quiet, but they were definitely singing a song that was confined to the small pile of stones. None of us humans in the lodge were singing—we were all sweating in silence, and the singing was clearly coming from the stones in the center of the lodge. Several of us gasped, and Buck just said, "Those are the Grandfathers singing to you—listen to them!"

After that absolutely remarkable experience, I've never doubted the existence of a spirit world beyond this physical dimension. I don't necessarily believe that it adheres to the organized religions of the world, but there is definitely something going on beyond the veil that we can't see. So when I see eagles flying in a circle, a red-tailed hawk starting a dive, or when the wind blows through the forest in a certain manner - I pay close attention to what the spirits are trying to communicate.

I'm saying all this at the outset of this final Verse because it's important to remember that if you're born in North America, you probably feel this ancient wildness in your heart. This is where the Wild West was born, where Crazy Horse and his Lakota warriors beat the US Cavalry in every single engagement; where Custer and his mercenaries got their karmic return; and where indigenous warriors still stand up to the Big Oil bullies on the Dakota pipeline and elsewhere. They might be fighting for their land and their sovereignty, but in spirit, they are fighting for you too. Honor them, because they are the original warriors of this continent.

As a rock musician, I've always felt a connection to the Native American worldview, because rock & roll is all about standing up to abusive power structures that hold people down. I know that many of my musical friends feel the same way, whether they are rock, blues, jazz, or hip hop artists. Even if we don't have the blood quantum to be official tribal members, the spirit of the Native American is in many American musicians, artists, and writers. And that is because we listen to the Earth, we channel that truth, and we know in our hearts that this is more powerful than anything we ever learned in a classroom.

Between the years 2014-16, I spent extensive amounts of time traveling, doing research, and completing the final verses for this book. During those three years, I also traveled through some of the most important ecological zones in Australia, North America, South America, and Southeast Asia. These included the Great Barrier Reef in Australia, the Brazilian Amazon, the Peruvian Andes, the Mississippi

Delta, and Alaska's Arctic National Wildlife Refuge. When you personally visit these places, it is immediately clear that global warming and humanity's heavy use of fossil fuels and extractive industries have radically damaged the natural landscape of our planet.

The Great Barrier Reef, which I have dived three times since 1991, is now bleaching white, its beautiful iridescent colors totally gone as a result of warming ocean temperatures and toxic chemicals from factories in Asia that drift down on the ocean currents.

In Brazil, we have an enormous country rich in natural resources, but the corruption in its government has prevented any real change from happening. Their economy languishes, even as pirate-industrialists exploit and destroy the Amazon Rainforest. This ravaging of the natural landscape goes utterly unchecked while Brazil's enormous military, (which has never been in a major war, yet occupies a huge part of Brazil's economy) stands by, utterly impotent and unable to protect its own precious Amazon Rainforest. The rainforest is predicted to be totally gone within 25 years at the current pace of destruction, meanwhile the Brazilian military polishes its boots and rifles.

The Upper Peruvian and Ecuadorian Amazon are also under threat from oil and timber extraction, and in the Peruvian Andes Mountains, the glaciers I saw in 2004 were almost totally gone when I visited again in early 2017. This is the direct result of global warming. On my most recent trip to Alaska in the far northwest of North America, global warming is even more apparent.

I've been to Alaska three times now, first in 2006 when I went (on crutches with a broken ankle no less) to see the dances of the Alaska Federation Of Nations. This is the annual drum and dance competition between the Alaskan tribes and it is astounding to watch. The second time I visited was in April of 2015 when I was a guest lecturer at the University of Alaska at Anchorage. On that trip, I drove as far north as Fairbanks to see the sacred Denali Mountain and the Northern Lights. Then in August of 2016 I went further north than I have ever been in my life, going about 200 miles north of the Arctic Circle, to a tiny village that the indigenous Gwich'in people call *Vashraii K'oo*, or Arctic Village. It's the last spec of human civilization before you reach the coast of the Beaufort Sea at the southern edge of the Arctic Ocean. All of this is right in the middle of one of the wildest and most beautiful places on Earth, the Arctic National Wildlife Refuge.

Perhaps because I was born in the Pacific Northwest I have always felt a natural affinity for Alaska. Separated only by the Canadian province of British Columbia between us, Alaska just seems like a much larger version of Washington State. My grandfathers, father, and now myself have all been drawn to Alaska either for work, or for the raw beauty of the natural landscape. Strange as it may seem, it was only a few months earlier, in 2016, when I was deep in the Brazilian Amazon on a river tour after an intensive recording session in Sao Paulo.

From the air, the Arctic National Wildlife Refuge looks exactly like the Brazilian Amazon, with its winding rivers and lagoons, and vivid green forests. The Amazon Rainforest provides 25 percent of the Earth's oxygen supply. It is a global oxygen and medicinal resource that is being utterly decimated by corporate greed, and most of it falls within the borders of Brazil. If the world is unable to stop Brazil from destroying the Amazon Rainforest, will the rest of us have the courage to stand up and prevent the destruction of our own natural wilderness from oil and gas exploration? This is a decision that will affect every generation of human beings from here on out, so we must weigh this heavily.

To start this conversation, we must first address our own oil and gas consumption, which has been proven by scientists around the world to cause severe environmental degradation, global warming, and a collapse in many biological ecosystems. I am as guilty as anyone because I was in a touring rock band for many years and the carbon footprint of a rock band on tour is about the same as a professional sports team. Airplanes, tour busses, vans, and cars burn an enormous amount of fuel, not to mention what the audience burns to get to a show, the plastic garbage generated, and other waste products. We all release a huge amount of dirty energy into our atmosphere every day. But that doesn't mean we can't reimagine our world and create a new way for us all. There are alternative energy sources that we can harness, they already exist, but as long as there is a demand for the fossil fuels, those corporations will hold sway over our economy—and our democracy.

And this brings me back to the Arctic National Wildlife Refuge, where I started writing this essay, in the chilly, quiet nights of the late summer, as I sat in my tent on the soft tundra Earth. I asked myself, why would we, as conscious human beings, let a handful of oil and gas corporations destroy the last pristine corners of our planet? It is estimated (by the oil experts themselves) that there is only about one year's worth of America's petroleum needs in this part of the world. Why would we destroy this incredible place for one year of oil? The answer is in greed and the whitewashing of the facts.

I say "whitewashing" because the oil lobbyists would have you believe that the Arctic Refuge is a snow and ice covered wasteland that is devoid of life, and therefore open for drilling and exploitation. But this is absolutely false and I can tell you, as an eyewitness to the place, it is exactly the opposite. True, for about 4-5 months in the dead of winter it is covered with snow. But so is Montana, Colorado and much of the Midwest and New England for that matter. The rest of the time, from about April until November, the Arctic Refuge is one of the greenest, most beautiful places I have ever seen on Earth. There is so much water, so many fish, birds, an enormous boreal forest, and caribou herds than number in the tens of thousands. It's also one of the main habitats for grizzly and polar bears, wolves, and a massive bird migration system that is unrivaled on the Earth.

The Arctic Refuge is where the vast majority of our planet's migrating birds congregate before they make their enormous journeys around the planet. They come here to gorge on the insect populations that live in the rivers and lakes, because here the birds can breed, raise hatchlings, and prepare to make transoceanic flights. This includes flying nonstop across the Pacific Ocean to Australia, New Zealand, Japan, and Asia, as well as South America, and even all the way to the Antarctic, as the Arctic Tern does every year. It is, to make a human comparison, the bird kingdom's equivalent of Heathrow Airport.

I came here with a few other adventurers in a 10-seat bush plane, where we were met by a fleet of 4-wheelers, mostly driven by Gwich'in women and a few boys, who helped to gather up our luggage and camping equipment. It's ironic that 4-wheelers are the norm here, and not 4-legged horses, as they were just 50 years ago. Trucks cannot even get this far north except on a river barge, as there are no roads to Arctic Village and gas is approaching $10 a gallon. Thus, 4-wheelers are a much more efficient mode of transportation. But how is it that gas in this northernmost part of Alaska is so expensive, when the oil companies are extracting millions of dollars a day in crude oil right out of their back yard, doing little to help the very people they are taking it from?

I spent ten days and nights in Arctic Village, where I stayed on the land of Sarah James, probably the most well-known Gwich'in person alive today. This is because Sarah, who was born and raised in the Arctic Refuge, has almost singlehandedly raised the story of the Refuge to a global conversation. She learned how to survive as a child by learning the qualities of love and respect, both for the land and her people, and this is her greatest power, a quality she exudes. Visiting her in her modest cabin in Arctic Village, I see pictures of her with world leaders, American presidents, and environmental awards from almost every agency that matters. She is the real thing, a literal force of nature, but she is ultimately a kind, generous, and loving person. She wins over everyone with her charm, but she also has the facts on her side.

On my first day in the village she gave me a copy of the excellent book, *Arctic Voices,* which is a series of essays written by notable scholars, travelers, and environmentalists on the Arctic situation. Every evening in my tent I read these superb essays, the light coming from the midnight sun, which only briefly dips below the horizon for about 3 hours every night, when the evening temperatures drop to freezing.

The ground is soft tundra, but it too is in danger because of the melting permafrost, and this is causing a myriad of problems in the Refuge. I go for a walk with the renowned Gwich'in hunter and outdoorsman Charlie Swaney. Tall, handsome, and about 60 years of age, Mr. Swaney has been interviewed by almost every hunting and sporting magazine that exists—he's a bit of a celebrity in that world. Today, he and his men have just brought in the last of 8 caribou that they've hunted to feed the gathering of Gwich'in people and environmentalists who have arrived in Arctic Village for the biennial meeting that is happening over the next 4 days.

Charlie tells me that when he is out in the Refuge, he sees a number of alarming problems related to global warming. The layers of permafrost, which date back to the last Ice Age, are melting under the topsoil of the tundra. This is causing the tree roots to become loosened, which then causes the trees to lean in all manner of directions. This "drunken forest" as they call it, is a disturbing sight to see because you can tell that something is very wrong with the landscape. He hands me his binoculars and I see an entire forest with formerly healthy trees leaning and tipping over in very unnatural ways. It's a terrible sight to see.

He also describes the huge upheavals in the soil, where giant mounds are emerging, river banks are crumbling, and this in turn is making the rivers and streams become wider, but also shallower. This is a real danger for the spawning salmon and other fish that swim in the innumerable waterways because there is less depth to the water. He remarks about it being over 80 degrees in Barrow Alaska a few days earlier, on the northern coast of the Arctic Ocean. I am stunned.

Charlie shows me some fast growing under brush, particularly the scrub willow. It used to be short and close to the ground but it is now growing taller, and this is confusing and disrupting the natural migration routes of the Caribou, the one animal Charlie has studied, hunted, and revered his entire life. The Caribou prefer open, clear tundra where they can direct the herd, but they are becoming confused by the growing underbrush, which blocks their vision, as well as the bizarrely tilting trees, and the encroachment of the oil refineries in Prudhoe Bay.

All of the things Charlie has described to me I would see firsthand from his hunting camp high up in the Brooks Range. I see more of the tipping forests, the upheaval of giant mounds of soil in the melting tundra, and the rapid growth of the scrub willow. The Refuge is still extraordinarily beautiful, but something seems wrong, you can see it, and you can feel it.

There are only about 200 people who live in Arctic Village on a permanent basis, and there are perhaps another 200 people here for the biennial meeting, most of whom are also indigenous. The Gwich'in are an Athabascan people who are closely related to the Navajo in the American Southwest, but they are more environmentally aligned with the Inupiat people who live near them along the Arctic coastline. The Gwich'in are Caribou and Moose hunters, whereas the Inupiat are whale and seal hunters, one group plying the land and the other the sea. It is a harmonious and respectful relationship that views both the land and the sea as the source of their livelihoods. Unfortunately, the abundant sea life is also at risk.

Elders and environmental experts from all over Alaska and the Canadian Yukon have come here to exchange their opinions and experiences on the changes in the environment their ancestors have inhabited for over 20,000 years. This awareness and activism came to a head just 30 years ago, in 1988, when the first Gwich'in leaders met to discuss the impact of the oil companies on the Refuge. It was one year later, in 1989, when the oil tanker Exxon Valdez ran into an Alaskan reef, spilling 38 million gallons of crude oil into Prince William Sound. That spill destroyed most of the sea life and the livelihoods of all the people who lived around that magnificent corner of Earth. It was a warning of what was still to come—in the Nigerian Delta, in the Gulf of Mexico, the Dakota pipeline, and other places around the world where oil spills have contaminated and destroyed previously healthy ecosystems.

Every afternoon there are talks and teachings by elders, and the young people speak too. It is inspiring to hear the next generation talking about preserving their Gwich'in language, their traditions, and the hunting practices that are linked to honoring and protecting the Earth. Ask any American hunter and he'll say the same things—hunting wild animals also means protecting the land, waters, and habitats in which those animals reside, because everything is connected and inseparable. This difference here is the American hunter who only takes what he needs, whereas the large corporations take everything they can get their hands on. This is the difference between the ecological hunter, and extractive, destructive greed.

On the third afternoon of the conference, two very powerful women speak, one of whom is a woman from the Sarayaku people in the Ecuadorian Amazon. She speaks about how her tribe successfully fought off the illegal invasion of a foreign oil company on their indigenous lands. The women went first in the attack, their men following behind. The women disarmed the guards, took all the men's clothing, and marched them out of their territory without a shot being fired. The Ecuadorian government was forced to admit their own corruption and collusion with the oil company, but these are the kinds of shady, illegal deals that happen all the time, where politicians are bought and sold like potatoes in a market.

Another indigenous woman from the Cordillera people in the Philippine highlands speaks about a mining company that is destroying her people's lands, who pay no royalties or reparations for the minerals they extract or the damage they cause, and who act with impunity as they destroy and pollute her people's lands. Again, it's the same pattern we hear about in developing countries all the time.

All of this legitimate frustration and anger is muted slightly in the evenings when the music starts up and the people begin to dance. At night in the large communal building, local musicians tune up their guitars and fiddles, people clear away the plastic picnic tables that have served as conference tables, and the floor is opened up. The music starts and it's roughly the equivalent of what I would call a Texas two-step. The warm up songs consist of Rolling Stones covers, and because the word has gotten around that I am a "famous drummer," I have been invited to sit in during the opening set. Unfortunately, no one dances to our rock & roll songs, but they leap out of their seats and dance ferocious jigs as soon as the fiddle music begins. It's a total Arctic hoedown.

The conference is now winding down and the village has begun to clear out. My flight leaves in a couple days and I want to get out on the land a bit more. I meet another gentleman, the Italian alpine skier Ario Sciolaria who, back in the winter of 2005-2006, skied the length of Alaska, from Valdez Sound all the way to the Inuit village of Kaktovic, about 4,000 kilometers north. He did this completely by himself, pulling a sled of camping supplies behind him, and he often snowshoed through the heavy snow when he couldn't ski. It was a slow journey and it took him about 5 months to do it, but Mr. Sciolaria did this to raise awareness about the Arctic Refuge. His book and documentary film are forthcoming.

In the few hours that I spoke with Ario as we walked around the land, he spoke with eyes of wonder about the magical quality of the Refuge, where he encountered a pack of wolves who followed him with curiosity, and as Ario believes, protected him from a stalking grizzly bear. When he finally reached the north slope of the Refuge, he encountered the enormous caribou herds that make that North Slope its primary calving ground. It is a sacred place, full of life, death, and rebirth. It is also where the oil companies want to drill, which will almost certainly scatter the herds, destroy the landscape, and permanently disrupt the balance of life that has existed here for tens of thousands of years.

Doing more research upon my return home I found that the Arctic is already far more polluted than people realize. This is because the Earth's ocean and wind currents flow to the poles, carrying with them the toxins that are generated in the middle of the Earth, all the way to the Arctic and Antarctic. Mercury from coal extraction, banned PCBs and other pesticides, and industrial chemicals from North America, Europe, Russia, and Asia slowly make their way to the Arctic and Antarctic poles, poisoning the air, the sea, the animals, and ultimately the people who survive on those animals and resources. Decades of burning oil and gas in the refineries here has created a toxic cloud that is referred to as the *Arctic Haze*, a mixture of fog, refinery pollution, and god knows what else, which gathers and never disperses from the Arctic. Ironically, as clean as the Arctic looks with its pristine white snow, it is becoming one of the most polluted places on the planet.

The modern message from oil companies is that they are leading the way in energy exploration. But what does that jingoism really mean? Absolutely nothing of course, because oil companies do not support any form of renewable energy that might put them of business. It's a façade of misinformation and it needs to be called as such.

Oil companies are famous for saying one thing and then doing another. For example during the Exxon Valdez oil spill in Prince William Sound, the spokesman for Exxon said, "We will make you whole again." Except they did exactly the opposite—they litigated against Alaskans, dragging it out for years in court, and in the end, they paid out as little as $100 in checks to individuals who had lost their entire livelihoods to the oil spill. This is all documented, it's in the legal briefs, and you can look up it up yourself if you wish. It's all in the public record.

When the Deep Water Horizon oil platform exploded in the Gulf of Mexico, dumping millions of gallons of crude oil into the ocean they literally said the same thing and the ramifications of that spill continue to unfold. In Nigeria, oil companies are notorious for their violence against Nigerian citizens who protest the pollution in the Niger Delta, and many people have been murdered and even executed by the Nigerian government.

As the famous saying goes, *The stone age didn't end for lack of stones,* and this is also true of the Oil Age. We may still have some oil left on Earth, but it's killing us and we have to evolve beyond it. We have to phase out fossil fuels and find renewable energy sources before it's too late to save our planet.

As Frank Zappa once said, "Without music to decorate it, time is just a bunch of boring production deadlines or dates by which bills must be paid." It's a sentiment I've heard many times during my life, and most artists have their own version of the quote. This is also because musicians and other artists are often the most capable of expressing the social, political, and environmental problems facing humanity. We use our art forms to express these complexities, and we have a moral responsibility to use that artistic power to change hearts and minds for the betterment of mankind. Music is one of the greatest tools for social evolution, because, as I wrote at the beginning of this book, it is essentially a survival mechanism. Rock & Roll, by its very nature, is a form of musical resistance against entrenched power structures, whether they be political, socio-economic, religious, or educational.

It also happens to be one of the greatest musical forms ever invented when it's done with real intention.

My musical career has allowed me to see and hear many other cultures around the world, including a good bit of time spent with indigenous people. Those personal experiences have shaped my worldview on humanity and our natural state of balance with the Earth, and it has shown me the power of music as a force for social justice and change. Some of the people who inspired me, might inspire you as well, and here's a short list of them.

In South America, the Chilean singer and poet Victor Jarra helped start the Nueva Cancion movement in Latin America during the 1960s as a protest against the right wing fascist governments that were seizing power through various military coupes. He ultimately gave his life for that anti-fascist belief, as so many others did, which is why Victor Jarra is a Latin American hero of the highest standing. Caetano Veloso and Gilberto Gil did a similar thing with their adventurous Tropicalia movement in Brazil in the early 1970s, and fortunately for us, their music helped topple a military dictatorship and they are both still making music today.

The Nigerian singer and activist Fela Kuti challenged the corrupt Nigerian government and its oil-backed military when he released his protest anthem "Zombie" in 1976. The song was immediately banned in Nigeria, but went on to become an international hit. In South Africa, the indigenous Mbaqanga songs helped bring about the end of apartheid by hiding coded words of resistance in its radio friendly "pop" music. Bob Marley did a similar thing with his many songs of resistance, perhaps the most powerful being "Redemption Song", released in 1980.

In Australia and New Zealand, popular songs written by indigenous and pop songwriters, such as Yothu Yindi's "Treaty," helped spark an indigenous land reclamation movement that is still ongoing today.

The country I have seen the most of is, of course, my own—the United States. I love my country and our people, and I have driven through all 50 states in the union, including Alaska and Hawaii. Sometimes it was in a van, other times it was in a tour bus, and a few times it was on a motorcycle. I've experienced America with my own eyes and ears, my own boots on the ground, and it's an incredible country with some extraordinary musicians and songwriters. Those songwriters have, over the decades, brought about great social evolution with their story-songs and political messages, which have literally changed the landscape of our country.

In the early 20th century folk movement, Woody Guthrie sang "Roll On Columbia" about the enormous Columbia River in my home state of Washington, expressing his love for the American West. When Pete Seeger wrote "My Dirty Stream," it was his alarm call to the industrial pollution that was destroying the east coast Hudson River. Mr. Seeger's song sparked the modern day clean up of the Hudson River Valley, which returned it back to the pristine condition it is today.

During the Civil Rights Movement, Billie Holiday sang about "Strange Fruit" hanging from the trees, as she decried the lynchings and abominations that were going on in the American South. People started to listen, and when the Movement gained steam in the 1960s, Aretha Franklin brought her gospel music out into the streets with marching protestors as they demanded "Respect," and ultimately won it. Curtiss Mayfield united everyone with his epic song, "People Get Ready," and Stevie Wonder continued that tradition with song after song that uplifted the American spirit.

The jazz musicians weighed in too, using song titles and instrumental melodies to get their social and political messages across. When saxophonist John Coltrane composed the mournful melodies of "Alabama," it was to honor the four little girls killed in the Birmingham church bombing. The drummer Max Roach composed ferocious albums that sounded like entire protest marches, and when Charles Mingus composed "Better Get It In Yo' Soul," man, he meant it.

In the late 20th century, Bob Dylan wrote one of the greatest anti-war songs of all time, "Blowing In The Wind," and the Canadian Native American singer, Buffy St. Marie, offered a similar message with her anthem, "Universal Soldier." When Crosby, Stills, Nash, and Young wrote the song "Ohio," it was a direct challenge to the National Guardsmen who murdered four college students protesting the Vietnam War on the Kent State campus. And when Iggy Pop and The Stooges recorded "Search And Destroy," it was as much a clarion call for American punk rock, as it was about the soul-destruction of the Vietnam War.

When I hear the poet and singer Joy Harjo sing about her Native American experience, I am deeply moved. Her poem-stories reach beyond the indigenous perspective and touch all of us who are willing to listen to another possibility, another way of life, in which justice is delivered to the oppressed.

One of the greatest American songwriters of all time, Bruce Springsteen, tells powerful stories about the everyman/woman who struggles for identity in an increasingly homogenized world, which is why he is so beloved in our country, around the globe. I often wonder, who will be the next Bruce Springsteen, Stevie Wonder, Billie Holiday, Bob Dylan, Aretha Franklin, or Iggy Pop? Why are we not hearing their young voices on the radio or television today?

One thing we do know, and its heartening to remember, is that music and progressive politics has led directly to environmental action, the civil rights of all men and women, movements against war and violence, and it has raised the voices of the working class and marginalized people. We now need to direct it toward direct political action once again. Powerful songs have always been the engine behind the greatest social and political movements — it is the soundtrack that unites people both in a march and at the voting booth, giving them the focus and resolve to make the most informed decisions.

The reason music works in this way is because music gets people thinking, talking, and then acting. I cite all of these examples above because, frankly, I am very worried about the condition of the world's environments, and decaying political systems that are rife with corruption, incompetence, and a rising tide of public apathy. We have education systems that are failing around the world; a profit-before-health medical system that is making people sicker and bankrupt; and a minimum-wage economy that keeps people in a "working poor" status while their potential wealth is siphoned off by a predatory financial apparatus. It is only through the immensely powerful spear points of music and the arts that our social awareness can be raised to the make the necessary changes in our societies.

In my lifetime, I have seen our world be radically transformed by global capitalism, and in most cases, it has not for the better. I've seen both the environmental and cultural damage of this colonial creation, and it is not sustainable. We have a literal handful of people controlling the world's wealth, while the Earth's environments are being polluted and destroyed, and most of the world's population languishes in debt or abject poverty. This is not an economic or environmental model that our species can, or should support. It is not sustainable. We are on the brink, and that's the hard reality we all must face. Now it's a matter of the decisions we make, both personally and within our collective societies, as we go forward in time.

As I've shown throughout these stories, responsible eco-tourism is a wonderful way to see and understand the world and her cultures. That is a real economy, which supports the people and their communities directly. Of course we still need responsible trade and commerce, but we also need to preserve and protect the indigenous cultures of the world and our shared Earth. Will these cultures be able to hold on to their sacred spiritual traditions, their incredible languages and music, and their ancient knowledge of the Earth's ecosystems? Will technology and the digital age enhance this knowledge or denigrate it? And how will we use these tools of technology for the betterment of humanity?

We must ask these same questions individually as well. Do we want to participate in the ruining of the natural environments of our shared Earth? Or is it possible that we can envision another way of life, a way in which we harness renewable energies, nurture our planet's magnificent environments, and cultivate the best talents of individual people so that we can develop sustainable economies?

We need a non-violent people's revolution, driven by music, to change things for the better. Probably, Thomas Jefferson and his enlightened contemporaries, past and present, would be screaming for it. We should be looking to the next generation of songwriters, producers, artists, and writers from around the world to show us the way. Those who have the courage to stand up and write it, speak it, and sing it. We are waiting patiently, listening for their voices to rise.

25. Joy Harjo & Barrett Martin "An American Sunrise"

CODA

ASIA, WHERE THE GONGS STILL RING

Balinese rice terraces, 2017

"If one should desire to know whether a kingdom is well governed, if it's morals are good or bad, the quality of its music will furnish the answer."

—Confucius

I'm writing this last verse, or Coda (a final musical statement), from Bangkok, Thailand, and Bali, Indonesia. It's the end of 2016 and the New Year's celebrations are in full swing here in Bangkok. Fireworks are exploding in the sky and young people are celebrating in the street. I can feel their optimism, their hope. After visiting five continents over 30 years for the stories in this book it seems appropriate to end with a new adventure on the sixth continent of Asia. This is the first time I've visited here, but being a percussionist, I've used various Asian gongs and Indonesian gamelans in my recordings over the last two decades. I am quite remiss in not having visited here sooner, and I am enchanted by the sounds I am hearing. These are truly magical countries with beautiful people, incredible music, and sublime spiritual practices. Its all quite beyond what I could have even imagined.

In Bangkok, I am amazed at this gleaming, modern city, which has skyscrapers that match anything I've seen anywhere in the world. There is a new rapid train system that snakes its way above the city's streets and I am surprised by the laid-back nature of the Thai people—their walking pace is much slower than a New York pace, despite the fact that Bangkok is about three times the size of New York City. No one appears to be in much of a hurry to get anywhere, and they seem happier for it. The police and security guards lightly bow and say *Ka* (thank you) after politely answering my questions. They rarely carry guns and I remind myself about the last time I approached an American cop to ask a question, only to see him place his hand on his pistol grip. Even though it is an ancient city, Bangkok is in many ways a more modern, friendlier city than most American cities. The fear of a gun-toting fanatic in the street isn't even an afterthought, because these people have wisely figured out that owning guns does not make for a safer country. I feel like I am in an enlightened city.

Bangkok looks like what the next century is probably going to look like—sleek, modern, and technologically savvy. Sure, the charming little *tuk tuk* motorcycles are still here for the tourists to take a joyride, right next to the new Mercedes taxis, scooters, and the occasional Harley Davidson. But prosperity is definitely here in Asia, slowly manifesting in its architecture, wide city streets, and a generation of young people designing new fashions—and new music.

While we are here, the current American president talks about leaving the Paris Climate Agreement and bringing back coal and oil production, which every intelligent person in the world knows is limited in quantity, extremely expensive to extract, and hugely polluting to the Earth's environments. The same week, China announces that it will lead the world in renewable energy research over the ensuing decade, moving away from oil as Asia inches ahead economically and the United States stays in the fossil fuel dark ages.

We leave for Bali the following week, deep in the Indonesian Archipelago.

I've been collecting Thai, Burmese, and Balinese gongs and gamelans for many years now. They are extremely hard to find in the United States because few percussionists use them, and those who do are usually in professional orchestras who commission their manufacture in these Asian countries. Bronze casting is an ancient, sacred profession here, and when a full gamelan orchestra is commissioned, it may involve dozens of workers. If they follow the traditional protocols, they will fast, pray, and even take on special secret names as they work, so that their bronze casting has the highest spiritual essence to it.

Here in Bali, the old animistic ways still hold sway, despite the fact that it is in the largest Muslim country in the world. Since the turn of the 20th century, anthropologists and musicologists alike have been drawn to the fascinating culture here. Social theorists like Clifford Geertz and Margaret Meade wrote incredible ethnographies that I read in graduate school, with stories that taught and entertained as much as they educated. They knew that Bali was one of the most unique places on Earth, a mixture of ancient Hinduism, and later imports like Buddhism and Islam, which came centuries later. But Bali, the island, holds closer to the ancient, shamanic traditions that honor the spirit of water that surrounds the island, the spirit of fire that fuels its volcanic activity, and the spirit of rice, which has fed the Balinese for millennia.

On our first night here, my wife and I watch an all-female gamelan orchestra of about thirty musicians, combined with a troupe of actors and dancers, also mostly women. They are reenacting the famous story of the Ramayana where the beloved couple Rama and Sita are separated by the evil king and his demonic helpers. What's most amazing in this utterly captivating performance is all of the cultural inversions that are at play. The usually male-dominated orchestra is, in this case, all female, and some of the male characters, are played by females. The audience loves it all. A few nights later, we watch a stunning performance of the Kecak, also known as the Monkey Chant, which sounds like a gamelan orchestra, but vocalized by dozens of males voices as they honor the monkey-king Hanuman. It closes with a performance of the traditional fire ceremony, where a dancer in shamanic trance dances through a bonfire, kicking red-hot coals with no visible pain or injury to his bare feet.

On another day, we hear, far off in the distance, a ceremony that has begun on the far side of the rice paddies near our hotel. We can hear a large group of men, women, and children, roaring back and forth in a call and response style. Something is being purged and cleansed from the collective village, and it is clearly another of the ceremonies that Bali is so famous for. A few dogs bray in unison, and then the cacophony fades away.

Bali appears, at least to my eye, to be an inversion of everything I have seen in the western world. Here the culture is more matriarchal, feminine, and generally organized in a more nurturing, community-based society. The power and musicality of the female musicians and dancers is clear to all who see them. By day, these woman work as mothers, teachers, shop owners, community leaders, and several construction sites we pass contain more women than men, all of them carrying bags of concrete and cinderblocks on their shoulders as they build new temple-homes. Indeed, the entire island feels like a temple to the feminine, a very shamanic and slightly wild one.

During our days in Bali, we visit several different parts of the island with a driver we've hired named Wayan Marjana. Like most Balinese, he is crisply dressed, clean-shaven, and his English is incredibly good. He drives us around in his immaculate SUV and our first stop is to visit women weaving the traditional Balinese fabrics. I am hypnotized by the rhythmic clatter of the old, wooden looms as the women weave, laugh, and occasionally sing a song. Their beautiful fabrics are as colorful and vibrant as their souls.

At another place—a community-owned rice terrace—we watch families tending rice paddies on ancient terraces built by their ancestors. We visit several temples that look equally ancient, as the people conduct ceremonies with their portable gamelan mini-orchestras. These ceremonies honor the elements of earth, fire, and water and I suddenly make the connection that their gamelans too are hewn from the Earth (brass and copper), melted in the sacred fire, cooled with water, and then hammered into some of the most exquisite sounds on the planet. This in turn propels the ceremonies with a perfect, rhythmic, hypnotic cadence that enchants anyone within earshot.

On another day, Wayan takes us to see a gamelan casting facility where he and I play a basic gamelan pattern together. It is gorgeous in its polyrhythmic complexity. Wayan then moves down to a Balinese drum with two heads on either end, and he begins playing ferocious polyrhythms, for which I cannot even count the time signature, much less play myself. I stop to watch and listen and suddenly realize that Wayan is secretly a badass drummer, who just happens to moonlight as a day-driver for tourists. I say it in this order, because Wayan considers music to be his sacred profession, and his day job is just a way to pay the bills—and buy more musical instruments. Music is the real job here, it is soul-work, and of course my personal karma is such that the man I hire to be our driver for the week is a far better drummer than I am, and I love him even more for it. For the rest of the week, all Wayan and I can talk about are the different ways to make gongs and gamelans, how to pick just the right one, and the addition of secret alloys to make special ceremonial gongs. We make extensive plans (still to be fulfilled) to find the best gong maker in Bali.

As I near the end of this first trip to Asia, I reflect on all the places I have visited over the years, all the people I have met, ate dinner with, played music with, and did sacred ceremonies with. It's as if every place I visited sprinkled a little dust on me, a sacred kind of dust that settled into the pores of my skin, my hair, and my eyes, allowing me to see the magic of this world. It has changed me at a molecular level. I am not just a man from Seattle in the United States who just happens to be a musician. I'm now a human being who loves the entirety of the Earth, her people, and their music.

As we fly out of Tokyo on our way home, I am reminded of what is perhaps Asia's greatest gift to the world—the spiritual philosophy of Buddhism. The idea that each person is a sacred being and each of us has the spiritual capacity to evolve ourselves into something we can't really see, but perhaps can feel. Each of us has that potential, and when we do this, we become more powerful than any single country or national identity. We become truly human.

It's the only thing I really believe in, evolution of the Self, and in that moment I realize a great truth that my Zen Buddhist teacher, Yuko Conniff, taught me so many years ago: There is no separation between us and the Earth, her musics, her many peoples, and her numerous environments. All of it is just One Thing, interconnected, intertwined, and inseparable. It's the most beautiful thing you can imagine—an enormous, roaring sea.

26. Balinese Nightscape
27. Gina Sala & Tuatara "God's Meditation"

ACKNOWLEDGMENTS

It would be impossible for me to thank everyone who helped, assisted, taught, counseled, or otherwise advised me on the making of this book. But I shall do my best to encapsulate their efforts here.

Firstly, I must thank all the musicians, singers, songwriters, poets, shamans, medicine men/women, and all the indigenous people who gave me their rhythms, songs, stories, poems, myths, and sacred teachings that enriched my musical and spiritual life to a degree that words can barely describe. This book simply would not exist without their wisdom and their contributions to this world.

I must also thank my various teachers and professors who, over the years, gave me great encouragement and direction in my research, writing, and spiritual practice—all of them extraordinary women: Carolyn Hartness, Joy Harjo, the Reverend Yuko Conniff, Dr. Maria Williams, Dr. Suzanne Oakdale, Dr. Andrea Heckman, Dr. Carole Nagengast, and Dr. Caroline Heldman.

And then there are all the bands I played with who certainly influenced my musical ideas and often gave me the opportunities to travel and do musical research in the field. So thank you, Thin Men, Skin Yard, Jack Endino, Screaming Trees, Alice In Chains, Soundgarden, Kim Thayil, Pearl Jam, Mad Season, Mike McCready, Tuatara, CeDell Davis, R.E.M., Peter Buck, Walking Papers, Duff McKagan, Queens Of The Stone Age, Josh Homme, Fred Drake, Dave Catching, and everyone at the Rancho De La Luna.

The extended Martin family gave me great love and support over the decades, and my wife, Dr. Lisette Garcia, took me on that first trip to Asia, which totally changed the conclusion of this book. Also, a deepest thanks to my dear friends and teachers in Los Angeles and New Mexico, with whom I have studied, sparred, laughed, and done ceremonies with over these many years: Mich Rogers, Rod Rowland, Davis Factor, Elliot Haas, Barnard Voorhees, Tony Hassett, and the incredible artist Erin Currier, who did the portrait on the book cover, as well as hundreds of other portraits of exceptional people from around the world.

The brilliant people who helped bring this book into its physical reality were Rachel Shimp and Dr. Bryan Tomasovich, who both did the copy editing, Tyler Jon who designed the cover, and again to Dr. Tomasovich, who did the beautiful layout and interior of the book. Also, a big thank you to Bradley Laina and Chris Hanzsek, who helped organize the book soundtrack.

Finally, and perhaps most importantly, I must thank the living landscapes of this Earth, whose jungles, deserts, and rainforests are the soundtrack of this book. Those forests and their animals do not have individual names, yet collectively they represent the immensity of life on this magnificent planet, and in fact, they represent the Earth's collective spirit. They must be protected at all costs.

—BHM

BIBLIOGRAPHY
(selected readings you might like)

Amira, John and Steven Cornelius. *The Music of Santeria.* White Cliffs Media, 1991.

Azerrad, Michael. *Our Band Could Be Your Life: Scenes From The American Indie Underground 1981-1991.* Little, Brown, 2001.

Bancroft, Anne. T*he Dhammapada.* Element Books, 1997.

Banerjee, Subhankar. *Arctic Voices: Resistance At The Tipping Point.* Seven Stories Press, 2012.

Barks, Coleman. *Rumi, The Big Red Book: The Great Masterpiece Celebrating Mystical Love & Friendship.* Harper Collins 2010.

Barks, Coleman. T*he Essential Rumi.* Harper Collins, 1995.

Barrio, Hilda and Jenkins, Gareth. *The Che Handbook.* St. Martin's Press, 2003.

Basso, Keith H. *Senses of Place.* School of American Research Press, 1996.

Basso, Keith H. *The Cibeque Apache.* Waveland Press, 1970.

Basso, Keith H. *Wisdom Sits In Places: Landscape And Language Among The Western Apache.* University Of New Mexico Press, 1996.

Beckwith, Carol and Angela Fisher. *African Ceremonies.* Harry Abrams, 1999.

Black Elk, Wallace. *The Sacred Ways Of A Lakota.* Harper & Row, 1990.

Blacking, John. *How Musical Is Man?* University Of Washington Press, 1973.

Boas, Franz. *Anthropology and Modern Life.* Dover Books, 1986.

Bramly, Serge. *Macumba.* City Lights Books, 1994.

Cage, John. *Silence: Lectures And Writings.* Wesleyan University Press. 1973.

Charry, Eric. *Mande Music.* University of Chicago Press, 2000.

Carson, Rachel. *Silent Spring.* Mariner Books, 2002.

Cleary, Thomas. *Shobogenzo: Zen Essays By Dogen.* University Of Hawaii Press, 1991.

Cowan, James. *Rumi's Divan of Shems of Tabriz.* Element Books, 1997.

Davis, Wade. *The Serpent and The Rainbow.* Simon & Schuster, 1985.

Debroy, Bibek & Dipavali. *The Holy Vedas.* B.R. Publishing 1999.

Deren, Maya. *Divine Horsemen: The Living Gods Of Haiti.* McPherson, 1953.

Deutschmann, David. *Che Guevara Reader.* Ocean Press, 2003.

Diallo, Yaya. *The Healing Drum: African Wisdom Teachings.* Destiny Books, 1989.

Dinwoodie, David. *Reserve Memories.* University of Nebraska Press, 2002.

Durkheim, Emile. *The Elementary Forms of Religious Life.* The Free Press, 1912.

Eakin, Laurialt, Boonstra. *People of the Ucayali.* International Museum of Cultures, 1986.

Eliade, Mircea. *Shamanism: Archaic Techniques of Ecstasy.* Princeton University Press, 1964.

Ernst, Carl. *The Shambhala Guide to Sufism.* Shambahala Books, 1997.

Fernandez, James. "Emergence and Convergence in Some Sacred African Places," in *The Anthropology of Space and Place.* Blackwell Publishing, 2003.

Fitzgerald, Edward. *Rubaiyat of Omar Khayyam.* St. Martin's Press, 1983.

Fischlin, Daniel. *Rebel Musics: Human Rights, Resistant Sounds, And The Politics Of Music Making.* Black Rose Books, 2003.

Fleet, Cameron. *First Nations, Firsthand.* Chartwell Books, 1997.

Foster, Byron. *Heart Drum: Spirit Possession in the Garifuna Communities of Belize.* Cubola Productions, 1986.

Fox, Aaron. *Real Country.* Duke University, 2004.

Frazer, James George. *The Golden Bough.* Collier Books, 1922.

Galeano, Eduardo. *Open Veins Of Latin America: Five Centuries Of The Pillage Of A Continent.* Monthly Review Press, 1973.

Garcia, Gabriel. "Garifuna Bicentennial." *Americas*, Volume 49, July/August 1997.

Gebhart-Sayer, Angelika. *The Cosmos Encoiled: Indian Art of The Peruvian Amazon.* Center For Inter-American Relations, 1984.

Geertz, Clifford. *The Interpretation Of Cultures.* Basic Books, 1973.

Giles, Lionel. *The Analects Of Confucius.* Heritage Press, 1970.

Guevara, Ernesto Che. *The African Dream: The Diaries Of The Revolutionary War In The Congo.* Grove Press, 1999.

Gumperz, John. *Language and Social Context.* Penguin Books, 1972.

Hale, Thomas A. *Griots and Griottes.* Indiana University Press, 2007.

Harding, Rachel E. *A Refuge In Thunder: Candomble And Alternative Spaces Of Blackness.* Indiana University Press, 2003.

Harjo, Joy. *A Map To The Next World.* Norton, 2000.

Harjo, Joy. *Crazy Brave.* Norton, 2012.

Harjo, Joy. *How We Became Human: New And Selected Poems 1975-2001.* Norton, 2004.

Harjo, Joy. *In Mad Love And War.* Wesleyan University Press, 1990.

Harjo, Joy. *The Woman Who Fell From The Sky.* Norton 1996.

Harvey, Graham. *Indigenous Religions.* Cassell, 2000.

Heckman, Andrea H. *Woven Stories: Andean Textiles and Rituals.* University of New Mexico Press, 2003.

Helminski, Camille and Kabir. *Jewels of Remembrance.* Threshold Books, 1996.

Hill, Jonathan D. *Rethinking History and Myth: Indigenous South American Perspectives on the Past.* University of Illinois Press, 1988.

Hymes, Dell. *Directions in Sociolinguistics.* Basil Blackwell, 1986.

Isaacs, Jennifer. *Australian Dreaming: 40,000 Years Of Aboriginal History.* Lansdowne Press, 1980

Jackson, Michael. *At Home in the World.* Duke University Press, 1995.

Jefferson, Thomas. *Autobiography.* Wilder Publications, 2009.

Johnson, Paul Christopher. *Secrets, Gossip, and Gods: The Transformation of Brazilian Candomble.* Oxford University Press, 2002.

Josephy, Alvin M. *The American Heritage Book Of Indians.* American Heritage Publishing, 1961.

Karade, Baba Ifa. *The Handbook of Yoruba Religious Concepts.* Samuel Weiser, 1994.

Keil, Charles. *Urban Blues.* University Of Chicago Press, 1991.

Khan, Hazrat Inayat. *The Mysticism Of Sound And Music.* Shambhala Books, 1996.

Krause, Bernie. *The Great Animal Orchestra: Finding The Origins Of Music In The World's Wild Places.* Little, Brown, 2012.

Ladinsky, Daniel. *The Gift: Poems by Hafiz the Great Sufi Master.* Compass Penguin, 1999.

Lamb, F. Bruce. *Wizard Of The Upper Amazon.* North Atlantic Books, 1971.

Langdon, E. Jean Matteson. *Portals of Power: Shamanism in South America.* University of New Mexico Press, 1992.

Lathem, Edward Connery. *The Poetry Of Robert Frost.* Holt, Rinehart, Winston 1967.

Lathrap, Donald W. *The Upper Amazon.* Thames and Hudson, 1970.

Levin, Theodore. *The Hundred Thousand Fools Of Gold: Musical Travels In Central Asia.* Indiana University Press, 1996.

Levi-Strauss, Claude. *Structural Anthropology.* Basic Books, 1963.

Levitin, Daniel J. *This Is Your Brain On Music: The Science Of A Human Obsession.* Plume, 2007.

Mails, Thomas E. *The Mystic Warriors Of The Plains.* Marlowe & Company, 1995

Malinowski, Bronislaw. *Argonauts of the Western Pacific.* Waveland Press, 1922.

Marx, Karl. *Selected Writings In Sociology & Social Philosophy.* McGraw Hill, 1964.

McKenna, Terence. *The Invisible Landscape.* Harper Collins, 1993.

Merriam, Alan P. *The Anthropology Of Music.* Northwestern University Press, 1964.

Metzner, Ralph. *Ayahuasca: Human Consciousness and the Spirits of Nature.* Thunder Mouth Press, 1999.

Meyer, Laure. *Black Africa.* Telleri, 2003.

Moberg, Mark. "The Garifuna Journey." *American Anthropologist,* Volume 100, December 1998.

Moore, Jerry D. *Visions of Culture.* Alta Mira Press, 2004.

Munn, Nancy D. "Excluded Spaces: The Figure in the Australian Aboriginal Landscape," in *The Anthropology of Space and Place.* Blackwell Publishing, 2003.

Narby, Jeremy. *The Cosmic Serpent: DNA and the Origins of Knowledge.* Tarcher Putnam, 1999.

Neihardt, John G. *Black Elk Speaks.* University Of Nebraska Press, 1972.

Neimark, Philip John. *The Way of the Orisa.* Harper Collins, 1993.

Nettle, Bruno. *The Study Of Ethnomusicology.* University Of Illinois, 1983.

Nettle, Daniel & Suzanne Romaine. *Vanishing Voices: The Extinction Of The World's Languages.* Oxford University Press, 2000.

Oakdale, Suzanne. *I Foresee My Life: The Ritual Performance Of Autobiography In An Amazonian Community.* University Of Nebraska Press, 2005.

Palmer, Robert. *Deep Blues.* Penguin Group, 1981.

Peddie, Ian. *The Resisting Muse: Popular Music And Social Protest.* Ashgate, 2006.

Pisani, Michael V. *Imagining Native America In Music.* Yale University Press, 2005.

Post, Jennifer C. *Ethnomusicology: A Contemporary Reader.* Routledge, 2006

Racy, A.J. *Making Music In The Arab World: The Culture And Artistry Of Tarab.* Cambridge University Press, 2003

Ralls-Macleod, Karen. *Indigenous Religious Musics.* Ashgate, 2000.

Reed, A.W. *Aboriginal Myths, Legends, & Fables.* Reed New Holland, 2013.

Reed, A.W. *The Raupo Book Of Maori Mythology.* Raupo Books, 2008.

Rodman, Margaret C. "Empowering Place: Multilocality and Multivocality," in T*he Anthropology of Space and Place.* Blackwell Publishing, 2003.

Roe, Peter. *The Cosmic Zygote.* Rutgers University Press, 1982.

Roessingh, Carel. *The Belizean Garifuna: Organization of Identity in an Ethnic Community in Central America.* Rozenberg Publishers, 2001.

Rosenberg, Donna. *World Mythology: An Anthology Of The Great Myths And Epics.* McGraw Hill, 1994.

Sacks, Oliver. *Musicophilia.* Borzoi Books, 2007.

Sapir, Edward. *Selected Writings of Edward Sapir.* University of California Press, 1985.

Saussure, Ferdinand De. *Course in General Linguistics.* Open Court Publishing, 1972.

Schultes, Richard Evans. *Plants of the Gods.* Healing Arts Press, 1992.

Seeger, Anthony. *Why Suya Sing: A Musical Anthropology Of An Amazonian People.* University Of Illinois Press, 2004.

Shah, Idries. *The Sufis.* Anchor Books, 1971.

Smith, Suzanne. *Dancing In The Street: Motown And The Cultural Politics Of Detroit.* Harvard University Press, 1999.

Sproul, Barbara C. *Primal Myths: Creation Myths Around The World.* Harper Collins, 1991.

Stewart, Kathleen C. *Senses of Place.* School of American Research Press, 1996.

Tanahashi, Kazuaki. *Moon In A Dewdrop: Writings Of Zen Master Dogen.* North Point Press, 1985.

Tang, Patricia. *Masters of the Sabar.* Temple University Press, 2007.

Tenaille, Frank. *Music Is The Weapon Of The Future: Fifty Years Of African Popular Music.* Lawrence Hill Books, 2002

Troutman, John W. *Indian Blues: American Indians And The Politics Of Music, 1879-1934.* University Of Oklahoma Press, 2009.

Turino, Thomas. *Music As Social Life: The Politics Of Participation.* University Of Chicago Press, 2008.

Turner, Terrence. "The Kayapo Revolt Against Extractivism." *Journal of Latin American Anthropology*, 1995.

Turner, Victor. *The Ritual Process*. Aldine Publishing, 1969.

Van Buitenen, J.A.B. *The Bhagavad Gita*. Element Books, 1997.

Veloso, Caetano. *Tropical Truth*. Borzoi Books, 2002.

Voeks, Robert A. *Sacred Leaves of Candomble: African Magic, Medicine, and Religion in Brazil*. University of Texas Press, 1997.

Wafer, Jim. *The Taste of Blood: Spirit Possession in Brazilian Candomble*. University of Pennsylvania Press, 1991.

Weatherford, Jack. *Indian Givers: How The Indians Of The Americas Transformed The World*. Fawcett Columbine 1988.

Weber, Max. *The Protestant Ethic And The Spirit Of Capitalism*. Routledge, 1992.

Whitman, Walt. Leaves Of Grass. Doubleday, 1926.

Whorf, Benjamin. *Language, Thought and Reality*. MIT Press, 1956.

Wilcken, Lois and Augustin, Frisner. *The Drums of Vodou*. White Cliffs Media, 1992.

Willis, Roy. *World Mythology*. Henry Holt, 1993.

Zinn, Howard. *A People's History Of The United States, 1492-Present*. Harper Perennial, 1995.

Barrett Martin is a drummer, composer, producer, and award-winning writer best known for his work with several prominent Seattle bands including, The Barrett Martin Group, Walking Papers, Mad Season, Screaming Trees, Tuatara, Skin Yard, and the Levee Walkers. He has played on over 100 albums and film soundtracks to date, and when he is not on tour, he produces albums that range from indigenous music, to jazz, blues, and rock & roll. Martin holds a masters degree in ethnology and linguistics and is a professor of music at Antioch University Seattle. He writes a music and culture blog for the Huffington Post, and in 2014 he was awarded the ASCAP Deems Taylor/Virgil Thompson Award for excellence in writing.